CAMELS ARE EASY
COMEDY'S HARD

ROY BLOUNT, JR.

CAMELS

ARE

EASY

COMEDY'S HARD

VILLARD BOOKS

NEW YORK

1991

The contents of this work originally appeared in the following periodicals and collections:
*Antaeus, Atlanta Journal-Constitution, Atlantic, Best of Business Quarterly, Bred Any Good Rooks
Lately?, Business Month, Condé Nast Traveler, Esquire, Food and Wine, A Garden of Earthly Desserts,
Gentleman's Quarterly, Harper's Bazaar, The Inc. Life, Light Year '87, National Geographic, The New
York Times, The New York Times Book Review, The New York Times Magazine, PC Computing, Rolling
Stone, Soho News, Southpoint, Special Report, Vogue.*

Grateful acknowledgment is made to the following for permission to reprint previously
published material:

KITCHEN SINK PRESS, INC.: "Nancy Is Herself" is reprinted with permission of Kitchen Sink
Press, Inc., No. 2 Swamp Road, Princeton, WI 54968.
SPORTS ILLUSTRATED: "47 Years a Shot-Freak" ("Couldn't Use Them in a Game") from April
20, 1970, issue; "And Now for the Resurrection" from the April 12, 1971, issue; "Yo Yo
Yo, Rowa uh Rowa, Hru Hru" from the November 13, 1972, issue. Copyright © 1970,
1971, 1972 by Time, Inc. Reprinted courtesy of *Sports Illustrated*. All rights reserved.
SPY MAGAZINE: The "UnBritish Crossword Puzzles."

LIBRARY OF CONGRESS CATALOGING-IN-PUBLICATION DATA
Blount, Roy.
Camels are easy, comedy's hard / Roy Blount, Jr.
p. cm.
ISBN 0-679-40053-2
I. Title.
817.54   PS3552.L687C36 1991
814'.54—dc20   91-9364

Text design by Beth Tondreau Design

Manufactured in the United States of America
9 8 7 6 5 4 3 2
First edition

TO MY TWO FAVORITE TEACHERS:
ANN LEWIS AND VEREEN BELL

═══ACKNOWLEDGMENTS═══

Of the word-editors I have worked with on these pieces, I would like to salute Joanne Gruber of *Spy*, Klara Glowczewska of *Condé Nast Traveler* and Corby Kummer of *The Atlantic*—good people to discuss choices and orders of words (not to mention, punctuation) with. And the same to Beth Pearson of Villard. But I would like to state publicly that *The Chicago Manual of Style* is a ass.

CONTENTS

ABOUT
THE
TITLE

It do not say, around *the needle. Nor* over *the needle.*
And it do not say a snake. Nor any small creeping *thing.*
IT SAY A CAMEL!
Through the needle's eye.
Now you say to me, "Preacher, how could that be?" **—FROM A RADIO SERMON**

What we need is affirmative action for *silly* people. They're everywhere, they vote (evidently). Uplift them. The trouble is, many of them have already been to, say, Yale. The other night I spoke with just such a one. He was a conservative, he told me, and the great achievement of his generation (people in their twenties) was to have realized that everything is bullshit.

"Well, you haven't achieved much then," I told him, "because everything isn't."

"What isn't?" he demanded.

I'm sitting here in my kitchen now, still trying to think where to begin. On the refrigerator is a photograph of my kids. *They* are in their twenties. *They* don't believe everything is bullshit.

How about that. My children don't believe everything is bullshit. I wouldn't mind that for an epitaph:

MOONLOVE CHAKHA CHAKHA
(1941–2020)
His children don't believe everything is bullshit.

I don't think they do. (Moonlove Chakha Chakha is the name I want to be buried under, as a reward for denying myself all mysticism here on earth.) At any rate you can't help but realize that everything isn't bullshit when you bring little children into this world. Because you have to convince them that everything isn't bullshit. Because if you don't, they will just lie there on the floor kicking and hollering "NO!" And the case you make had better not be purely materialistic, or they won't ever call or write you once they have their own money.

But this person the other night wasn't the right age for that argument. Next to my kids' picture on the refrigerator is one of me on a camel.

"Camels," I could have told this absolutist. "Not even camel *dung* is bullshit. I take it you know how bullshit goes down. Whereas camel evacuation, I have observed, is like the bottom just dropped out of a bag of marbles."

But that would have been too easy. What is there to cling to, nowadays? What is there about which it can be said, "You can take *that* to the bank"? If there were any such thing today, of course, you would not want to entrust it to today's banks. The reason so many young people profess to be conservative today is not that there is so much to conserve, but that there is nothing reliable enough to rebel against.

I'll tell you what kind of book I believe in: one that makes people say, at first sight, what the first person who ever saw a camel must have said: *"What in the world is that?"* And then, after a while, "Yet it seems to fit together some way."

This book incorporates warthogs, a nose-eating hyena, hippos, a tiger, piranhas, goaway birds, threatened ferrets, a rescued greyhound, sled dogs, bugs, literary lions, a rubber chicken, an agonized sloth, a stricken father gazelle, an envisioned bear, a minuscule weasel, fugitive raccoons ("A coon can make the walking rough"), a dauntless marmoset, a man-wrestling deer, more than one serpent and a self-declared fox.

And yet I wouldn't call it naturalism. It is part travel writing (Dierks, Arkansas; Kampala, Uganda; Atlantic City, New Jersey; Esperanza, Peru), part short story, part reminiscence, part sportswriting, part book review, part abortive serial novel about gigantic earthworms, part essay, part famous-persons-I-have-known, part political outcry, part crossword puzzle (you can *work* part of this book), part neoBiblical playlet, part cartoon criticism and part verse (may I say that reviewers sometimes use the term *doggerel* too loosely?).

Of the sixty-four pieces in this book, sixty-one first appeared (many in different form) in twenty-eight different publications. The longest (down the Amazon) is about ten thousand words, the shortest (in which jelly speaks), twenty-three. Most are hot off the griddle, but a few have been acquiring patina for ten to twenty-one years.

That much is easy.

Fitting it all together is hard. And that is something this book is bound to leave to the eye, and other parts, of just such a person as, by definition, yourself: the reader. You being so damn coherent.

If you want to read these pieces in your own peculiar order, or even just to flip through them picking out the vital new concepts for the Nineties (aerobic guilt, flaggot jokes, the debt/date ratio, etc., etc.), it's up to you. Comedy calls for a happy ending—getting married, gaining paradise, something. But there can be no guarantees.

"Have you ever considered writing something serious?" people ask me. Many is the time I have thought to myself, "Well, maybe I'll make this one tragic (loosely speaking). Heaven knows it wouldn't be hard." But then I say, "Nahh."

CAMELS ARE EASY
COMEDY'S HARD

═══HOW A CAMEL GOES═══

"Eeeeurghgr'gl'gl'gblglglglghg'blegh."

That's not it. It's richer, more crowded in there. More *b*'s, maybe—*b*'s and *g*'s and *l*'s on top of one another.

The cry of a camel being cinched up.

For four days it awoke me at dawn. I was on a camel safari in central Kenya, just east of where, scientists tend to believe, human life began. Though Kenya still has vast open spaces and more elephants than automobiles, it is not, by general agreement, what it used to be. Depending on your point of view, paradise began to go downhill when human life began, when the British took over, when independence was won, when Americans saw *Out of Africa.* To the area's camels, creation went out of joint when the idea arose that the camel was a "beast of burden."

That idea dates back to time immemorial, and yet camels are freshly outraged each time someone starts loading them up. Every camel seems to be thirty centuries old and yet to be confronting its role in life for the first time at that moment. So many things are done to a camel behind its head. What in blazes is going on back there?

Eeeurngh' glablalala'bleagh'l'leh.

The perfect protest. The noise I want to make when I get out of bed or sit down to work. But I don't have the chops.

A camel's long, not-quite-droopy lips are usually loosely pursed, except when they move old-yokelishly side to side in cud chewing and when they curl and gape enormously for a teeth-baring, tongue-baring *eeeoounh'g'blagl . . .* A camel's dark, heavy-lidded eyes, with luxuriant, dark, sand-resistant lashes, make it a highly aloof (its head, of course, may be eight feet above the ground) yet strangely come-hither animal. I am thankful that you have all seen at least pictures of a camel, because if you hadn't you wouldn't believe me when I say that a camel looks a little like a giraffe, a little like a dinosaur, a little (when folded up) like a grasshopper or frog, a little like an ostrich, a little like a horse and a little like a librarian.

I highly recommend a camel safari. Fifteen of us travelers—American, English, French, Canadian and apologetically South African, ranging from late teens to retired—spent five days covering twenty-three miles with one white hunter, Julian McKeand; his top Masai assistant, Barsula Lemaidok; twenty-four spear-carrying, red-wrapper-wearing, trinkets-in-their-earlobes Masai warriors, who had their hair in long braids dyed with red ocher and who protected us from the elephants that charged us and the bandits that might have; two Meru cooks; and forty camels. For four of the days we rode camels or walked with them over red dust and chunks of volcanic rock in near-desert country northeast of Isiolo, part of what used to be called the Northern Frontier District of Kenya (four hours from Nairobi). We saw warthogs and the greater kudu. We ate delicious stews and tarts and even a cheese soufflé cooked in a tin-box Dutch oven on open fires. We slept on camp beds under mosquito netting. The Masai set up shower and loo tents for us every evening. And let me tell you something else about camels.

You have heard that camels stink, balk, spit and bite. These are stereotypes. Julian McKeand's camels have acquired a certain crucial (to Westerners) propriety. A camel spits only when it feels threatened, but when this does happen it is even worse than you might think—the cud is ejected at the perceived threat, and a camel's breath, while not foul, as I had been led to believe, is so profoundly funky in a vegetarian way that I am thankful these camels apparently never felt threatened, although I went so far as to try petting them. (Only one of them liked it.) You can see the cud rising up the four-foot-long throat, but in the case of McKeand's camels that just means the camel is in a mood to ruminate.

A camel bite entails crunch and gnash, and is extremely hard to disinfect. A male camel gets sexually aroused only occasionally, but when he does don't get in the way, because such a camel has been known to bite the top of a man's head off. McKeand's camels are all gelded males, however. "It keeps the party clean," he says. And they are well trained. None has ever bitten a customer. All the Masai have to do is say *"oop oop"* and the camels fold majestically—first onto the front knees, then onto the back knees, which collapse, and then down onto the chest callus.

FOR EONS CAMELS have been kicked, whipped and fitted with bits that make their lips bleed, but McKeand's camels—the gelding aside—

have been treated sympathetically. At first, McKeand said, the Masai he hired saw no point in safari camels, because you can't get meat or blood from them. Masai are cattle lovers. Their traditional diet is mostly milk, sometimes mixed with blood tapped from their cows' jugulars. But safariing is a good enough gig that they can buy more cattle (or put more money in the bank, now that drought kills so many cows), hire other Masai as herdsmen, and subsist on goats' meat, cornmeal and vegetables provided by McKeand. They continue to believe that people who pay to walk around with camels are crazy, but they have acquired a taste for camel milk and an affection for camels as wholes. They deal with camels' deep disinclinations deftly and with good humor. They remove ticks from the camels' eyes tenderly. At night, when the hobbled camels hear lion noises (lions passed within a few yards of our beds), they crawl close to the Masai, who sleep around them.

Once a camel gets under way, you wouldn't think it was outraged at all. It has an easy gait—back left foot, front left foot, roll, back right foot, front right foot. Dah, dah . . . dah, dah. It is a bit as if the camel were two extremely long-legged bipeds, yoked in tandem, taking turns walking. I tried to walk in step with either side of a camel and then with either end of a camel, and I could never quite keep it up. Length of stride aside, there is a differential involved that no one person can master.

On camelback, I found myself singing, "How mild, how mild, how mild can a cigarette be? Smoke Camels and you will see. . . ." Was this just a cheap joke on the part of my subconscious? The "How mild . . . how mild" part fit the camel-gait rhythm, and it is true that a camel—when it is being led by a Masai, as ours were—is a mild ride. The only person who has fallen off a camel in the twelve years McKeand has led these safaris was a man who fell asleep.

In dry and unoppressive hundred-degree-plus heat we passed through country that proved how grand scraggliness can be. The sky was hugely blue, the rubbly terrain was ruddy and untampered with, the blue-gray-green mountains were abrupt in the distance, and the plant life was rigorously minimal. There had been no rain in twelve solid months. The vegetation was thorn trees—varieties of acacia, like the tiny-prickled, tenacious wait-a-bit tree—and poisonous Sodom apple bushes whose leaves are so abrasive that the Masai use them to smoothe ornaments with.

Camels thrive in such terrain, not only because they can go a week without water but also because they can eat twigs, thorns, abrasive leaves and probably birds' nests. As to birds, we saw the orange-bellied parrot, the sulphur-breasted bush thrush, the speckled mouse-bird, the red-billed hornbill, the goaway bird and the superb starling. A superb starling appears to be wearing an electric-blue suit. A go-away bird hollers *"Gawn, gawn!"*

"You're a goaway bird in a wait-a-bit tree. Why do you do what you're doing to me?" I sang, but it got no rise from the camel I sat on.

Then I began to listen to the young Masai behind me in the procession. He was leading the last camel, which, like the lead camel, wore a euphoniously clonking wooden bell. This Masai had been circumcised only recently, we had been told, which meant he had just begun his seven-or-so-year apprenticeship as a warrior, during which time he would avoid the company of women. But the young Masai behind me did not sound horny. He sang in a soft, sweet, highly uncamelish voice:

> *Ah yah yih hoyoy*
> *Ah yah yih hoyoy*
> *Ah yah yih hoonh*
> *Hoy yoy*
> *Hoy yoy*
> *Hoyyyy yi-no*
> *Heh-gung*
> *Heh-gung*
> *Hoymoy*

only longer and more complicated.

ON THE LAST evening in the camp the younger Masai danced for us. They gathered in a tight bunch and jumped straight up and down, *high*, continually, in unison, almost flat-footedly, just bouncing. And singing. By turns one man in the bunch would *not* jump; he would stay down to lead the singing, so there was always this one pair of feet on the ground in contrast with all the others that rose to the level of his knees, and went down, and back up.

"Hing hindera. Hing hindera" was the jumpers' principal chant, but the grounded man would usually weave in longer lyrics: *"Aya nanaro, wawa wimmido. . . ."*

"What are they singing about?" I asked Barsula.

"About what they have been doing since their circumcision. Whether they have been brave."

"What do they say they've been doing?"

"Being with camels, and fifteen whites."

MAN CHEWED

BY

MANY ANIMALS

"I vividly remember his left-hand tusks through my leg and my foot jammed between his molars. I could feel all the whiskers of his chin on the back of my thigh."

How's that for a lead? Alan Root on being bitten by a hippopotamus, which isn't the half of it.

In my own travels, I have been bitten by a spring lizard, a piranha and (in the Memphis zoo) a rhea, which is a kind of ostrich. I know a plastic surgeon in London, Dr. Peter Davis, who once made a new nose for a man who'd had his bitten off by a hyena as he slept (or, more precisely, woke) in a tent in the wilds of Zaire. Worth mentioning that hyenas are said to have, literally, the worst breath in the world.

"Was he in shock?" I asked Dr. Davis.

"Oh, no no. He was a real colonial. He didn't mind. Said, after it was over, he thought I'd given him a better nose. That's all."

Dr. Davis also maintains that English youths put ferrets in their pants, competitively, to see who can stand them in there the longest. "One wrote in to the newspaper that he'd been bitten on the left testicle. He wanted to know, 'Is that all right?'"

Far and away, however, the person I've met who knows the most, firsthand, about being chomped is Alan Root.

"Came chomping through the water chomp chomp chomp. Shook me around like a puppy with a stick. Banged me on the bottom several times. I wasn't aware at the time but people on the side said I appeared out of the water several times."

Root on the hippo incident again. Root may well be the only person in the world who has been bitten not only by a hippo but also by a leopard, a gorilla and a puff adder, and lived to tell about it with relish.

Root is a lean, fifty-two-year-old Kenyan bush pilot and balloonist who makes distinguished documentary films on East African wildlife. *The Great Migration: Year of the Wildebeest. Serengeti Shall Not Die. Mysterious Castles of Clay* (about termites and their mounds). He's won an

Oscar and a Peabody Award. And no one can accuse him of having done all this from safe removes. When the hippo got him, he and a cameraman were underwater filming a hippopotamus fight.

"All the commotion had stirred up so much mud I couldn't see anything. I sat there waiting for the water to clear. The guy who had lost the fight was fifteen feet away. He probably saw all the bubbles coming from our breathing gear and thought the other male was coming after him. He got more and more uptight about the bubbles."

That's when he came chomping. "I remember sickening crunching feelings. What bothered me was the idea he was going to go up my body, going to do a job on me. But he let me go—he wasn't after me, just felt threatened, and that was bad for his image."

Root was in the hospital for weeks recovering from that one. The vegetable debris that a hippo's bite transmits kept working its way out of the wound. The infection was terrible. "I sweated through not only sets of sheets but whole mattresses." But it was clear to Root that a prudent person's being set upon by a hippopotamus was unusual, so as soon as humanly possible he was back in the water amongst those huge purple blimps with maws like watermelons' nightmares.

"You always have a monkey, always get bitten by them—or you get bitten by your friend's monkey. That's part of growing up in East Africa," reminisced Root as we dined on inoffensive, indeed delicious, small sea creatures at Nairobi's Norfolk Hotel. Root is craggy, clay-colored and calm, the very picture of a man who moved from London to Kenya at the age of seven and has spent few daytime hours indoors since. As a boy he collected snakes and was bitten by them from time to time, and he knew that exploratory naturalism was the life for him. Nor did he doubt it years later when the leopard got his bottom.

"That was just a silly accident. I'd had a picnic lunch. Shouted and clapped my hands to frighten away any cats. Saw an owl fly out over the top of a rock nearby. Thought I'd see whether anything was there. Got to a ledge and looked down, and a few feet below was a dead jackal. Should've put two and two together. But I went down to investigate. Under the overhang, a leopard was crouched out of sight. I jumped down right in front of him and presented him with an offer he couldn't refuse. He grabbed my left buttock and chomped on it a couple of times. I reached back with my arm and hit him. Probably more frightened than I was. Almost always it's that you've violated their space, they feel threatened. Give you a quick bite to send you on your way.

"Blood was streaming down my leg and squelching in my shoes. I drove to the warden's office and squelched in. The warden was Miles

Turner, a dry character. I told him, 'One of your leopards has just bitten me in the arse.'

"He said, 'You've been around here long enough to know you can't feed the animals.' Cleaned it out with hydrogen peroxide. Just fang punctures, she bit and let go, wasn't ripping around."

The puff adder was a nastier matter. "There was an American guy who wanted to do business with Joy Adamson, so I flew him up to her camp. My wife, Joan, and I went for a walk along the river. Saw a very big female puff adder, and I caught it to show the guy; he had only forty-eight hours there, I thought I'd show him something exciting. Grabbed it by the back of the neck, got its mouth open, made it squirt venom, showed the teeth—did the whole Cook's tour of a puff adder, then let it go. Joy said, 'Oh, no, I didn't have film in my camera, could you do it again?'

"By this time it was a bit fed up with being shown to tourists. Not as sleepy as before. When I tried to grab it again, it just turned and got me.

"With a puff adder, you have about forty-eight hours. The venom makes the walls of the blood vessels porous, they start to hemorrhage, and it spreads to your kidneys and essential bits. Fortunately, there was another aircraft there faster than mine. When I'd been bitten by a burrowing adder at eighteen I'd been given antivenom made with horse serum, and I'd become allergic to it. But Joy had some in her fridge and halfway to Nairobi in the plane I became very sick, my hand was swelling enormously, and we decided I'd better have twenty cc's. Joan gave me the injection. I reacted very badly—vomiting even worse, fainting, blacking out.

"A taxi was waiting to take us to the emergency ward. By then I was semiconscious. When we got there Joan had to pay the driver—it only took her thirty seconds—but in that time the hospital people decided to give me antivenom without waiting for my history. Another twenty cc's, this time intravenously. It more or less killed me. 'I've got this incredible coppery taste in my mouth,' I said, and the nurse realized what was happening.

"They hauled in a very good lady doctor who . . . Clinically, I died. She shocked me back with cortisone and adrenaline. She had a very butch, I'm-in-charge kind of voice, and I was just clinging to that voice.

"They wanted to amputate my arm. There was a huge cushion of internal hemorrhage—the vessels leaking—over the whole arm and down to my waist. I did lose one finger, and a lot of the use of my right hand. All the tendons were crumbling."

Still, Root likes snakes, and he is even more enthusiastic about the gorilla who picked him up and chewed him.

"That was a bit shaming in a way. Gorillas are meant to be such gentle animals, and indeed are, but not all of them. I was asked by Warner Brothers, who were filming the Diane Fossey movie, to get footage of gorillas charging. We'd showed Diane her first gorilla, got her started.

"It's difficult to get gorillas charging now. In Ruanda, with the increase in tourism, they sit around signing autographs. So we had to go looking in Zaire for wilder groups. I was told about one male who was just a habitual charger.

"In my very first meeting with him—with hindsight I realize how many things were wrong. He was standing in a swamp, very untypically ankle-deep in water. I had a huge thirty-five-millimeter camera on a shoulder mount, which looked threatening to him.

"One of the youngsters came and sat near my assistant and me. He stayed and stayed, had breakfast with us—then let us get too close, and it bothered him, and he turned and fled past this male. This male, I later learned, was known as Mukamuka, Swahili for "The Boiling One." Big silverback. He saw the youngster running, and he just came—there was this terrible scream, which had a slightly harder edge than usual.

"Usually it's a mock charge, they get up high, make themselves as big as they can, run past you showing their stuff, how big and noisy and earthshaking they are. When we went back later we used a lower camera mount, which gave us a more submissive posture, and we got some very good footage of him suddenly coming right among us, swinging his arms, knocking over saplings, going after my assistant, Bruce Davidson, wearing a Diane Fossey outfit complete with ponytail. Some days he seemed to get a kick out of it, the gorilla. He's an amazing animal. Grumpy old bastard. He's a great animal.

"But this first time, I didn't even know him yet. He wasn't bluffing anything, he just came along the ground, he was going to get me. I had the wrong lens on—telephoto. I switched the camera on anyway but all I got was a black blur. But I had a very vivid picture of what was happening. He grabbed me with his hands like a man grabs a leg of lamb, at my knee and waist, and chomped me in between. I was thinking, 'Christ, he's gutting me,' but it was just his fingers I felt at my waist, not teeth. He gave me a couple of chews, basically just saying, 'Why don't you piss off?' When I found it was my leg I just burst out laughing, with enormous relief.

"It was a pretty ragged wound, an enormous flap. Tore up my

assistant's shirt to hold it together. Had to walk for two hours to get out of the forest, then drove an hour and had two hours on the airplane and another drive to the hospital.

"I was laid up for about a month, getting the infection under control so I could have the skin graft. Quite a lot of meat was missing."

None of which was heart. Let us remember this, we travelers, when mosquitoes get on our nerves or a customs official is snappish: Alan Root went back, as soon as he could, and got to know that gorilla better.

EATING OUT OF

HOUSE

AND HOME

"**W**hy is it that things taste so much better outside?" is a question that people are always asking, and unlike most questions that people are always asking ("Do you really love me?" "What is truth?"), this question springs from satisfaction.

Outdoors your senses perk up. And the smells of pine, honeysuckle, grass and woodsmoke are like extra spices: outdoor sauce, which isn't fattening. And you have so much more room to eat in. A mouthful becomes a heartier proposition.

I don't say there is no downside to eating outdoors. My daughter Ennis, who lives in San Francisco, notes that it takes some of the zest out of a picnic in the park when you see, and are seen by, people who are living in the park.

Another thing that will mar outdoor eating sometimes is rowdiness. Once I was attending an outdoor event called the Steeplechase in Nashville, Tennessee, with my friends Slick and Susan Lawson, when a man with no shirt on fell into our lunch, where we had it spread out there on plates on our blanket, and he got up with the bulk of our cold cuts sticking to his upper body. That was awful. It wasn't anybody the Lawsons knew well. I didn't know him at all. That wouldn't happen indoors.

Eating outdoors is somewhat like going naked outdoors. Animals do it. You know why Manet's *Le Dejeuner sur l'herbe* is so sexy, don't you? Not just because one of the people in it is outdoors naked—I wouldn't be surprised to learn that half the people in the entire history of French painting are outdoors naked. It's because she is outdoors naked *eating lunch*.

Sexy, and perfectly natural. Most foodstuffs come from outdoors, and cookfires had to be outside originally. In the scheme of things, more eating goes on outdoors than indoors even today. "The whole of nature . . . is a conjugation of the verb *to eat,* in the active and passive," said William Ralph Inge. Here is another outdoor eating poem I wrote, in case you are interested:

END OF THE LINE

The smallest meat-eating animal is the least-weasel. **—THE HARTFORD COURANT**

On what creature, then, does the least-
Weasel feast?
Let us say a herbivore,
Which furthermore
The least-weasel
Cannot, at least, eat easil-
Y. Still, such a meal
Must feel,
When finished,
Greatly diminished.

Take a hike up a hill and get out your ordinarily ordinary sandwich and look around at the bird with its worm, the frog with its fly (and here come the ants for your crumbs), and what do you think?

My. (What a good spot on the food chain *I* lucked into.) This is a *fine* sandwich.

One thing you want to look out for, eating outdoors, is that you don't eat bits of the outdoors itself. Bark, pinestraw, dirt. I ate a fly once, in some baked beans. Until you have bit down on a live, beans-sated fly, don't talk to me about knowing what it is to have a kind of trash-greasy taste in your mouth. It lingers. I realized what was happening before my molars quite meshed, but that was too late. Actually it might have been better if I had briskly chewed and swallowed and then realized. But, as I say, I realized just before I quite finished biting down completely. A buzz, some movement.

I'll tell you what's *good,* though. Baked beans without a fly in them, outdoors. Even the memory of having eaten a fly in them is not enough to put me off of outdoor baked beans. Or deviled eggs. Or potato salad. (I am from Georgia. My friend Lee Smith, who is from Virginia, says, "Northern people on a picnic take whole things. A whole chicken. A whole loaf of bread. Southern people have to have things that have had things done to them.") When I was a boy I would eat baked beans, and deviled eggs, and potato salad, and barbecue chicken, and homemade peach ice cream, in quantities that—well, I bet I could eat more outdoor food in one meal back then without feeling *unpleasantly* stuffed than I could eat in seven, now. And I can eat a lot of food in seven now.

On the island of Lamu, off the coast of Kenya, I have had just-caught fish roasted whole on the beach on a grid of green twigs.

Oo.

Say you do find a little something in your outdoor food that you wouldn't have found if you and your food had stayed indoors. I am reminded of a time in a Paris restaurant when I cast a warm eye on a raw oyster and saw a tiny wormish life-form swimming in the liquid.

I called the waiter over, but by the time he arrived I was unable to point out any swimming thing *("those nageuse")*. It had evidently succumbed to the lemon juice I'd squeezed on the oyster.

I approached a second oyster, and there was another one of those things. I summoned the waiter again, and this time he had to admit that he saw the thing swimming.

He shrugged and said, *"C'est la mer."*

You want to be mindful of what you're eating outdoors. I know a man who was eating potato chips out of a bowl at night in a semi-enclosed picnic area, and somebody said to him, "You're bleeding all out your mouth, there."

It turned out that he had been eating handfuls not only of potato chips but of light bulb fragments, from a bulb that had broken in an overhead fixture.

That wouldn't have happened if he had been *entirely* outdoors. Then too he had been drinking a great deal. He doesn't drink at all now, and that's one of the reasons.

Anyway, say you are serving something outdoors and someone complains that there is something unexpected in it. A bee wing or a windblown seed. Here is what you could say (I looked up the French for outdoors):

"C'est le grand air."

I don't know why there have been so many French references in these remarks so far. Perhaps because *picnic* comes from the French *pique-nique* (as opposed to the English *pyknic*, which means round and fat). I had better bring in reinforcements of Americana.

So here are some alfresco cooking hints from Slick Lawson, who has been deeply involved in such outdoor food affairs as annual goat-roasts featuring goat gumbo, nude swimming and helicopter accidents:

"Things cooked inside are cooked with elbows up; things cooked outside, the elbows are on a table.

"Inside you stand up and stir, outside you bend over and peek.

"Inside, guests tell you how famous chefs do things. Outside, they tell you how they do things. They have secret recipes that they share with everyone.

"Inside they help with the dishes, outside they help with the ice.

"Inside or not, women always help with the bread. Instead of nice hot French bread that you break off, they are compelled to slice it and put garlic and butter on it, wrap it in foil and turn it into a mush of dough that won't sop anything.

"Outside, men want to pick up things. (Chairs, beer coolers and your best client's wife.)

"Inside, people try to make interesting conversation and are dull. Outside, they remember the most deplorable things you did in the good old days.

"Outside, if you discard a chicken lip or the left front paw of a hamster (hamsters have more dark meat than gerbils), someone will tell you that you threw away the best part.

"Outside, someone you don't much like will leave a dish and follow up with three messages on your answering machine while you are in London.

"Outside, it's hard to clean up after dark.

"Boy scouts and girl scouts are forced to eat outside.

"Outside, anything that falls to the ground legally belongs to the dog.

"Outside, medium-rare has a wider latitude.

"After you finish eating from the grill, someone always points out that the fire is just now getting right."

In San Francisco my daughter Ennis teaches three-year-old kids who have various handicaps: Down syndrome, deafness, parental sexual abuse, drug addiction in the womb. When the '89 earthquake hit, her workday was over and she was at home, but many of the kids were still at the school. After the earth stopped rippling, the teachers on duty took the kids outside while someone checked to make sure the building wasn't about to collapse. It was suppertime. The next day Ennis wanted to give the kids a chance to talk out any traumatized feelings they might have.

"Okay," she said to her class, "now what happened yesterday?"

"We had a picnic!" the children exclaimed.

THE VANITY
OF
HUMAN DISHES

Being hot is nice, but that
Don't mean you're in control.
The jelly said to the butter pat,
"Hey, we're on a roll."

TAN

When I was a little kid, of course, I was brown all summer. That's because I was free as a bird—nothing to do but catch bugs all day—and didn't care what color I was. Whatever didn't wash off handily at night was the tone I took.

Puberty ended all that. As we know, puberty alienates the skin from the mind and both skin and mind from the young person involved. If I had it to do over I would go through puberty again, but I would do it where no one could see me.

Spring vacation when I was fourteen I traveled sourly with my parents—the last people anyone would choose to go through puberty with—to Daytona, Florida. On the beach I met a strange girl, named Lu, from Racine, Wisconsin. She spelled it out for me, in a provocative tone of voice: Lu. I had never met anyone named Lu or from Wisconsin, let alone Racine, and I had certainly never met a girl who was cute by popular standards (by any standards—her hair was bouncy and the color of lightly buttered toast) and yet would be the one who approached me on the beach—*because she saw me reading an anthology of stories of horror and the macabre.* There must have been something wrong with a girl who had perky lips and also admired the stories of H. P. Lovecraft ("The Cult of Cthulhu," "The Rats in the Walls"), but to my way of thinking at the time, borderline schizophrenia was the only thing that seemed to pull everything together. When I met her there on the beach she was more or less my color. I turned my back for a moment and when I looked again she was already butterscotch.

I didn't want Lu to sink deeper and deeper into sepia without me. And, hey, I was only a couple of years removed from brown boyhood. So I abandoned myself to the sun. Chuckled when Lu wondered, in a provocative tone of voice, whether I wasn't rushing it. Did take certain precautions, like keeping my arms akimbo so as not to run the risk of white stripes down the sides.

The next morning I woke up (to use a word that often appeared in stories of horror and the macabre) *eldritch:* a pulsing salmon-pink, with tiny white blisters all over.

You'd think there'd be more to this episode, but there isn't: since my first instinct at that time was to be ashamed of being seen in any condition, I was not about to return to the beach, even for Lu, especially for Lu, looking like I'd been covered in garish chintz. Lu surely found other fish to fry—her father was a big dairy magnate, she refused to eat ice cream for that reason, and she had been to seven high schools. When I got back to my school, my new color had nearly all scaled away. What traces remained did not move anyone to ask me, "Mmm, where'd you get all that tan?" However, a naturally platinum-haired senior majorette, whom I had never had any pretensions to being on the same level of reality with, stopped me in the hall. "Who do you go to?" she said.

For a wild moment I thought she had said, "Who do you go *with.*" I was astounded to find that I was larger than she was physically. I answered, "Whuph?"

"Your dermatologist," she said. She thought I had been undergoing dry-ice treatments.

Officially, my complexion is "Ruddy." It says so on my draft card, which was issued in October 1959. In the fall and winter months, when other Caucasians (my race would have unstable coloring) tend toward the peaked, I look healthy, at least by noon. But often in the summer, by comparison to more seasonal people, I pale. And showing my draft card does no good. In summer, sometimes, my draft card looks tan next to me.

It would be one thing if I were a roofer, but the kind of work I do—this, for instance—doesn't get me out into the sun *regularly.* I travel, type, talk. On a given Fourth of July I may have Juned where it isn't sunny—for instance, in departure lounges. I may have spent June *losing* a tan of some interest.

The last great tan I had was one recent March. I got it in Africa, riding camels. A camel-riding tan is an honest tan, especially if it has been achieved despite eighteen-power sunblock.

Sunblock is a great invention for people who want to make it clear that their purpose in life is nothing so superficial as tan. If you happen to get tan while putting all your effort into (a) learning to imitate the cry of a camel (an amalgam of moose gargling diesel fuel, clubman being goosed by steward, and outboard motor going BWORP in too-shallow water), for instance, and (b) not getting burned so badly that you don't end up looking odder than the camel, then fine. If someone, say a senior majorette, should ask you where you got such a tan, you can say, "Hm? Oh, let's see. Zanzibar?" Getting tan has not been your pursuit.

However. A cool, incidental tan may well be a head, arms and knee-to-ankle tan—which should be enough for decent people, but then you turn up in a bathing suit somewhere and you look like one of those 1940s shoes. In fact your tan may begin halfway down your forehead, because you have been wearing a practical hat, a hat appropriate to camel-riding, say.

There are only so many things you can do, as an adult, in a bathing suit. In fact there is only one thing you can do in a bathing suit without being largely covered, like the earth itself, by water. That one thing is sunning.

I hate to be just . . . sunning. Sunned against is more like it. Lying smeared with lotion on sand in the hot sun is like being rolled in cornmeal and dropped into a hot pan of Crisco, only less dramatic. "Soaking up the rays," sunners call it. I would rather soak up gravy, thereby replenishing, not depleting, the body's essential oils. (I say that, but of course I've had to lose my innocence about gravy, had to learn the malignity of it, as we all have, in these health-conscious times. We have to live more naturally and wholesomely, stop eating the things we love.)

One spring in my late twenties I was in Florida, covering the baseball training camps. I was new to sportswriting and hadn't made many sporting friends or started to drink much yet. I was in Florida for a month, and I had to do something. For some reason I decided to take another shot at tanning. I applied myself systematically. Anointed my limbs. Held to a schedule. Within a week I possessed, for the first time since the age of twelve, a good deep hamburger-bun glow over every mentionable part.

A consummation, but also a responsibility. It isn't easy to cover spring training, what with the games being played in prime sunning time, and maintain your tan too. Driving to ballparks, I would roll my left sleeve up awkwardly high and hold my arm and shoulder out the car window at various angles, to catch the sun all around. The police pulled me over and accused me of giving intentionally farcical hand signals. I didn't care. I got so transcolored after a while that in the light of my motel bathroom I was orange. After that nothing was enough.

I developed new fears. One day I went to Flamingo, Florida, in the Everglades, and sat on a dock watching pelicans and eating a po' boy sandwich. Observing. Getting outside myself. Pelicans are like snowflakes, in that no two of them are alike. But no given pelican is like any snowflake, either.

Suddenly a blackbird, which I hadn't been watching, swooped down and literally grabbed my sandwich from my hand, with his feet.

The po' boy was too heavy for him to fly very high with, so I ran after him a few steps and grabbed it back, scarcely damaged. I liked it. I had paid eighty-five cents for it, which would be a couple of dollars today. I was still hungry. Ignoring the blackbird's cries, I started eating the po' boy again.

But then I began to worry. I might catch some kind of rare tropical disease from a South Florida blackbird's feet. Who knew what the symptoms might be. What if my tan fell off! I might have to take it back to New York in an envelope!

My last day in Florida, I overbaked. I turned a peculiar, sizzling shade of rust. I sat in my hotel room fascinated by the color of my own stomach. What had I become? Fiery chills ran through my thighs. At length I slept, and tossed, and dreamed that I had fallen off a speeding bicycle and was skidding over concrete.

But as I flew north, burnt sienna, I was under the impression that it had all been worth it. I went straight from airport to office.

No one said anything.

I dropped hints.

No one took them.

Finally I worked my tan into an editorial conference. When someone said, "That's a good line," I sprang up, tore open my shirt, tugged at the top of my pants and said, "Speaking of lines. . . ."

There it was, visual proof. The line where my bathing suit had left off and the rich, dark gold began.

Only no one seemed impressed, favorably. I looked down. It was gone.

Airport X-ray machines, I now believe, neutralize tan in some cases.

"Oh," someone said, grudgingly, at last. "You got a little color."

You can "get a little color" drinking! Which is what I worked on that year as the spring gave way to summer. I found I had a knack for it. Years went by. Drinking is more active than sunning, and it makes you feel no worse in the morning than sunning does. And it recalls your innocence.

The girls that I caught bugs with back in the old days were so easy to talk to. No, not easy, fun. Because that was when summer was summer, you were out of school, you didn't have to do anything most of the time (back when time was *time*), the pavement was hot but your feet were tough and the air was sultry but you were out moving, creating a breeze, and you could treat yourself to an unhealthy soft drink of some kind and it would be sweet, refreshing, exactly what you wanted.

And the bugs were for the taking. Bumblebees to trap between jar-lid and jar, roly-polies to roll up into hard grey BB-sized balls lined with little curled legs, lightning bugs to snatch in midflash and get that funny smell on your fingers, grasshoppers in your fist like vaguely pulsing stem-wads and then you'd open it and feel them ping off. You wouldn't torment bugs but you wouldn't care how they felt either; if they died they died, the sun shone on them and you alike.

Drinking was like that, to some extent. The way I did it. But it's changed. I don't know whether it's my forties or the Eighties, but lately I have so many forms to fill out. And I don't feel as fluid as I used to in my joints. My very children are borderline adults. And I need to take niggling, conscious measures to shore up my everyday health. And I tend to wake up before I want to. And money is so much more of a *consideration* than it used to be. And I find drinking gets irksome. Who has time for it anymore? Not even reporters. Recently a campaign-trail press veteran was quoted as saying of his new, young colleagues, "They don't even drink at *night.*"

O temperance! O mores! You start thinking about why you are drinking, and how much of it you ought to be doing, and it gets to be too much like sunning. So I am drinking less and less, and the days get longer and the nights earlier and I suppose as a matter of course I will be spending more time wholesomely in the sun.

That last sentence surprises me. But it could well be true. Last night on television I saw an international fashion model being interviewed. She looked a little hard, you know, but ravishing. She said tan was passé. What she was at pains to maintain now, she said, was just "a blush." Which is what I have long maintained by way of natural embarrassment. Now, if tan has become unseemly, my life can be expected to adapt. At noon today I noticed I was outdoors mowing the lawn in nothing but athletic shorts. By the time I am elderly I may be back to running after bugs (Nabokov did it), brown as a berry.

GILDA: "THIS STOFF

————————CAME————————

OUTTA *ME?*"

AFTER THIS *piece appeared in* **Rolling Stone** *in 1978, Gilda called me up and said, "When I read it I fell down on the floor and sobbed and then all my friends called me and said, 'Gilda, it's you exactly, and it made us love you even more,' so I said, 'Oh,' and I like it." This is the best response I have received from any famous person I have written about (most have not responded at all, except by not hitting me). We had dinner a couple of times after that, and she sneaked my then-little kids into the* **Saturday Night Live** *audience (which apparently had a minimum age) and kept promising to visit us in the country, but we lost touch. When I heard that she was dying of cancer I kept putting off calling her up, because it had been eight or ten years since I'd seen her, and I couldn't think what to say. As if she weren't tough and nice enough to be funny about whatever lame thing I might have blurted. (According to accounts I have heard, Bill Murray's speech at a memorial gathering of her close friends was a masterpiece of death-defying indecorum.) In 1989, shortly after her book about struggling against dying appeared, she did die. When you want to call someone up, you should.*

"You know that stoff you find in your eye?" Bushy-haired, outgoing (*bushy-haired! outgoing!* pale words!) TV newsperson Roseanne Roseanadanna extricates from the corner of her eye some of that strange, crusty matter—that stuff that we all have known intimately, which our mothers may have referred to as "sleepy dust," but which we have never really faced up to the dubious mystery of, and which we never expected to hear mentioned on *national television* . . .

Roseanne looks at this stuff, makes a luminous face of distasteful fascination, and exclaims: "You look at it and you say, 'What *is* this? This stoff came outta *me*!?' And you hold it between your fingers and you roll*llll* it around, and roll*llll* it around, and you think, 'What amma gonna *do* with this? Where amma gonna *put* it?' And you roll*llll* it around and roll*llll* it. . . . And then it don't matter what you do with it. It's *gone*."

Before I made Gilda Radner's acquaintance, I doubted it would be too good an idea to roll around and roll around whatever stuff it is that comes out of her when she becomes Roseanne—and Emily Litella, Judy Miller, Rhonda Weiss, Lisa Loopner, Baba Wawa and all kinds of other awful but peculiarly fetching characters on *Saturday Night Live.* I was afraid Gilda would be less redoubtable than her characters, that she would be neurotic, mostly, and would let slip that she is so funny because she used to be fat and has never gotten over it (I got this impression from research); and then she would run and throw up; and there we would be—she explicated, I brought down.

But no. Fat is a factor, and Gilda is a waif, but her stuff will stand some rolling around.

She is walking down Sixth Avenue in her strange tip-tip-tip . . . tip-tip . . . tip . . . tip-tip-tip teeter-wobbling fool's-progress manner, which is accentuated by high heels and tight Levi's. She has just left a place where some of her oldest friends in New York can be found: her dentist's office. Many a time she has sobbingly confided her non-dental problems to Dr. Paul Scheier (who on request will do Swedish-dentist and Indian-dentist dialect) and his assistants. And once, after Dr. Scheier had temporarily removed her many caps, she ran outside on Central Park South wearing her drool bib, flashing her tooth stumps and holding two of those absorbent cotton cylinders in her mouth like fangs, and banged on his ground-floor window, and cried in a demented voice, "Give me my teeth! Give me my teeth!"

But before we go on, let me just summarize briefly what Gilda Radner looks like in person going down the avenue:

(a) all of her characters

(b) a fresh-faced, young, good-looking woman

(c) a regular, more-than-ordinarily sympathetic person you would have no reservations about going up to on the street and asking if you had some spinach caught in your teeth, or something, if you had to know

(d) a second grader who (1) has just been told she can have a puppy, and is pleased as pie and (2) has just been told that her puppy won't live, and she can't understand why.

She squints a lot and has a scratchy voice and she chews: "I'm on gum. Sugarless, a whole pack. And if I can chew all this sugarless, I can throw in one stick of sugared. I have very bad teeth," she adds. "It's something about the saliva in my mouth. . . ."

"Hey Gilda!" "Hey Roseanne!" young persons along the avenue are shouting. She responds nicely, not as a star, but as a fellow young

New York pedestrian who *happens to be* a star. And sometimes celebrity can be a nuisance.

"I've had people get mad at me when they see me on the street. Like, 'What are you doing out here?' They're going, like, 'Oh, a star,' but with resentment. Kids come screaming after me down the street, and I tend to forget—you know, I'm on my way home or just going for cigarettes, just doing my life? And they all want autographs, and I say, 'Isn't it enough that you *saw* me?' I mean, I'm ambitious, I'm greedy for attention . . . , but, isn't it enough that they *saw* me?

"I'm a big starer. I went to read for that movie *Girl Friends,* and while I was waiting there was this girl who had on this Marimekko print dress that matched the color of her tights *exactly,* and she had the biggest tits I ever *saw,* and I stared at her so long I didn't get prepared to read and I gave this terrible . . . I just murmured the lines.

"And now everybody stares at *me.* When you take away a comedian's opportunity to observe . . .

"But I don't understand people who say they can't be funny in real life because it would use stuff up. That's like saying you can't write but so many songs because there's only so many notes. I can always make that choice—I mean, when somebody comes home and asks what went wrong today, I can either tell him the truth, you know, I'm depressed, I'm . . . Or I can say, 'Well, the maid had jury duty and couldn't come in today and her brother-in-law from North Carolina came instead. . . .' You know, and make up stuff. Making that choice. Because I have lots of energy.

"I saw Woody Allen at a party, and I couldn't *stand* it, because he was just standing there, not talking to anybody, and I don't know him but I love what he does so much, and I went up to him and *pushed him in the chest.*

"And it was awful. Because *he didn't like it.* He didn't say anything. . . . And I said to people who knew him, *please,* tell him I was just . . . And he probably—the terrible thing, he probably didn't even notice. You know what I mean? I say 'You know what I mean?' a lot.

"But . . . Sometimes . . . One morning I changed clothes eight hundred times, I really did, I really wanted to look attractive. I really wanted to look sexy. And I went out and a guy went by in a truck and yelled, *'Hey. You're funny.' "*

She makes a pained face. "Hey Gilda, why do you walk funny?" asks this young guy who comes up behind us.

"I have a very uncertain walk," she says. "But that's all right. So does my brother; he's in real estate. Hey, you walk pretty funny yourself," she says to this guy.

"Yeah, I'm in the *Guinness Book of World Records* for it," he says. "I walked like this all the way from Hartford." And he disappears, walking that way, into the distance.

"Hey," she says. "That wasn't bad."

GILDA GREW UP in a comfortable suburb of Detroit, the well-loved daughter of a man who did so well in real estate and investments that she inherited serious wealth herself, I am told, when she turned twenty-one. Her father dreamed of being a song-and-dance man and took Gilda to Broadway shows, and he died, of a brain tumor, after years of just lying there, when she was fourteen. She has never gotten over it and doesn't like to talk about it. Her mother was a frustrated ballet dancer and a great beauty who gave Gilda the impression that she might have been expected to be more beautiful herself. For one thing, Gilda was a fat girl. She went to girls' schools and camps where she was the funny fat girl with a heart of gold.

At the University of Michigan in the late Sixties, she worked in theater and avoided politics. "My friends would try to get me into things and I'd say no, I have to do this play. In fact I moved to Canada when pepper gas came through the window."

She lived with a sculptor in Canada, trying to be a homemaker, but it didn't work out. Many boyfriends have come and gone, including actor Peter Firth and fellow *Saturday Night* star Bill Murray. "I don't know whether it's me . . . sometimes, or it's them. . . ." She doesn't like to talk about it. But she keeps saying she wants to be a wife and mother. "And pretty soon I'll be over thirty-five and I'll have to find a man who's willing to father my mongoloid children."

She got into comedy professionally with Toronto's Second City improvisational troupe, then the *National Lampoon Radio Hour* and in 1974, the *National Lampoon Show* onstage.

"In London, Ontario," says Bill Murray, "we were supposed to do the show twice a night to two different audiences. But there was only one audience's worth of people in the whole town. And they hated us. But one night, all of a sudden as we turned around, we heard this cackling. This girl in front was laughing! And we looked out and it was Gilda. She had sneaked away from us and down into the audience. And we realized that if *we* were watching us, we'd be funny. She gave us the will to go on against this nasty, ugly crowd.

"In New York we did the show to a really hostile crowd. Came to curse at the actors. Gilda was great. She did 'Rhoda Tyler Moore,' playing a blind girl trying to make it in New York. John Belushi was her boyfriend, and he'd change his voice and pretend to be these thugs hitting her. Beating her, cuffing her around on the stage. Then he'd change back to the boyfriend's voice and pretend to be saving her from the thugs. Then he'd pretend to be a big dog humping her, and then he'd chase the dog off. . . . It was really funny, and she'd die with this wonderful blind face, this wonderful smile. She'd run, with a cane, full speed into this wall. To get a laugh. She was covered with bruises. You had to admire her."

By this time she was thinner. Lorne Michaels was forming *Saturday Night Live,* and he hired her without an audition. "I had known Gilda in Toronto and thought she was real special," says Michaels. "She was the first person I picked for the cast. At first, she said, 'I don't do characters,' and I said, 'Well, I don't do windows.' Now I think she's right there between Charlie Chaplin and Lucy—and I don't mean to say she's got one foot in the grave."

"She's probably the best physical comedienne ever," says *Saturday Night* writer Marilyn Miller. "She can do literally anything. Doing the 'Judy Miller Show,' she fell off the bed and smashed her ribs up and kept going."

The "Judy Miller Show," scripts by Marilyn Miller, is a running *Saturday Night* feature wherein Gilda, in a Brownie suit, is acting out in her bedroom a major one-person entertainment. No jokes, just this eerie re-creation of a five-year-old disporting herself, murmuring, "and then I go . . ." and "ta-da-ta-daaa," and sort of singing and sort of dancing, all alone.

"Gilda is very much in touch with her child self," says Miller.

"Yeah, sometimes almost too much," says Gilda. "When I'm doing Judy Miller, it's amazing how my mind clears away. I have to just completely forget about whether people are looking up my skirt, and just flop around and be five."

A skinny five. "Funny is the thin side of being fat," says Miller, who, like nearly all of *Saturday Night*'s women writers and performers, used to be fat and constantly worries about being fat again. "If you've ever been heavy, there's always a fat person standing behind you saying, 'You're fat, you're fat.'

"I wrote a song for the show, 'Goodbye Saccharin,' when it looked like saccharin was going to be taken off the market. That was written by me in utter panic. And sung by Gilda, as Rhonda Weiss, in the same way. Linda Ronstadt heard we were going to do it and volunteered to sing backup because the subject was so close to her heart. Even

Laraine Newman, who's eighty-three pounds, holds the tops of her thighs and says, 'Ewwww, *jodhpurs.*'

"As girls, we were all fat and loud. If you can talk real loud, maybe people won't notice you're fat. It's like one side of the world is thin and attractive and the other side is fat, loud, and funny. We look toward a new world where everyone can be thin, attractive, fairly loud, and rather amusing."

Gilda even seems to prefer her *material* thin. "The worse the material is, the better she does," says Murray. "She's really fearless with stuff. We sent her out there as Howdy Doody's wife, Debbie Doody. That was it: just being Mrs. Howdy Doody with some strings hanging off her. *Deadly.* And she was *great.*"

Gilda has gotten thinner and thinner—to the point now of fashion-model skinny—and more and more prominent. Since the departure of Chevy Chase, she and Belushi have become *Saturday Night*'s best-known regulars. It's to the point now that she is getting movie and TV-special offers and is recording her own comedy album. On her album cover, she says earnestly, she wants to look like Donna Summer.

"SOMEBODY SENT ME a toenail, okay? In the mail." She is sitting at her desk—she has a desk—at NBC. The toenail was a response to the Roseanne routine in which she talked about toes—"you know how your baby toe looks like a canoe, and . . ."

On her desk is *Julie Eisenhower's Favorite Stories,* selected from *Jack and Jill* and other children's magazines. But what Gilda is looking at is *TV Guide,* which has just come out with her on the cover. "I'll be like a coaster in millions of homes of America. All week, people will be putting their beer on my face."

Another thing that has just come in is a new comic book in which Gilda and the rest of the *Saturday Night* cast are rescued from terrorists by Spiderman. "Hey, I don't even look Jewish as a cartoon. I look like kind of a neat girl with big tits!

"When I started out in the show, I told Lorne, 'Every character I do is going to be this Jewish girl from Detroit. I don't do dialects; they all come out like Swedish.'"

But one day she and her friend and co-star Jane Curtin "were fooling around," and Emily Litella came out. Emily was based on a woman named Dibby who took care of Gilda when she was a girl. Emily, supposedly responding to Jane Curtin's editorial, would go on at great length demanding to know why people were making such a fuss over, say, "Soviet jewelry," until someone would break in to tell her that it was "Soviet Jewry."

"Oh," she would, of course, say, "Never miynd." A great sound in that "miynd." The *wangy,* ratchety tones of Gilda's characters linger earphone-deep. Who of her fans cannot summon immediately in his mind's ear the last note of Roseanne's recurrent exclamation, "Ah thawt ah would *dah.*"

But the Roseanadannaism Gilda thought would prove most catchy is what Roseanne says her father always used to say to her: "He used to say, 'You know, mah little Roseanne Roseanadanna, it's *alllll-*ways *som*thin.' " That is what Gilda's father always used to say to her.

Gilda's characters have a wonderful imperviousness. Especially Roseanne. Writer Rosie Shuster got Roseanne started in a "Hire the Incompetent" bit—Gilda was the blithe, overwhelming, bewigged incompetent talking about making hamburgers, and you know how sometimes an armpit hair will get into the patty?

After that, Roseanne became one of the "Weekly Update" newscasters, but somehow her reports always swung around to some new bodily grossness. Gilda and writer Alan Zweibel work out the Roseanne skits together, often over lunch, so that facial-sore references and phrases like "rectal eclipse" mingle in with their sandwiches.

I always assumed that Roseanne's name, at least, came from Roseann Scamardella, the unWASPy coanchorperson on New York's Channel 7 news, and rumor has it that Scamardella was recently given a raise because she had become identifiable to the point of Roseannadannafication. (When I caught her on TV the other night she was saying, "Amid the rats, dead cats, garbage and feces . . .") But Gilda says the name grew out of "The Name Game," a favorite song of hers whose refrain goes "Bannana-banna-bofanna," and that she developed Roseanne as an antidote to "all these women reporting the news on TV; they always look like they're so frightened to lose their job. You know they're saying, 'We're women and we have credibility to report the news, we don't go number two, we don't fart'—they're like these perfect . . . And Roseanne, she's a *pig.* Under the table she's wearing the highest pair of heels and white socks, she's Jewish/Italian/Puerto Rican. . . ."

And she is nice. She has a magnetism. She accepts her body. Gilda's characters are people you enjoy knowing.

"Yes," says Gilda, "I'm always there. I'm thirty-two years old. I like people. I like my job. That person who loves doing it is always in there. And I don't want you to miss the joke. I'm in there taking care of you while I'm doing the job."

She says that Michael O'Donoghue—the *Saturday Night* writer and occasional performer whose quintessential bit was his portrayal, with the assistance of backup singers, of Tony Orlando and Dawn having their eyes put out with red-hot needles—"gets on me for being cute. He says it's all right now, and it'll be all right when I'm old, but when I'm middle-aged, it won't work."

Saturday Night Live might tip too far toward the mean and spacy, however, without Gilda's niceness. Her "Baba Wawa" takeoff on Barbara Walters, though biting, is hardly nasty. Baba has such a presence, even if she does say "weewee" instead of "really."

Gilda put Baba's voice and mannerisms together not by studying Walters directly, but by asking other people, "What does she do?"— focusing on "the things that stand out about her for other people. One time I saw her at a party. I went up to her and said, 'I'm the girl who does you on TV.'

"And you know, she's very tiny—but very tough; she's on top of everything. She took me over into the corner and said, 'Okay, what do you do?' And I did some Baba Wawa and she watched, saying, 'uh-huh, uh-huh,' you know, and, 'Yeah, I'm working on my *ehw*'s and *ahw*'s.'"

Saturday Night Live is right down Gilda's alley, and its personnel are, to a great extent, her family. During the *Saturday Night* season, Gilda is around the studio all week and all hours, studying the camera blocking, helping writers work things out, making people rehearse with her, bringing them into her personal crises (once she put a notice on the bulletin board: "Lorne: I'm happy"). When she goes home, she sleeps with her phone in the bed so she's ready when a writer calls up in the middle of the night to tell her he's figured out a line.

But even though the show's ratings are great and it has won an Emmy, its people live in some anxiety that each year will be its last. The cast is mindful of the fate of so many old *Laugh-In* stars: occasional daytime-panel shots. "Whenever we do something really cheap in rehearsals," says Gilda, "Lorne starts whistling the *Laugh-In* theme."

Gilda is surely well enough established that she will go on to do her own shows. But if she is to aspire to the level of Lily Tomlin, Gilda will have to develop her independent repertoire further. She is working on that now for her album, with a mind to taking the same material on the college circuit.

"But comedy albums—that's one of the saddest sections in the whole record store. They don't even have fingerprints on them. What I'd like would be for my album to be played in a supermarket—if they would play my album over the PA system and people would shop to it."

She could see getting into movies, but so far her only film role has been a bit part in *The Last Detail.* She appeared, plumply, in a scene where a group is chanting a mantra and meditating and talking things out. She was supposed to stand up and say something about a breakthrough she had made in playing the clarinet. But by the time the cameras started rolling she had come to like the Nichiren Shoshu group so much that she arose and gave a testimonial to the chanters' supportiveness.

"So finally the group chanted that I would remember my lines, and I did."

Her first love, she says, is the stage. Two summers ago she appeared at the Berkshire Festival in *Broadway,* a play starring William Atherton and Chris Sarandon. "I was enjoying their acting so much I was just leaning back being lazy, thrilled that I was getting to be an ingénue with them."

"She was camping it up," says a prominent critic who caught her performance.

Gilda says: "After he saw the show, Lorne told me, 'Don't you ever embarrass me like this again.'

"I guess it will come down to doing some kind of television. I grew up in front of a television, I guess I'll grow old inside of one."

"How OLD AM I?" she asks her makeup man.

"Oh . . . , early thirties," he says.

There is a silence.

"I look my age," she says.

"No you don't, no you don't," cry the makeup men and the hairdresser and I.

We are in the dressing room of Francesco Scavullo's studio, where that famous glamour photographer is to shoot her for the cover of *Rolling Stone.*

There are pictures all around the walls: *Cosmopolitan* girls, various eminently glamorous or decadent personalities, Arnold Schwarzenegger naked, a man with a skewer in one cheek and out the other. This man has his mouth open so that you can see the skewer passing through, and he appears to be smiling. There is a small, vaguely shaggy dog running around everywhere. "He's a King Charles spaniel," says a woman who works there. "He's Oliver Twist. Isn't that right, Oliver? You're twisted."

The makeup man and the hairdressing man are devoting over an hour and a half to preparing Gilda for her portrait. She had arrived nearly an hour late, with no makeup on and her hair just washed and floating, looking keyed up and saying, "I think I look ugly today." Now she is having her eyebrows plucked and her hair layered so that it sort of tendrils out exotically in various directions, and her face layered painstakingly but thickly with paint.

"What *is* this?" Roseanne might say about all the different tubes of junk in the makeup man's kit. "This stoff gonna go onto *me*?" But Gilda is avid for glamorization. The idea had been for her to pose as Roseanne, but she insisted on being shot as herself, as beautiful as possible.

The girl her mother wanted. Gilda says she and Laraine Newman have the same kind of mother—beautiful. Their mothers didn't want them to have blemishes. They went into comedy to protect themselves, she says.

"My mother was exactly the same," says the makeup man. "That's what messed me up." He catches a look of himself in the mirror and sighs, "By this time of day I look worse and worse."

"Did you want to be a movie star when you were a little bitty girl?" I ask.

There is a silence.

"Are you talking to me?" Gilda says.

The makeup man and the hair man, who are the only other parties present, smile.

This is the first time I have seen her without her green jacket with the teddy-bear pin on it. She really is skinny. "I saw myself on TV and couldn't stand it, I looked chubby," she says. "So I lost weight, and now people say, 'You look awful'—my arms and everything—but now I look normal on TV." She holds up her arm, which looks underfed, and flexes it, so that it looks anatomical. "I like it! I can see all my muscles and everything."

"Can one of the boys, uh . . . ?" The hairdresser asks a woman who works there, indicating all the hair on the floor. "There aren't any boys," says the woman.

"Here, I can get that for you," says Gilda—only kidding, only kidding, but seemingly the most amenable person around. She wrinkles her brow, forming four horizontal lines. "Draw in those lines and draw on a clef," she suggests.

There's an idea! Let's use all this makeup to bring Gilda's real stuff out! Let's paint a pointedly exaggerated but still amicable smile on her mouth and that musical-worry design on her forehead and a well-earned bruise on her chin.

Or let's step back and let her move into some kind of makeup freak character, who cries, "More! More! I can still see my nose! I hate my nose! Cover up my nose! Do something with my tongue! Here, let me eat some of that! Pour it down my neckline! Eyes! More on the eyes! *I want more languorous eyes!*"

But Gilda says she hasn't "reached the point where I can tell people what to do yet," and anyway, she is not going to pass up a chance to look divine. Like a cute little car with a lot of chrome on the front, she enters an all-white room and lies on the floor, and Scavullo shoots and shoots.

WE GO TO dinner. She eats her own four courses and portions of my last two. I tell her people want to know how she lost weight. I have heard that one thing she does is eat and then throw up. She hasn't been looking forward to this question. "Here it is: I had a cyst removed from an ovary and lost ten pounds and kept them off. So tell everyone: chew a lot of gum and have major surgery. And I do jumping jacks. And pretend I'm jumping rope. If you use a rope, you miss and it breaks the flow. I put on records and dance."

Roseanne might be more forthcoming. But Gilda is intent upon keeping some stuff private. "I want people to like me," she says, "But the more people who like you, you realize how you want just a few people to like you. Who you can phone. Having the world love you is not gratifying. Because you don't know their phone numbers.

"They all applaud, but none of them will come home with you and look at your back someplace to see if you have a pimple.

"Show business is an opportunity to pretend. And to get scared. And to not be mediocre. Get everybody to look at you. And you get to make people feel stuff, you know. I've got to work just as hard at that with one person as I would with forty million people.

"I'd get real scared if it started being *only* for forty million people." She looks real scared.

"I have a boyfriend now who's an actor, who I'm going to see tonight after his show. Wait . . . I'd better make a phone call to see if . . ." She begins to rise. "No," she sits back down, "it's all right. I do have a boyfriend."

Even Roseanne makes Gilda uneasy. "People want to peg you," she says. "I don't care if I ever do Roseanne again. I'd rather force myself to come up with someone new."

When I ask her about the disadvantages of being a woman in her line of work, she rolls earnestly into a girl-power statement: "When I was a little girl, I said, 'Gilda, are you glad you're a girl or do you wish you were a boy?' I said, 'Boys have to go in the army, get in mud, wear heavy stuff, and kill people.'

"I love being a woman. You can cry. You get to wear pants now. You can *always* sit and think when you go to the bathroom. If you're on a boat and it's going to sink, you get to go on the rescue boat first. You get to wear cute clothes. It must be a great thing, or so many men wouldn't be wanting to do it now.

"One great thing about not being superior, you get to change yourself. Wear high-heel shoes, make yourself taller, put makeup on.

"And you get to give up.

"That's all."

However all this stuff may look in print, on hearing it I wanted to adopt her, order her another meal, buy her beautiful fuzzy bathroom slippers. What I did was blurt out, *"Gilda, I thought you looked pretty when you came in, before they put all that makeup on."*

She makes an I-could-just-cry-except-it-would-seem-maudlin-in-the-story face.

"Bill Murray says you would run head-on into a wall, being a blind girl," I say.

"Yeah," she says. "I'd throw myself into it. *I don't want to die.* I have a real strong will not to bomb. I want to do the job well, not waste anybody's time on the job, not waste anybody's time who's watching. And not jerk off."

After dinner she leaves in a cab, looking worked up, and I stand there on suddenly less intense Second Avenue, reflecting that I would like to see her run at a wall sometime and it would dissolve and she would go right through it and sail off to some better place where blemishes are jewels, weight is immaterial, *Saturday Night* is immortal, and she is loved duly by the right number of people.

I reflect that, but I don't really mean it. I want to see her bounce.

NANCY IS HERSELF

I can't remember ever being unaware of Nancy, or ever knowing what to make of her. And yet, how can you *not* know what to make of Nancy? (I mean the late Ernie Bushmiller's Nancy, not the regrettable, decadent, Nancyesque strip that runs in newspapers today.)

My friend Vereen Bell and I once had a long conversation about the rocks in Nancy. Those bland hemispheres, halfway out of the earth. Vereen is the author of *Robert Lowell: Nihilist as Hero.* I say we had a long conversation about them, those rocks, but now that I think about it, we didn't.

What we did was, Vereen said: "Those *rocks.*"

"Yes," I said. "Yes."

And then we just sat there for a long time.

The less said about Nancy the better, probably. And yet.

There is a poem by Gertrude Stein:

> I am Rose,
> My eyes are blue.
> I am Rose,
> And who are you?
> I am Rose, and when I sing,
> I am Rose like anything.

Nancy is simpler than this. Nancy doesn't care who we are, and she need not sing. The very idea of Nancy singing. . . . The very idea of Nancy doing anything is almost incredible—almost, in fact, monstrous. However, we know that Nancy does do things, and knowing this, we go on doing things ourselves: dreaming, blowing bubbles, visiting museums. Nancy has done all these things before, and done them more definitively.

There is nothing more obvious than Nancy, and yet when we think about her, if by some chance we do, it is hard to get her in focus.

She seems to be scarcely over toddler-sized, in relation to adults and doorknobs, and yet she reads books, has crushes, and goes places by herself. (The children in Henry James are also anomalous.) Her skirt length, it would appear, could be spanned by her opened hand, and yet when her friend Janie says "We're supposed to wear a dress that matches our boyfriend's hair," Nancy pictures Sluggo's baby-bottom baldness and she blushes, perspires, and says "WOW."

We can imagine what the characters in *Peanuts* or *Dick Tracy* would be like in real life. But Nancy?

Would she be like the eleven-year-old girl of Negaunee, Michigan, who in 1989 twice traveled to Panama to visit her pen pal, General Manuel Antonio Noriega, who called her a "meritorious daughter" of Panama and an example of "the truth of the United States, purity not hatred"? That girl, for her part, observed that Noriega was "very nice" and that she did not believe "the bad things papers in the United States say about him."

"If it was my daughter, she wouldn't be going," averred a Negaunee councilwoman, and the girl's congressman took this position: "To have one of our little citizens go down there and be treated well is kind of an embarrassment for our government."

Well, there is no doubt that Nancy embodies a kind of purity. And if by any chance she were to become involved in international relations, she might well do or say things that the United States government would have a hard time explaining. But to picture Noriega and Nancy together is impossible. The two may share, and derive strength from, a kind of taking-oneself-as-one-finds-oneself disposition; but Noriega next to Nancy is indistinct, transitory.

Noriega may delight in disorder, for dictatorial reasons, but one way or another he crumbles in the end. Nancy will always love to spin on the piano stool, although it leaves her feeling awful.

Noriega grows old. Nancy grows or shrinks only in passing. In dreams. And when she is splashed by reducing cream, in one open-ended (and itself shrunken) concluding panel.

And in funhouse mirrors.

Nancy walking toward the carnival is one together little girl. That pleased little line that is her mouth is by no means forced. In the next panel we see her from an angle that conceals all her features, but we know she still has that look. (Over her head is a small, benign cloud.) Then in a series of mirrors she sees herself misshapen in many ways. "I love to come to this place," she says, and we (including Nancy) see her smile reflected in a distortion of herself. And then she gets up onto a box to see herself in a straight candy-machine mirror and she says, "I always feel so GORGEOUS when I come out."

Which would be sad, if she weren't so comfortable in her own skin to begin with. She is startled out of her composure often, but never for long. In that, she is a kind of ideal child. (Compare Calvin of *Calvin and Hobbes.*)

My daughter Ennis, who is twenty-three and works with abused or otherwise impaired children in San Francisco, was dozing on her couch when the October 17, 1989, earthquake hit. She thought she was having a dream. Then she realized what was happening—if "realized" is a word that can be used in connection with what happens during an earthquake. She knew that she was supposed to go to the nearest doorway, but when she looked at the nearest doorway, as she recalls it, it was changing back and forth between rectangular and triangular. She ran outside, as did most of the other people in her neighborhood. Down the exact middle of the street was a line of dogs and cats.

Very like a Nancy strip. But Ennis and her friends (and, vicariously, her father) were still bent slightly out of shape months later.

The pavement and the high-rise slabs had shuddered like people and rippled like flags. Even that jewel of the mind, the baseball diamond, had been thrown out of whack temporarily—*during the World Series*—and (as sportswriters were still complaining months later) residually.

Nancy's kilter persists. The gags that engage her may seem to be beneath us, but they always challenge *her* sense of things, and she always snaps back. And we are comforted.

When Ennis went out into the street she saw a crowd of people gathered around a girl about eight years old. Ennis went to see what was going on. The girl had torn out the page in the telephone book that tells you what to do in an earthquake, and she was reading it aloud.

I asked Ennis if she thought the girl's parents had given her this task to keep her from being afraid.

"No," she said. "I think she was just one of those little smart kids who always have to know everything."

I don't think we would call Nancy one of those kids. Yet she knows what she knows.

There is a poem by Marvin Bell that includes this line: *I, or someone like me, had a kind of vision.*

There is no one *like* Nancy. So it must be she, sheerly, who is having the visions—nightmares, misapprehensions, ideas—in this book. Lord knows they don't seem like anything a grown man would have. But to say that is not to sell them, or Ernie Bushmiller, short.

COULDN'T USE
THEM
IN A GAME

World's Greatest (doubtless only) Freak Shot Expert Wilfred Hetzel, who was discharged from the Army in 1943 "for nervousness," is nervous now. In the assembly program at Ladysmith (Virginia) High School this morning, the kids were restless, and his performance ragged. True, he hit over 70 percent of his gallimaufry of shots—with eyes shut, with legs crossed, with legs downright entwined, on the bounce off the floor, from one foot, from one knee, from both knees, from behind the backboard (frontward and backward), from up on his toes, from back on his heels (toes in the air) and in various combinations of the above. The kids responded with a gleeful shout, as he says they almost always do, to his "goofy series," in which he suddenly assumes a fey, exaggeratedly knock-kneed or bowlegged stance and then lets fly.

But the days of his sixty-foot and seventy-foot peg shots, which he used to make off ceilings or over rafters or simply from one end of the court to the other, are gone. Now, fifty-eight years old and weakened by an operation for TB, the man who bills himself as "Thrice Featured in *Believe It or Not* and Twice in *Strange as It Seems*" can shoot the ball only underhanded (except on his bounce shots) and seldom from farther out than the foul line. And in fourteen tries at Ladysmith, his eighteen-foot dropkick, his most spectacular remaining shot, was in and out once but never quite swished. The kids cheered frequently and came up for autographs afterward but, as Hetzel says, "If I can't impress them as the *best*—well, that's the point."

Now, sitting in the boys' dressing room of Louisa County High School in Mineral, Virginia, thirty miles from Ladysmith, he is shaking, and drinking his fifth cup of coffee to counteract "spots of fatigue." He got only four hours of sleep last night because the pills he has been taking for his sciatica since 1949 keep him awake in spite of Sominex. The principal of this just-integrated 580-pupil school has consented to move Mr. Hetzel's performance up from 2:30 to 1:00 so he won't have to sit around getting tenser.

"Nothing terrifies me more," Hetzel says, "than for the ball to be falling just short by inches—because these students don't know, they don't realize the handicaps. And then maybe some of the students start laughing, and I try harder. What some people can't understand is that I'm governed by averages, too."

He is stooped. He is gaunt. His crew-cut hair is white.

He sheds his traveling clothes, gray suit and greenish tie, revealing himself in the maroon shorts, the gold sleeveless undershirt lettered WILFRED HETZEL on the front and FREAK SHOT SPECIALIST on the back, the worn black-top shoes and the straggly strips of tape on his knees (kneepads shift too much when he kneels to shoot) that constitute his working uniform. He has worn this outfit underneath his clothes on the road since 1962; he had read that Esther Williams kept her bathing suit on underneath for quick changes during her appearance tours. Distractedly, Hetzel proceeds to the gym and takes a few practice shots as the kids file in. Then he presents himself and relates, in an absorbed, recitative voice, a brief history of his involvement in freak shooting.

Not the comprehensive history, because he hasn't the time. If he were to include all the material he is more than happy to bring forth in conversation, he would go back to 1924, when, in Melrose, Minnesota, at the age of twelve, he nailed a barrel hoop to the side of the family woodshed and took his first shot. If you start counting then, Hetzel has said, "and if you include all the times with a baseball, a kittenball, a soccer ball, a rag ball, some socks tied together in the form of a ball, a tennis ball, a football—I had to learn to shoot the football end over end so that it would nose down at just the right moment and pass through that small hoop"—if you count all those shots, along with the thirty thousand hours he estimates he has spent shooting a regulation basketball through a real basket, says Hetzel—"I have probably shot more goals than any man in history."

In his backyard there by the woodshed he shot them year-round, in rain, snow, in tricky gusts of wind ("It was a thrill to have the wind pick up the ball and blow it six or seven feet through the hoop") and in temperatures down to twenty below. He pretended he was the University of Minnesota and also its opponents, which meant, since he did his best for both sides, that Minnesota lost half the time. He would plan out a complete schedule in advance, but when the Gophers had lost too many games to hope for a Big Ten crown, he would start over. When he tells audiences this, Hetzel says, it gives the coaches present a good laugh "because they wish they could start a season over. Of course, it's so much easier the way I do it, all make-believe."

The first time young Wilfred tried shooting with a real basketball, "it went straight, three feet under the basket, like a pass."

"Gee whiz," remarked an unkind neighborhood boy who was watching, "if I couldn't do any better than that, I'd quit."

"He was one of those boys," recalls Hetzel, "who move away a few years later, and you don't know what happened to them." One of those boys, in other words, who do not go on to become the world's greatest anything.

Somewhat later, Wilfred started doing a little shooting in the local gym—but it wasn't easy. "There were some boys there, after school, who were good at clever fakery, dribbling, passing and that, and they would hog the ball. I might have to wait two hours, from 3:30 to 5:30, until they went home and I could get in five minutes of shooting before the janitor locked the ball up. Or maybe he would lock it up as soon as they quit. I'd think nothing later of shooting five thousand times, because I'd been deprived of it for so long."

There was no question of Hetzel's going after one of those clever-faking boys one-on-one and taking the ball away, because ball handling has never been his forte. It has never been even a part of his portfolio. The truth is that Wilfred Hetzel, who has made 144 straight foul shots standing on one foot, who bills himself as "One of Basketball's Immortals," has never learned to dribble.

"I realized I would never be good at the game one day in PT class when I was a freshman in high school," he says now. "We were supposed to do what they called a figure-eight drill. I'd be a forward, and the center would pass it to me, and I would pass it to the other forward and then I wouldn't know where to go. They never explained it to me in detail, never diagramed it or anything. After I fouled it up twice, I knew I'd never play. I was too slow and kind of awkward in other ways."

Hetzel did serve the high school team briefly as a scrub, and "I made a few shots against the first team, and I'd pass it pretty well, but I never did dribble. And I'd be open for a shot and very seldom would anyone pass it to me. There were cliques on the team—they'd pass it to their friends."

He got into one unofficial game against a local telephone-company team, didn't shoot, and committed two technical fouls by neglecting to check in with the timekeeper each time he went in. The year before, his uniform was stolen twice. He decided to quit organized basketball forever (except for a brief exhibition game appearance with Western

Union College in Le Mars, Iowa, many years later, when he was inserted to shoot two foul shots and hit one).

In fact, young Wilfred found that he had no great knack for any competitive sport. In baseball he could hit fungoes with precision and catch fly balls gloveless in his big, long-fingered hands, but he was too slow to play the outfield and couldn't get the bat around fast enough to hit pitching.

But that just meant more time for shooting basketballs by himself every day, including the day his father, a Bavarian immigrant and railroad man, was killed. The water tank for which the elder Hetzel was responsible was out of order, and evidently he went up to its rim to investigate. No one saw him fall in through the layer of ice, but when sixteen-year-old Wilfred came in for lunch, his father's hamburger was overcooking on the stove. Finally Mrs. Hetzel took it off. "The ice froze back over," as Hetzel tells it, "and they had to get special permission from division headquarters to go in and see if he was there. And he was."

It is easy enough to see a fateful symbolism in the mode of the father's death—the son doomed to act it out with a basketball over and over again—but Hetzel says he has never seen any irony in it. By the time his father died, at any rate, he had already devoted hundreds of hours to what was to become his vocation.

Pretty soon Hetzel was making ninety-eight out of a hundred from the free-throw line. But he never had any witnesses, "and people thought if I really had a talent like that I would be on the team." So one day, as a high-school senior, he put on an impromptu lunch-hour exhibition in the school gym. That was his first show, in 1929. "I've thought about writing Ed Sullivan," he says, "and saying they're all talking so much about the sports stars of the Golden Twenties—Red Grange and so on—and here I am, out of the Twenties and still performing."

But in those early days he had no tricks, just free throws, performed at no charge. Upon graduation from high school he moved with his mother, who had remarried, to nearby Sauk Centre, Minnesota, and began to do some sportswriting for local daily and weekly papers. In the line of duty, he would attend Sauk Centre games, and while the players were dressing he would seize the opportunity to take the floor in his street clothes and shoot before a crowd. He went so far as to write himself up in one of the papers, in the third person: "Wilfred Hetzel of Sauk Centre, in a recent practice session, hit 467 free throws out of 500."

Meanwhile, the local team was doing well to hit 40 percent from the foul line—and he reported that, too. "The fans in Sauk Centre were so hateful to me in those years," he says. "Maybe it was my fault because I slammed their team in the paper. Maybe I was like a prima donna. But once I made 120 of 122 before a game, 82 straight, and I walked off the floor, and there wasn't a single handclap. But you know, they've never had a bad team since? It kind of woke them up when I slammed them."

And then one night, in the visiting cheering section, someone woke up to Wilfred Hetzel. "This very beautiful girl came down and made such a fuss about me," he recalls. "The home people never made any fuss. The principal's son would take a couple of shots before throwing my ball back to me, and they would laugh at my embarrassment. But this beautiful girl raved about how good I was. Well, the next night Sauk Centre was to play at that girl's school, and I planned to ride with the team over there in hopes of seeing her again. But at the last minute they took only one car and didn't have room for me.

"So, rather than waste the day, I got in through the window of the gym in Melrose and practiced. I'd make seventeen in a row several times, and then I'd miss. I got disgusted. 'I could do better than this with my eyes closed,' I told myself. So I just tried it that way. I shot a hundred with my eyes closed and made seventy-four. That was my first trick. I never did see that girl again."

Gradually Hetzel's reputation spread, and he was able to talk several area schools into letting him put on a free-throw show before a game or at the half. The Depression bore down, and he couldn't find much work, so he lived at home and kept on practicing his shots. When he was twenty he tired of pretending he was the University of Minnesota and began to work more on variety. He practiced for seven or eight years. After a few fans complained that free throws tended to grow monotonous, and after he lost a free-throw contest to an expert named Bunny Levitt who was traveling with the Harlem Globetrotters, he introduced his eyes-shut trick and a couple of other "unorthodox shots" to the public.

In 1937 Hetzel enrolled in the University of Minnesota and was able to work out in the gym and book himself, occasionally for a two-dollar or five-dollar honorarium, into shows at high schools, colleges and military bases throughout the state and beyond. He hitchhiked from place to place, persuaded sixty businesses in Sauk Centre to chip in on a sweat suit with SAUK CENTRE, MINNESOTA on the front and WILFRED HETZEL, STUNT SHOT SPECIALIST on the back, and it was not long before he was popping up in *Ripley's Believe It or Not* and in *Strange as It Seems*. "Wilfred Hetzel, Minneapolis Basketball Star, Shot 92 Baskets Out of

100 Tries with One Hand, Standing on One Leg and Blindfolded!" right alongside "Mrs. M. J. Wellman, Oklahoma City, Has Worn the Same Set of False Teeth for 45 Years." "Wilfred Hetzel Shot 66 Straight Basketball Foul Shots from His Knees!" right alongside "Musical Teeth! For 4 Months After Having Dental Work Done, Mrs. Fred Stutz, Indianapolis, *Could Hear Radio Programs Without Having the Radio Turned On!* Her *Teeth* Formed a Receiving Set!"

Then, in the early forties, after he mastered the long peg shot and the dropkick, Hetzel's career reached its fullest flower. In those years, aside from ten months in the army during which he experienced severe trouble with his teeth (not involving radio reception) as well as with his nerves, he spent September through May traveling the country, performing for around twenty-five dollars a show, sometimes four or five times in a day. In 1941 he appeared at the Clair Bee Coaching Clinic at Manhattan Beach, New York, and was invited by Ned Irish to perform in a clown suit in Madison Square Garden, but that latter deal, to Hetzel's great regret, fell through. In the 1943–44 and '44–45 seasons alone, he traveled forty-two thousand miles, passed through forty-seven states and performed over 150 times. He remembers all his best performances from this heyday in detail, especially the ones in Oklahoma. "I've done an extraordinary amount of spectacular things there," he says. "In Davis, Oklahoma, on February 29, 1944—which I remember because I thought at the time, 'This is an unusual day, it comes along once in four years, I wonder what feat I'll accomplish that will make me remember this day?'—I hit forty-foot, fifty-foot and seventy-foot shots, all on the first try. All straight through. In fact, I lost the thrill of the seventy-footer because the netting moved so barely, I thought at first the ball had just brushed it underneath. In Okmulgee, Oklahoma, on a sixty-footer, the ball hit the inside of the rim, bounced way back up diagonally, hit the junction of a rafter and the ceiling, rebounded right back to the goal, bounced around the rim, and went in. That was for a girl's gym class. It was funny, I had told them my superduper was coming up.

"In Miami, Oklahoma, I made a shot over two girders at once that the coach remembered there ten years later. In Jenks, Oklahoma, there was just a narrow opening to throw the ball through to get it over two crossbeams. I tried it eight times before I even got the ball through, and then it missed the basket by a foot. But I've always thanked my lucky stars that I had guts. I kept at it, and on the very next try the ball went through the opening and right down into the basket. Fifty feet. Unbeknown to me, Mickey Mantle was in junior high school in Commerce, just a few miles away, that very year."

During these cross-country tours, Hetzel would book himself for three weeks in advance. As he traveled he would write to other schools, advising them to address their replies to him in care of the school where he would be performing at the end of that period, and when he reached the school he would check his mail and map out another three weeks.

It was a grueling routine, traveling by bus or train at night (he had no car, and anyway he finds that driving impairs his touch), often getting too little sleep, lugging around his two bags (one containing clothes and the other his ball and pump), casting about in each town for a room "in some respectable place," struggling through snowstorms so as not to miss a date.

Albuquerque; Dodge City, Kansas; Forest Grove, Oregon; Homer, New York; Ferndale, Michigan; San Luis Obispo, California; Augusta, Georgia; Manassas, Virginia; Muncie, Indiana; Louisville; Leechburg, Pennsylvania; Ogden, Utah; Akron; Morgantown, West Virginia; Hagerstown, Maryland; Maywood, Illinois; Tombstone, Arizona. It was a thorough way of seeing the country, but it paid Hetzel only about enough to keep him going, and the travel took its toll on his health. Not until years later did he realize that he had contracted tuberculosis, which lingered until his operation—the removal of a rib and part of a lung in 1968—but he knew he did not feel up to any more full-time barnstorming, so when he found himself in Washington in the spring of 1945, he decided it was time he got a regular job. In 1942 he had applied for a defense-plant job in Chicago, but "they watched me for a while and then they rejected me. I asked why and they said I didn't have no coordination. Well, if they'd known that coordination was one of the things I was famous for! I've always attributed my success to the three C's—confidence, coordination, and concentration. But then, you can be coordinated in one thing and not in another. I never did learn to dance." This time, in '45, his touch qualified him as a civilian typist for the Marine Corps, a job he holds to this day.

Settling down in Arlington, Virginia, where he lives now as a roomer in a private home, Hetzel kept up his shooting career through the Fifties and Sixties by spacing out his leave time in bits and pieces of two or three days. His job has not paid enough to support a wife—or so he concluded after meeting the woman of his life, a toe dancer, on a bus. He confessed to her in a letter, "I kissed you when you were asleep on the bus," and she confessed in reply, "I wasn't asleep." They saw each other for some time and still exchange letters, but she married someone else. "I guess that's why I've never married," Hetzel says. "I didn't want anyone to replace her."

It was not until 1947 that he started taking off his sweat jacket to shoot—"Before, on account I was so slender, I was afraid there would be more people laughing at me, and the jacket made me feel a little fleshier." The greater freedom of movement helped him to keep up his distance shots; but he made his last seventy-footer in '54, his last thirty-footer in '67. In the Fifties he began to find it hard "to get my pep up," and sometimes when that happened he got "snotty" receptions and reviews. "Those few times when maybe I wasn't in form, no one asked for autographs," he says. "They looked on me as a fake or a cheat or a has-been. I get emotional when I think about the time, in Jeffersonville, Indiana, some people were saying, 'He's not much,' and the coach there stood up and fairly exploded and said, 'I wish I could shoot half as good as that man.' "

In recent years he found that small, out-of-the-way black schools in the South were a fertile field, though once "they were envious—one of the boys came up and asked if I could spin the ball in my hands. I said if I could do those things, I'd have been a Globetrotter. But usually there's no resentment of me because I'm white. Without my saying it, the Negro kids come up to me and say, 'You're better than Alcindor.' Now that don't take no glory from him. He's still one of the greatest centers that ever lived. It's not the same competitive field."

In 1936 Hetzel heard Dr. James Naismith, the inventor of basketball, make a speech. "He said if you're doing something for humanity, don't think about getting a reward now, you'll get it later. I thought then, 'If I don't get a million dollars for it, I'll just enjoy it.' I do envy those football players. You know that commercial: 'Remember, Charley Conerly, such and such a day when you threw three TD passes,' and then they show the replay? I wish that on my best days they'd had TV cameras running. And I wish the people back in Minnesota that hated me and made fun of me and said, 'If there was money in it, somebody would be better at it'—I'd like to get all those people together in one gym and do all the greatest tricks I ever did."

But now, at Louisa County High School in Virginia, his audience is some five hundred rural kids who have been charged twenty-five cents apiece by their student council for the benefit of a Korean orphan. And what Mr. Hetzel is saying now to the kids, in reference to all those doubters back in Minnesota, is "if they'd believed me back there in the beginning, when I tried to tell them I had made ninety-eight out of a hundred, I might not be here now."

And he is advancing, in his gangly yet almost formal walk, to the foul line, where he begins to hit his underhanded shots, blim, blim, blim, coolly, crisply, now cross-legged, now on his toes, now on his heels, missing one occasionally but in command, running through his repertoire, down on his knees, up on one foot, and the kids are paying him mind. Mr. Hetzel's manner of shooting is memorable in many respects, but its most noteworthy feature is that when he releases the ball—even routinely in practice but especially when he knows he is going well—his face is lit by a proud and affectionate smile. The first time Wilfred Hetzel has ever tried a shot from behind a Louisa County backboard, over the crossed wires that raise and lower it, he scores. On his second try at that same shot backward, over his head, he scores. He scores on one more backspin bounce shot from his knees. And now, in closing: the dropkick.

Short. Short. Off to the right. Short. Off to the right. Short. Short. Off the rim. Off the rim. Off to the left. Off the rim. No, way short. A pause before the thirteenth try and then it is up, off the backboard, swish.

"Yaay!" "Aw-*right!*" "Sign him up!"

WHAT IS FUNNY
ABOUT THE
NATIONAL GEOGRAPHIC?

(AN ANALYSIS THAT APPEARED IN THE ONE-HUNDREDTH
ANNIVERSARY ISSUE OF THAT MAGAZINE)

This is an odd question to be exploring *here*. In the *Geographic*. I feel certain that Mr. Baird Orey, the person who had more back issues of the magazine than anyone else I knew when I was a boy, never looked in them for the answer to such a question. When the Oreys would have us over for supper, Mr. Orey would go to his shelf packed full of *Geographic*s and look for the issue where he had once read something, all the details of which he couldn't remember.

"I believe you'll find that the natives of Micronesia live on poles," he would work into the conversation, unexpectedly.

"On poles?"

"Poles—I remember . . ."

He would get up and begin pulling out issues.

"Huts on poles?"

"Not *huts,* so much as—it was in, what year? Look! Here's a two-headed turtle!"

That was the part I liked, when Mr. Orey would start finding things he didn't remember at all.

"This twin-headed turtle," he would read to us aloud, "shows why such freaks, though not uncommon, rarely escape their natural enemies for long: each head controls the two legs on its side."

"Imagine," Mrs. Orey would say.

"Often the right head sounds 'Retreat!' while the left orders an advance. Result: the turtle gets nowhere."

"My stars," Mrs. Orey would say. "Baird . . ."

". . . has a single blood stream, shell, and lower intestine, most other parts are dual. The heads often fight over food and seldom agree on a common objective."

"Whole families just on poles?" my father would say. He liked to get Mr. Orey going. By that I mean he liked to pin Mr. Orey down.

"I think you'll find," said Mr. Orey, moving on from the turtle reluctantly, "that the family structure there is not at all what we . . . Hazel, which issue was it . . . ?"

"I just don't know, Baird. Don't look for it the whole rest of the evening, now, Hon."

But he would keep sneaking looks over there, and my father would say, "I can't see how poles would hold a whole family up. Just poles." And he and Mr. Orey would argue about it without either of them having a clear picture of what they were arguing about. Which certainly wasn't the magazine's fault. Nor was it my father's, as he would not refrain from pointing out. Meanwhile I would be on the floor getting a clear picture of the turtle. I have remembered that turtle for thirty-six years. I was relieved, recently, to discover that I hadn't made it up. I found it in the library by looking through all the issues that came out in 1951 and '52, when I was ten and eleven.

No one I knew back in Georgia when I was that age had ever, except in the army, traveled anywhere farther away than Washington, D. C., which is where *National Geographic* staffers start out from. But we all knew of jungle life, fezzes, desert islands, lumberjacks and igloos, largely from two sources: the *Geographic* and, in other magazines, cartoons.

The cartoonist got it all from the *National Geographic.* I feel certain that no person working for this magazine has ever actually been boiled in a pot—which is perhaps one reason why it has been the source of so much humor. You never saw any boiling-man cartoons in publications my mother received from the Missionary Society.

The *National Geographic* gives off a sense of security. "These fur-hatted Kirghiz admired the way the author packed a yak with diamond hitch, but disliked his boots (too cold, they said). Quolan Larh, who never heard of the U.S., learned to sing 'Oh! Susanna.' "

If someone named Quolan Larh could learn "Oh! Susanna," I could learn about yaks in good humor. Re-perusing those issues of the early fifties has taken me back to my childhood, which was strange (being childhood) but by no means exotic, at least for its place and time. I was prepared to believe anything, as long as it made sound American sense.

By that I mean, I suppose, made sense to my father. He preferred such information as was found in the July 1951 article about wood. The whole wood picture, worldwide. "Versatile Wood Waits on Man." (Nothing in it about people living on poles—I checked.) The

National Geographic wasn't out to shock me, so I could cheerfully accept that in New Guinea natives wore marsupial fur in their ears.

There is something funny about an institution that juxtaposes marsupial fur in foreign ears with the story of wood, but I don't know how to put my finger on it. You might as well ask what is funny about cats, uncles, plumbing, breakfast, lawn mowing, Thanksgiving, Pikes Peak, television sets or monsters under the bed. In any staple of national life there is bound to be comedy.

You notice I haven't said anything about breasts. Neither did my father. Or Mr. Orey.

CAESARS
FOR THE
BATH GEL

"**W**e're full," said the woman at the Atlantic City Caesars Hotel Casino reception desk, referring to her computer. "But we have plenty of rooms." She took another glance at the computer. "It's about half and half." She looked up and smiled in a nonobjective sort of way. "Seventy percent occupancy."

According to the literature in our suite, "The Caesars experience is unique. Caesars world famous casinos throb. . . . It all adds up to *Excitement Maximus.*"

I'll tell you what it all added up to: two *virtually free* three-hour bus rides through New Jersey for $420. Not counting room and meals. The $420 is what the woman then in my life and I lost during six hours of blackjack and roulette in places where, as a fellow tinhorn put it to us, "money ceases to mean anything."

I think things *ought* to mean something.

And indeed Atlantic City seemed a perfect spot to sum up the Eighties—glitz and debt and homelessness hand in hand in hand. To reach the glittery seaside slabs of throbbing excitement—Caesars, Trump's Castle Hotel and Casino, Bally's Grand and so on—where the whole point is meaningless lucre, we passed the rubbly vacant lots and garish billboards and defunct storefronts and crumbling flophouses and innumerable stoplights that added up to Atlantic City proper.

How could we complain about being bused through these ruins? It almost didn't cost us anything, in a sense. In fact you could, in a manner of speaking, come out on top. Atlantic City was so eager to welcome excitement seekers that every half hour from 7:30 A.M. to 9:30 P.M. daily, buses departed New York's Port Authority terminal bound for casinos where passengers were given coupons redeemable for more—in rolls of quarters and buffet privileges—than the ride cost!

On the bus that the woman then in my life and I took, most of the passengers were elderly, and none of them were high rollers. They looked like people you stand in line with at the prescription counter of a discount drugstore. In nice weather, the trip might make for a gently pleasant outing—a nap on the bus there, a free meal, a stroll on the boardwalk, and a nap on the bus back, all for less than nothing. How could these casinos stay in business?

For one thing, the window where we picked up our quarters was very near the slot machines. To me, the sight of someone's neglected grandmother pumping quarters into a one-armed bandit, and pulling down the lever, and watching as cherries and sevens and other symbols of fortune whirred and settled into patterns, and pumping in more quarters and pulling the lever again until some combination of those symbols stirred the bowels of the machine to loose a rattly shower of quarters into a metal tray, and then reaching into those quarters to make further deposits, on into the night, was as exciting as watching a hospital patient struggle endlessly with a capricious vending machine. Oh, I forgot: lights flashed and from time to time you got a *bee-OOOP-be-OOP-boop.*

Atlantic City's slots are required to pay off a minimum of 83 percent of the overall amount deposited into them. Once every few blue moons some machines pay off a million dollars or so—not, I suppose, in actual quarters. All I know is, whenever we asked a slot machine fancier whether he or she was winning, he or she looked at us as if we must never have been there before.

"Why do you keep doing this, then?"

"I just enjoy it" was the most flavorful answer.

A little low on cash? The casinos are fitted out with cash machines that accept all manner of charge cards, and you can also visit cheerful credit departments.

But don't think you can just say, "Here is a picture of my family in our rumpus room. Can you give me fifty thousand against them?" No, you have to fill out an application, giving employment and bank account information. This form has to be processed.

"So I can't lose my house?" I asked the smiling credit woman.

"Not tonight," she said.

Once you're in a casino's computer and you've established that you're willing to play, say, fifty-dollar-a-hand blackjack for three hours at a stretch, you can get not only credit but also complimentary rooms and meals and—if you've proved yourself to be such a solid citizen that several thousand simoleons a night is no big thing to you one way or the other—a free Gotham-to-Sodom-and-back helicopter ride.

I say Sodom but I don't mean it, because to me veritable cities of sin suggest a good deal of pitching about and sloshing and yelling and guffaws and lamentations; whereas everything boils down to numbers in Atlantic City.

We caught a 6:30 P.M. bus out of the Port Authority, arrived at the Showboat at 9:30, got our quarters, hailed a cab for Caesars, gambled until 4 A.M., grabbed five hours of sleep, took quick bubble baths in the Jacuzzi and got the 10:30 A.M. bus back to where we started, the Port Authority (which *does* seem like Sodom, but that's another story).

The most exciting part was the ten minutes I spent in the tub. Swallowed by a monstrous head of Jacuzzied-up Caesars foam, I felt the full potential of complimentary hotel bath gel for the first time. That bath *really* gelled. I got out of that tub, looked at myself in a vast expanse of bathroom mirror and thought I had become a polar bear. And the bus we needed to catch was leaving in half an hour. It would have taken that long to get the foam out of my hair alone. Tufts of it floated about as I dressed. Have you ever pulled your socks on over suds?

Blackjack and roulette, on the other hand, did not transform me. As I observed above, everything boils down to numbers. At the roulette table, I tried to personalize these numbers by thinking of them as football players.

Doug Williams of the Washington Redskins had just become the first black quarterback to play the Super Bowl and had been named that event's most valuable player. His uniform was number seventeen. Since seventeen is black, I must have put $500 on it during the course of the evening, and it came in once, with five of my one-dollar chips on it, paying me $175. I also played quite a few other numbers, thinking of them as Pittsburgh Steelers of that team's glory years. This enabled me to root.

The woman then in my life had no system. Each of us at one point had a big pile of chips, and that was sort of fun because it raised the level at which we began to lose again.

What can I say? We played at both Caesars and the Trump Plaza Hotel and Casino, we were surrounded by brass and marble and cocktail girls in little bitty costumes. We didn't see anyone expressing any emotion to speak of. We lost more money than we could afford. We didn't see anybody winning very much, except maybe one wizened guy in a tracksuit who sat hunched over his chips and a tiny piece of paper that he kept making tiny notes on and who did not seem to be having any more fun than Scrooge in his crabby period.

"This is not gambling!" I exclaimed as we took a vodka-and-grape-fruit-juice break at a bar where it was impossible to avoid watching MTV. "Buying a house is gambling! Getting married is gambling! Having children is gambling!" Then I changed the subject.

WILD FISH

RIPPED

MY FLESH

Let me qualify that.

A wild fish ripped my flesh. If there is one point that Ney Orlotegui, Amazon guide, would like to clear up ("When I had a agent, I was going to swim in a twenty-thousand-gallon tank with thousands of piranha at Circus Circus in Las Vegas, but the guy who had contact with my agent say, 'You commit suicide?' "), it is that people go overboard when they talk about man-eating fish.

To tell the truth, when people ask me what the Amazon was like, it is not man-eating fish that spring to mind. It is the mud. Strange gray-green-blue-brown mud. But I tend to steer clear of the mud.

One small man-eating fish ripped my flesh. "You tell about that, nobody gonna want to come," said Ney. It probably wouldn't have ripped my flesh at all if . . . It's a long story.

Traditionally, stories told by explorers back from the Amazon are hard to swallow. Those fierce women warriors for whom the Amazon is named? Fabricated by a sixteenth-century Spaniard. Those three-hundred-pound catfish that will drag children to the bottom of the river and gulp them whole? Well, those do exist. We ate part of one. And we found out that the Amazon is where Hollywood finds models for imaginary beasts: the wookies in *Star Wars* and the gremlins in *Gremlins,* for instance. We *owned* a gremlin, on our raft. It kept jumping into our meals and nestling in our armpits. And we could have picked up a wookie, but we didn't, we left it in the muddy village of Santa Maria, moaning.

The mud is what sticks with me. Two episodes in the mud. Ney, my son John and I in the mud twice—once wallowing like little kids, and once when I thought: "Someone could die like this."

The thing is, you probably want to hear about the man-eating fish. Okay. But I refuse to sensationalize it.

There I was, dog-paddling in the Huallaga, an Amazonian tributary in northern Peru. Our raft, the Yacu-Mama (named by Ney for a legendary Amazonian monster that is said to abduct people, down into the depths), was at anchor. Several of us explorers were in swimming. Ney had assured us that we needn't worry about what he referred to as "my piranha."

As long as we kept moving, he said, the kind of piranha that frequent this stretch of the river would rather eat something dead. "People come here, they make a documentary out of the piranha. They take a cow, they shoot pictures till they drown the cow. They use special pipes from the United States to blow bubbles. They buy one of the stuffed piranha, put it in the water and make its jaws move. Then they strip the cow, so it look beautiful, to the bone. That's false. That's why my piranha have gained so much fame."

Special pipes? This did not dispel footage of cow-devouring that held me rapt in my boyhood. But another explorer was asking about something even worse: the candiru, a toothpick-sized fish that introduces itself (strange phrase) into one or another of a swimmer's orifices, spreads open its set of spines, commences to grow in said orifice and cannot be removed except by surgery. Was it true, in fact, that the candiru had such a soft spot in its heart for any old human entrance that it was capable of swimming up the stream of a person urinating into the river?

"Oh, yeaahhhh," said Ney. "They do that. Can . . . *dee* . . . ru. But thass just if you not wearing a bathing suit."

Room for clarification there, too. But deep down, in the Amazon, how much clarification could we stand?

So there we were, treading water, energetically, in the brown-green, pleasantly warm, unhurriedly inexorable current. And I felt a nibbling on my upper thigh.

I had been pecked at by fish before. I grew up being pecked at by fish, in waters of northern Georgia that were about this same color and temperature. I swam a few feet away.

I felt a sharper nibbling, in the same spot on my leg.

I thought to myself, this is just a hysterical piranha attack. I won't give in to it.

Then the nibbling got *fierce*.

And I hydroplaned back to the raft, yelling, "Fish! Fish!"

Nobody else had been attacked by fish. The others were still bobbing around, and now they were laughing.

I sat on the side of the raft. I pulled up the leg of my bathing suit.

And behold: ten or twelve spots of blood, growing.

People saw these! Heinz Kluetmeier, my fellow explorer, took pictures! Did anybody take pictures of the warrior maidens? No. But photographs exist of my bites.

"Sabalo," said Ney. A sabalo is not a man-eating fish. It is more or less what I would call a shiner. "This time of year, the dry season, those fish are starving," Ney said. "That is why. One hungry fish!"

I took his word for it. I had been attacked by a baitfish. At least I had demonstrably been attacked. When you wiped off the blood you could see the teethmarks. What kind of river was this, where you weren't safe from the *bait?*

At any rate, this boyhood rule applied: got to get back on that horse. I stood, semivindicated, and prepared to dive.

And something moved on my person. A cooler explorer would have said, "Heinz, get the camera." I said, *"Aauughhh!"*

And it jumped out of my pocket! People witnessed this! It glistened red, blue and voracious in the Amazonian sun! Eventually even Ney admitted it was a small piranha. (Later Julia Huaman Nolasco, his assistant, took me aside and confided, "Jou were very lucky. That was the fish that introduce himself into jour body." But I think she was just trying to make me feel better about having hollered "Fish! Fish!")

Flip, floop, it bounced off the side of the raft and disappeared into the murk of the Great Brown God.

I had a live Amazonian piranha in my bathing suit pocket for five solid minutes and lived to tell about it!

That is the kind of thing an explorer wants to dwell on. Not the mud.

WE WERE THE Emerald Forest expedition. Seven hundred miles in ten days along the Peruvian headwaters of the Amazon, through the heart of the rain forest, from Chasuta to Iquitos, on a raft handmade out of balsa logs, cane poles, wood poles, chainsawn planks and palm fronds.

Eight Peruvians. Ney, Julia, Ney's brother Aldo, crewwomen Lidia and Alicia, and boatmen Fermine, Antero (also known as Jack) and Nelson.

Nine gringos. Fred Bonati, former Marine pilot now a Northern California contractor and sailboatman. Hannah Carlin, British fashion consultant living in Houston. David Flint, graduation-picture photographer from Cincinnati. Fred's boyhood friend, the ominously named (for those who had read "Heart of Darkness") Jim Kurtz, now in investments in Arizona. Stephen and Carol Tatsumi, a cheerful young Southern California couple. Heinz, who taught innocent Amazonian children to point at me and say "Uooogly." My son John and I, at the time seventeen and forty-four respectively, awkward ages. I figured he and I needed an adventure together before he left the nest. He didn't seem to be so sure.

Most of us gringos had booked the trip through Sobek Expeditions, a California outfit that specializes in adventure vacations, but this particular tour was owned and operated by Ney, forty-seven, who grew up along the Amazon, lives in Florida now, and is nimble to be so stocky. Dressed in a pith helmet and khaki shorts-and-shirt ensemble, and moving through the jungle in an odd preoccupied scuttle, with his head down into his shoulders and a look on his face of possible shrewdness, he invited comparison to Tattoo of *Fantasy Island,* but he was a larger man than that and his face suggested a rounder, browner, vaguer Vince Edwards. Not an easy man to figure.

When our plane landed in Lima it was after the 1:00 A.M. curfew, the streets were empty except for soldiers with rifles and machine guns. Meeting us, Ney said we would be taken to a different hotel from the scheduled one, because of a revolutionary bomb threat. This said, Ney and Julia left the airport-to-town bus and scooted off into the darkness—standing an excellent chance, Ney said, of being shot.

The next day we flew to Tarapoto, where we banqueted on excellent fish and hearts of palm and danced to pisco sours and the music of an eerie drum-and-whistle combo. "Now we a family," Ney said. On the third day we took minibuses to Chasuta, where the paved road ended, and the river was the highway.

NEY FIELDING THE inevitable gringo question, whether we would acquire any authentic shrunken heads:

"Indians won't shrink your head anymore. Missionaries told them it was illegal. Now they wait till you die and then shrink your head.

"You go to the tourist hotel in Iquitos, white-man trader come to the hotel, says, 'I been in the jungle, got a shrunken head for five hundred dollars,'—it made in Japan! Says 'Taiwan' on the bottom!

"But if you tell the witch doctor *why* you need a head . . . if you're patient with 'em, stick around. . . . Don't be mean with 'em. . . . And give 'em silver dollars 'cause they think paper money rot in the jungle. . . .

"But if you come into the jungle, *bambambam* shoot them, they prob'ly shrink your head."

I wrote that down, thinking it would be clearer later. We never met any witch doctors. Bad mechanics, yes; and John had the experience of bribing a policeman. But such headhunters as may be left in the Amazon have retreated deep into the jungle, away from the sounds of motors and the promotions of such outfits as Green Hell Tours, which in the Seventies (according to Alex Shoumatoff in *The Rivers Amazon*) brought tourists by the boatload to see a ceremony called "the plucking of the virgin's hair."

Native dress in Chasuta was pretty much the standard for villagers along the river: jogging shorts, patched T-shirts and either holey sneakers or flip-flops. I'm not saying we saw no primitivity: many of the villagers could not be dissuaded from shaking newly-snapped Polaroid pictures vigorously, which hasn't been necessary for years.

Then too, they lived in one-story huts whose walls were of flat, vertical three-inch-wide strips of cane (it grows broad in Amazonia), or occasionally of corrugated metal, and whose roofs were palm fronds or tin. Inside, the decor was pictures of Jesus and just about anything torn from newspapers or calendars: modest girlie photos, a two-page spread on Cheryl Ladd, a Mum deodorant ad, "The Anatomy of an Echinoderm." Along the main dirt street, Chasuta was in its second year of municipal electricity, which would come alive at dusk.

These villagers were predominantly old or middle-aged, or young mothers, or prime candidates for young motherhood, or little kids. Older children had to go to larger towns if they wanted to attend secondary school, and most of Peru's young men are drafted by the army and taken into the big cities, where they discover boots, motorcycles and ice cream and lose their taste for the simple life. The villagers dwindle, the big cities swell, terrorists blow up a train or kill some policemen every so often (one of Ney's tour groups came trekking out of the jungle into an unprepared town and were taken for guerillas, had to lie on the ground with shotguns and machine guns held on them for a while), and the vast majority of people are poor.

But in the country fruits are handy (try and find an unpicked ripe banana near a trail). Jute, maize, rice, sugar cane and yucca grow quickly with little tending. People go out in canoes and return soon with ten-pound zebra-striped catfish. And piles of brilliant feathers next to charred spots mark snacks of opportunity. "Everything these people see, they kill and eat," Fred said.

Very appealing people, though. Clear handsome faces with smiles for us everywhere. At one time in history, the agency charged with protecting the Indians fed poisoned candy to inconveniently situated Indian children, and the kids in one village ran from us, saying (according to Ney) that we were Germans who would kidnap them for their fat. They were giggling, though. Uncorrupted-looking smiles abounded.

Chasutans led us up a mountain to swim in the pool below a fifty-foot waterfall (further along the river we would shower in falls warmed by a defunct volcano), and on the way down, as evening fell, one of them, named Marylou, got herself and Fred and Jim and me lost in the jungle.

Heinz and John and some local youths, full of beans, had *run* down the mountain toward the village, and Ney was shepherding other explorers. Fred, Jim and I assumed we were being led by Marylou. Every now and then she would stop and chuckle. Jim knew some Spanish (which nearly all the villagers spoke, proudly calling it *Castiliano*—it is not cool in the villages to be regarded as Indian). He asked Marylou where we were.

"Yo no conozco," she said. That meant she didn't know. It didn't seem to bother her as much as it did us.

My first impression of the jungle was bananas and houseplants. Only way too big for a house or even a cathedral. A philodendron large enough to swallow a child, a forty-foot ficus tree and something that seemed to touch Fred: pothos. Pothos on an enormous scale. Among us gringos Fred was the most into nature. He took offense when a Peruvian threw rocks at the only snake (an unimposing green one) we saw on the whole expedition.

Fred was the only one of us with jungle experience. He had bombed it during the Vietnam War. "The Southeast Asian jungle puts this to shame," he said. "Vegetation a hundred feet high. Beautiful country. We destroyed a lot of it. The jungle will come back, but I doubt the tigers and elephants will. I loved the flying. I didn't even mind bombing people. I just hated the dirty trick the system played on us. My father was in World War II. The president then, the system then, was pretty much ideal. That's not what I saw when I was in Vietnam. And then there was Watergate."

There we were, the houseplants closing in, darkness approaching, and personally I would have been glad to see Richard Nixon, if he knew the way to Chasuta. The path (or was it a path?) would peter out, Marylou would seem amused, and we would shout and not hear any animal sounds, even. (We were days further down the river before we heard jungle cries.) Two hours later we somehow made it to Chasuta's mini-outskirts. Marylou's mother was waiting with a machete, but I, at least, was so obviously grateful to see her—she was standing next to a man-made structure—that her suspicions were allayed. By this time John was dancing to a scratchy Stevie Wonder record with the daughter of the lieutenant governor. (There seemed to be a governor and a lieutenant governor for every forty or fifty people along the river.) I had the feeling this was not going to be one of those over-packaged tours.

"MY FATHER LEFT me with the Campas Indians when I was thirteen," Ney said the next day as we jounced through rapids in a thirteen-meter-long dugout canoe (mahogany bottom built up with planks on the sides). There were twenty people on this boat, including a nursing mother and another hitchhiker, and three chickens and a dog. We were headed to where the raft awaited us.

"He got into hot water with the chief of the tribe. My father cheated him, didn't give him the merchandise he promised. My father traded with the Indians, and he would take me on trips. 'If you don't trust me,' my father said, 'I'll leave my son here, and I'll be back.'

"I waited six months. I was one of forty-eight kids my father had with different women. He was sixty-four when he kidnap my mother, when she was sixteen. She was a Brazilian native, civilized. He came over from Spain in a small boat in 1922. He came to get the gold.

"Only good thing about him, he a gold prospector, a merchant, a lawyer, and he always got his way. We were wealthy people in the jungle. He put the gold in beer bottles under the house, and every two years he sell his gold and go to Spain and buy the most beautiful things for his wife and children. We lived at our gold mine in the headwaters of the Pachitea River, thirty days upriver from here. He never panned for gold, he held a shotgun on a hundred Indians while they panned for gold. There was an Indian who swallowed a nugget. My father stood there with a shotgun and said he was going to wait until that Indian passed that nugget. He did, twenty-four hours later. Then he took all the Indian's clothes and fired him.

"My father carry about five or six dynamites in his pocket, just for kicks. Sometimes he fish with it. Sometimes we fish with Indian poison. Take mashed potatoes, put a little poison in them, toss them on the water, the fish hit them, Pow, they jump around like crazy and you scoop 'em out before they die and cut their heads off so the poison don't get in the meat.

"I only had two years of school. My father teach me first grade. I wouldn't pronounce one word right, he come on top of me with a belt. He beat his kids—oh!

"When my father got to be eighty he wasn't right in the brain anymore. There's a legend about cutting the bull's ears and gold will come out. My father say, 'Ney, go get a saw, you take one end and I'll take another, bring a sack, we cut the bull, we have enough money to take the whole family to Spain.'

"My father travel the whole jungle here cheating people. He was so knowledgeable about the law. He name me for Marshall Ney, the French general at Waterloo. He was a fanatic about Waterloo. He could care less about another son. He left three of my brothers before me. I got scared with the Indians because this witch doctor, they would come to him, and a lady came with colic—she ate a lot of sugar cane and bar sugar. He tell that lady lay down, you got bad spirit in your stomach, and he cut a hole in her for that bad spirit to come out. With that the lady died.

"When I left there I was scared to death. I escape on a two-log raft. I went probably fifteen hundred miles, back home. My father wasn't there. My mother took all the gold and my brothers, and we abandon our ranch, we head to the big cities. We never saw lights, we never saw bicycles, never saw white people before. That was sad. I said, 'I want to go back.' I crossed the Andes by foot, came back, but it wasn't the same anymore. I missed my father, missed my mother, I missed my brothers, I was underage, I couldn't employ the Indians. I didn't have capital. So I started to a-benture."

He explored, he lived off the jungle, eventually he found his father in Iquitos. "He was amazing in his beliefs. He never believed in God. In his dying breath he said in Spanish, 'In God I shit.' To me he was a great man. He was my father. Only difference between me and him, I am a very principled, religious, loveable man. I love people, I help them.

"He never tried to get back and see how his kids were doing. I found him when he was in the hospital dying. He was eighty-eight. He said, 'Which one are you?' I said, 'I'm Ney, the one you left with the tribe.' Out of the forty-eight kids he had, his sisters, brothers, not one would be at his bedside but me. I called them, they said no, because he was a mean man. They bring up the past.

"Then a missionary took me to Vicksburg, Mississippi, in his boat. Hired me to be the youngest sailor in the ship. On the way we stayed in Liberia for a year, thousands of Negro people pulled our ship to the shore.

"I worked till my contract was over, then he sent me back to Peru. That wasn't fair, after I see the United States. I stow away in a merchant ship, three times. One time I didn't know which way was America, and I wind up in Italy. Every time in America I turn myself in to Immigration hoping they'd be nice people. Finally a man said do your service in your army, and if your intentions are honorable, you'll get into America. So I went to be a parachute, and I got seventeen jumps, and in 1967 the first letter came from Washington, that I had been forgiven for stowing away. In 1980 I became a citizen. I know it is not impossible to get anywhere a man want."

BEFORE WE REACHED the raft we met some men who were getting ahead in, alas, what is currently the most cost-effective way in Peru. Nominally they were salt miners, idling on the river bank. They shared with us their *aguardiente,* which means water with teeth and is home-made sugar-cane rum, an intensely agreeable drink. They offered to sell us twenty-four kilos of cocaine, presumably unrefined coca paste, for nine million soles, about five hundred dollars. They said they had the stuff under chunks of salt there on the shore. Thanks to the coca trade, Ney finds it hard to hire boatmen for a dollar a day.

"These men offer this drink to people on small raft going by," Ney said after we declined to do business with them. "The man on the raft got cocaine. They get him to talking, they take his cocaine and send him on or kill him."

By 1968, Ney says, he was a-benturing in the U.S. In an aluminum canoe, he started out on the Yellowstone River near Billings, Mon-tana, and three months and five days later he was in New Orleans. Along the way he heard a speech by Ronald Reagan in Kansas City and painted R. REAGAN, EL HOMBRE OF TO-MORROW on the side of the canoe. "I told the Republicans, 'If you want a sign on there it cost you three thousand dollars,' and they paid."

He was back and forth between his new home and his old. After Eric Fleming, the trail boss in TV's *Rawhide,* drowned in a Peruvian rapid, Ney found the body. He says he took a raft from Belém, Brazil, across the ocean to Trinidad by himself. He did some guiding, kept going back to check on his ancestral gold mine, one thing and another.

Now, he says, "There are no more a-bentures. People gone every-where. People gone to the moon! People go across the Atlantic in a bathtub! If I had twenty people to put up twenty thousand dollars each I'd do the original Kon-Tiki trip again."

There must be something nobody's done in the Amazon before.

"In the Amazon?" he says. "Commercialize."

The Amazon resists *constructive* commercialization. It can be ripped off for ores and coca, and in fact its flora and fauna are being cleared away by leaps and bounds, in the interest of profit. Enormous stretches of jungle are being burnt off to clear land for cattle to provide American fast-food hamburger meat. The smoke threatens to disrupt the ozone layer around the earth, which would change weather patterns disastrously. In the early Eighties an ecologist predicted that the entire rain forest of Brazil, Peru, Ecuador and Colombia, the largest wilderness in the world, could be reduced to mud by the Nineties.

That unarable mud, which lies a few inches below the enormously fertile but shallow layer of soil, swallows up planned long-term development. The American billionaire Daniel K. Ludwig realized a loss of eight hundred million dollars when he pulled out of his Amazonian forestry-rice-and-mining project, which covered land the size of Connecticut.

So Ney has his work cut out for him, making a go of about eight tours a year along the Huallaga to the Mananon to the Ucalali to the Amazon proper, in Peru and sometimes on into Brazil. The economics of this operation are a mystery to me, especially after discussing them with Ney. All I know is that our expedition, whose price was $1,995 including airfare, was undercapitalized. Ney borrowed over four hundred dollars from us gringos in the course of the trip. He paid the builder of our raft a little over a thousand dollars. He sold it at the end of the trip for three hundred dollars. When his Coleman lantern broke down, Heinz and I bought a used one (which broke down) for about sixty dollars. Ney complained that Americans drank an awful lot of instant coffee at eight dollars a jar. And we kept running out of flashlight batteries, which meant that sometimes we traveled at night without navigation lights, because those lights were rigged up from flashlights appropriated from us explorers at unwary moments.

But none of us got sick—thanks to scrupulously prepared food and Ney's insistence that we take two Pepto-Bismol tablets a day. We hadn't even started feeling mutinous yet as we approached the place where the raft awaited.

"Donde está la balsa grande?" we cried to everyone we passed along the river as darkness fell, and then, at a place called Pellejo Island, we came upon her: the Yacu-Mama.

We clambered aboard. Eight meters wide by fifteen meters long, she floated on huge balsa logs, and she was made of *balina*-tree poles and planks, with rails of capirona wood, walls of *cana brava* cane and a thatched roof of just-dry *yarina* palm fronds. There were fifteen-foot-long oars, the paddle-ends hand-carved from *renaco* wood, for steering. There was a kitchen area—a handmade cookstove, mud laid down on poles so that wood could burn on top of the mud—and even a privy, with a real toilet seat and a tablecloth for a door. Most of this was lashed together with bark, though there were some nails.

Inside were two semiprivate bedrooms, a big open area and a dining room with a tabletop that showed the marks of the chainsaw on its surface. Up top, reachable by ladder, was a bridge. Ney kept saying the Yacu-Mama was modeled after the Kon-Tiki raft, but what it looked like was an ark, a houseboat, a shaggy treehouse. What I would have called it when I was a boy was *neat*.

"This is the best raft I had!" said Ney.

It was neat.

We lived on it.

It floated on the four-miles-per-hour dry-season current, with intermittent push and positioning provided by a *peque-peque,* which is what Ney called the sixteen-horse, rope-cranked Briggs and Stratton motor with a ten-foot drive shaft attached. Ney kept saying, "I want to hear the *peque-peque.*"

"That's right," Fred would say. "We were just beginning to hear birds. That noise really offends the sensibilities of a sailboatman."

So the *peque-peque* would fall silent. But not for long. But then too it wouldn't work for long either. Nor would the supplementary forty-horse Yamaha outboard that finally arrived from somewhere to replace the one that Ney said was stolen before it reached us.

"*Ha*-ha-ha!" Ney said when both motors were going at once, but that was seldom, because they kept breaking down and it is hard to get things fixed in Amazonia. There was an endless delay in the village of Lagunas as we waited for a mechanic to arrive and then as he cut a gasket from a cardboard box, a gasket that worked for a shorter time than it took to install.

It was never clear what our schedule was. "In Peru," Ney said, "you tell a guy you going to meet him at seven, he show up at nine, you have a fight. From that fight is born ten fights, everybody want to help. Now each of those guys is late to meet somebody else."

Here are some things I remember about our life on the water.

Our chickens clucking and scratching on the roof. We acquired these chickens for the equivalent of nine dollars each in the market at Yurimagua (where chicken feet and chicken *heads* were being cooked as snacks on braziers). One by one we ate them. We didn't eat the rooster—who crowed early in the morning, when Heinz didn't grab him and throw him in a sack first—until the last day. Ney identified with the rooster, and pouted when Heinz sacked him. When the rooster crowed Lidia would always echo him: "Chi-chimaraaada."

It wasn't just chicken we ate. Huge filets from horrible-looking catfish of various kinds, some fresh and some dried (the only portion I had trouble warming to was from a batch of insufficiently dried that I'd seen Lidia scraping maggots off of). Potatoes and potatoish yucca, mangoes with lime juice, beans, rice, a vivid beets-and-peas-and-potato salad, various hearty soups (one of which was augmented by quantities of melting gnats one unusually buggy evening) and some red meat that Julia, when asked, said was "bief."

"It monkey meat," said Ney. "They change the name to protect the innocent."

From then on, David, who wouldn't eat the gnat soup on the grounds that he was unaccustomed to such things, wanted to know what everything was.

It wasn't just chickens we kept, either. I bought a monkey named Blanca for two hundred thousand soles, a turtle who never got named for fifty thousand, a little green parrot named Rosita for one hundred thousand, a puppy named Tipico for sixty thousand (to replace the puppy named Inca, who got so sick we left him with the coca-dealing salt miners), a marmoset for one hundred thousand.

The marmoset needed no name. He was a pistol. In the face he looked exactly like a movie gremlin. He was smaller than an explorer's hand but had more attitude than any four whole explorers put together. He would jump down onto the dinner table, wade right through somebody's beans and go headfirst into the lemonade. So during meals we kept him in a bag, where he expostulated like an arrested diplomat. One night he sat on the rafter above Jim's hammock and screamed, as if hailing a cab, until Jim stuck up his hand and the marmoset ran down his arm to his armpit, where he spent the rest of the night. The marmoset and the little green parrot were about the same size. Finding themselves on the same rafter, they fought toe to toe like King Kong and the dinosaur.

There were two macaws. They were purchased, on credit, by Ney, because macaws sell for over a thousand dollars in the States. The macaws kept to themselves on the roof. Their wings were clipped, but they kept escaping into the river, where they would be on the verge of drowning when John or Heinz or one of the boatmen would save them. One night there was a cold windstorm and the macaws were brought in and placed under my hammock. I didn't mind the marmoset in my underarm—if he tossed and turned I could always throw him over toward the next hammock, where Lidia and Alicia slept together head-to-toe—but macaws under my hammock gave me nightmares, and I woke up completely disoriented, thinking things had changed somehow, I'd been shanghaied; I woke up wild, prepared to fight, it was pitch dark, I stumbled to the side of the raft and there was Ney.

"Where are we?" I asked him.

"The Amazon," he said. The boatmen who were supposed to keep us going all night had gone to sleep (they huddled without sleeping bags along the raft's edge, drinking *coosiwassi,* a formidable bark-and-sugar-cane liquor, to ease their rheumatism). The wind had slowed us down, we had run aground, we only had four more hours of gas, and Ney needed to borrow 380,000 soles from us to get two more barrels of gas.

I was glad I wasn't in his business.

"They all crooks on the river," he said. "The governor of a town in Brazil one time sold me two barrels half gas half water—the water goes to the bottom. I report him."

To whom?

"To the other governor."

THERE WERE LONG slow periods when we were drifting down along the wide brown-green, scum-flecked water, catching sight of gray or blue freshwater dolphins, looking at mud banks brightened by lime-green strips of young rice plants, waiting for Ney to give us a straight answer as to what we were going to do next.

During one of those periods Ney was lying on the bridge in the midday sun. Then he was up pacing, planning a crow's nest for the next raft, worrying about not going fast enough, making general business-administration statements: "I used to work for pleasure but I learned not to do that. Got to have capital." Then all of a sudden he was down the ladder and off the boat.

And wading to the riverbank. John and Heinz went off with him. Heinz ran ahead to get pictures of the raft from a distance. By the time I changed into my bathing suit the raft was a hundred yards from the shore. I swam in, and pretty soon Ney, John and I were in mud up to our ribcages.

This was great mud. Like modeling clay only thinner, like cake icing only thicker. There was firm footing underneath, and if we walked briskly the surface would just support our weight, so we could squooch in and out at will. We daubed each other, we turned ourselves into mudmen, we pretended to be descending into and then emerging from the primeval ooze.

"Now *this* is fun," John said. "What other guide . . . ?"

We never knew what to expect. "What other guide . . . ?" remained the essential question, but it acquired less approving connotations.

To us gringos, with our support systems, the Amazon itself wasn't maddening. Repellent kept mosquitoes from being much of a problem to anyone except Stephen, who for some reason was a martyr to them. The heat wasn't punishing. There were card games and plenty of opportunities to stop and acquire beer and rum and Inca Cola. At night we could sing "Vaya Con Dios" and "Cielito Lindo" with Julia, Lidia and Alicia.

To us it was Ney who was maddening.

Ney, Jim, Fred and I are hiking through a stretch of jungle with a man from the nearest village (Ney knows a lot of people). The local guy hits a rubber tree with his machete and latex runs down. Ney hands Jim a guava fruit, he bites into it, passes it back to me without looking at it, I see it is crawling with worms. Local guy chops down a forty-foot palm tree at Ney's behest to get one heart of palm for salad. (I hit it a couple of licks and it's as hard as a railroad tie and clangs like metal.) We pass by a thorn tree with an orange impaled on it.

"What's that tree?" Fred says.

"Orange tree," says Ney, who seems to be in a hurry.

"With thorns? What's that, over there. *That* looks like an orange tree."

"Thass an orange tree," says Ney.

"But the fruit are yellow," says Jim.

"Yes. Grapefruit," says Ney.

"Oh," says Fred, picking one of the fruit. It is as big as a grapefruit. "But it smells like lemon."

"Yes, lemon," says Ney.

EVERYONE IS GRUMBLING. I talk to Ney on the bridge, ask him to brief us more often.

Granted, it's difficult for him, because various of us explorers have various thresholds of adventure, but if he'd just . . .

"I gonna really walk those waitresses," he says.

"Waitresses?"

"Yes. *Alpiniste.*"

"Alpinist waitresses?"

"Waitresses, bartenders, *all* walks of life. Gonna be my next group."

"Oh. What . . ."

"I had all kinds of animals on the raft one time, capybara, ocelot, but the police say I got to register them. Where I gonna get birth certificates for all those animals?"

"What are we going to do next?"

"Three days off the raft, in the jungle."

"Three days?"

"Yeah. I never did it before."

"I'm not sure everybody—"

"We try it. If somebody don't like it, it's only an hour walk back to the raft."

"Well, you ought to tell them all that, then."

"Only thing, won't be any food on the raft."

"Well, then, how—"

"It's a spermint."

WE GOT OFF the raft at a village called Esperanza and walked two hours into the jungle. Bromeliad growing on trees. Vegetation finally closing over our heads. A cypress big around as any California redwood, whose top we couldn't see and whose roots grew above the ground for tens of yards in all directions, because the soil was too shallow for them to grow downward.

Then we took dugout cedar canoes down the Rio Yanayaquillo. Along the way, some of us caught piranha—panfish-range in size—on cheap rods and reels (not nearly enough to go around), malfunctioning plastic bobbers and hooks so flimsy the piranha bit through them. (Cut-up savalo, or piranha, for bait.) I'll say this: Ney caught a strapping piranha on a hook that had no barb or point and hardly any crook left on it. I don't know how he did it. Ney could fish. Arranging for everybody else to catch fish, or to be happy while some caught fish, was another matter.

They were good fish to catch, the bigger ones fat and game as crappie, and sautéed with lemon they were good, if oily. (I'll also say this: thanks to Ney, I am the only person I know who has caught, and eaten, and been partially eaten by, piranha.) Ney would cut their lips away with a knife so we could see their teeth. If you held a leaf in front of its mouth, a caught piranha would take a semicircle out of it clean as a cookie cutter.

But we were out into some rough country now and we had no idea how long we were going to be there or under what circumstances. Suddenly Ney pulled us up onto a bar. We scrambled up it through sucking mud, and a whole new group of Peruvians materialized. In half an hour, with machetes, they had cleared a camping space and built a shelter for us. Impressive.

But what are our sleeping arrangements? We've brought sleeping bags, but now that we're not moving the mosquitoes are more intimidating, and Ney has been pooh-poohing talk of netting.

Time now to go off into the darkness hunting cayman. John, Fred, Jim, Stephen and I, in two dugouts with one paddle between us. I hold on to the second dugout so that it's pulled along by the strokes of a Peruvian in our prow, who holds a flashlight in his teeth, trying to catch the glint of cayman eyes along the banks, and a shotgun in his lap. And it's beginning to rain, so hard that before long the dugouts are within an inch of being filled with rainwater, inside, and the river water is within an inch of the gunwales, outside. I'm bailing with one hand, holding the other dugout with the other, my boots and the copious lap of my rainpants are full of water, and we don't see any cayman. Which are alligators. Nor do any of them see us, thank God.

We go back to camp. This is the dry season, but this is also a deluge. And the army-ant venom is beginning to kick in. Army ants are a good inch long. While the shelter was being built we saw a bunch of them running up a tree, and Ney said, "Less burn 'em up" and poured kerosene on them and tried to light it. I jumped in with David's cigarette lighter, and the ants got on me, biting me on each knee, through my rainpants, and on every knuckle of the left hand except one.

"Nothing in the jungle will bother you unless you bother it," Ney chose that moment to advise me. "I used to sell these ants. Suuuure. Six dollars for two of them. I advertise them in *Argosy* and *Field and Stream.* First you have to spray them once, with liquid starch, and they go into a comeback posture. Then you have to spray them again and they stay that way, only they fall all apart. Then you have to glue them together. I sell thousands of them. But they make me stop. I have to register, they say. . . ."

Each of my army ant bites, when we come back from hunting cayman soaking wet, feels like I have been hit on that spot by a small ball-peen hammer.

There are nowhere near enough mosquito nets to go around, let alone hammocks. "If there's a hammock for everybody," says Ney, "where's de 'benture?"

He has a hammock. He ties it to our shelter, and gets in. The whole side of the shelter caves in.

I don't want to discuss that night's sleep any further. Sharing one single-size mosquito netting with John, wet, lying on palm-frond stems, mosquitoes getting in, ant bites throbbing . . . I have slept in a foxhole with a moth in my middle ear, I have slept in an English Ford with angry dogs jumping up at the windows, I have slept under a desk on industrial carpet in a tweed suit and tie, but I think that night's sleep in the rain forest is the worst I ever had.

But when the night is over, it is no time to fade. This is our deepest penetration into the jungle, and Ney says if we keep going further up the Yanayaquillo we could see capybara (the world's largest rodent, big as a boxer dog only short-legged and portly), jaguar, who knows?

Half of the party returns to the raft, but John, Heinz, Fred, Jim, Ney, Julia, Fermin, the lieutenant governor of Esperanza (who serenades Julia with a song called "Culpado"), one of his constituents and I go on further. At last we get into country that approximates the Rousseau painting I'd imagined the Amazon to be: the waterway narrowing down to a lurky closeness; the vegetation arching over; the awful ratcheting noise of uncaptured macaws; a sound like wind or distant traffic that Ney says is monkeys; huge blue butterflies flashing artificially vivid, like the animated bluebirds painted onto the film in *Song of the South*. The unelected Esperanzan reaches abruptly under a stump and pulls out—what? What is that? A needle nose, an obscene (to my way of thinking) neck, a prehistoric aspect generally: the matamata turtle, which Hollywood hasn't caught up to yet.

In our dugouts, sitting on jammed-in sticks of cane, we limbo under limbs that lie a foot above the water, we keep floating forward as we step over logs, all the while catching the odd piranha and untangling the more frequent backlash.

And Ney keeps conferring with the lieutenant governor and then saying that further on, maybe an hour further, there could be anaconda, there could be pure Indian villages where they don't wear shorts . . .

And our fellow explorers, not to mention the whole kitchen operation, are back at the raft now, and we're not as far along toward Iquitos as we should be. If anything is clear, it is that we are not going to spend three days in the jungle; we are going back to the Yacu-Mama.

Fred said later, "I think we weinied out a little bit on the jungle." So did Daniel K. Ludwig.

Not that weinieing out, in itself, is a piece of cake. We canoe back to where we have to walk seven miles through mud, carrying packs, along a trail that we can't get lost on because Ney marked it on the way in. Right.

My feeling is, let's all stick together on the way back. John's feeling is, he wants to go full-tilt. Over a trail which, after that rain, is like the inside of an exotic alimentary canal—dank, dully glistening, sloshy, contracting, ingestive.

John and I have hung out with Steelers together, been to spring training together, swum in Georgia waters together, and one night when he was a little kid we walked on the tops of cars together, after *Singin' in the Rain.* Walking on cars together is when you are out with all your loved ones and feeling so good the sidewalk won't hold you. But forty-four and seventeen, father and son, are awkward ages. And I was damned if I was going to let him get lost in the jungle, on the one hand, or outwalk me, on the other.

John and I beat everyone else out of the jungle by half an hour. Everyone else except the anonymous Esperanzan, who caught us just as John was hurtling into a wrong turn. "We're in Peru!" I was reminding John at the top of my voice, "Wait up!"—breaking my neck to keep him in sight or at least hearing, *sprinting* through foot-deep puddles and over thigh-level logs. At the point of the nearly-taken wrong turn, there was an altercation, loud on my part. Semi-vindicated, and pumped, I threw what might well be my last effective (*I* led the rest of the way out of the jungle, and just as—or just about as—fast) paternal tantrum. Sometimes you'd think I was as crazy as Ney's father.

Or at least that's one way of looking at it: I went wild because my son, whom I have proudly watched tackling people half again his size, was not afraid enough of the jungle to suit me. Not as afraid of it as I was, in other words. By the time he's my age the jungle may have been devoured, indirectly, by the customers of McDonald's, and I cost him a chance to be alone in it.

Or you could look at it this way: had I not been so obnoxiously paternal, my son would have been swallowed by that wrong turn. To my way of thinking, this view was supported, inadvertently, by Ney: *he* got lost on the way back. Granted, he made it back to the raft after a while. Fermin got so lost that darkness fell on him and we left him behind. The way Ney looked at it, Fermin had abandoned us. But some of us explorers imagined him thrashing around in circles in the dark. "He is not a jungle boy," said Julia. Granted, he caught up with us a couple of days later, down the river.

If a father could stay in touch *and* a son could be on his own. Life is muddy. I'll say this: I'll bet we picked up that Esperanzan's pace a little.

For the next two days John and I weren't on speaking terms, except when I congratulated him on saving one of the macaws from drowning. He and Heinz would swim alongside the moving raft, or man the steering oars, and do photography together, and in the villages John petted all the dogs (many of which looked almost as bad as the matamata turtle) and ran through the streets with flocks of little kids.

Ney had one more trek in mind. We were to walk a couple of hours across a neck of land and meet the raft, coming around the peninsula under brother Aldo's command, at the village of Nauta.

We disembarked. Moved easily over a long mud flat, through some farmer's rice field, to the high ground, where it struck Ney that we had disembarked in the wrong place. He ran off hollering, "ALDO!" Aldo (who, incidentally, believed he had malaria) eventually heard, and brought the raft back to the bank half a mile downriver.

So we cut across toward him, shaking our heads: Ney had done it again. John, Fred, Jim and I were ahead of the others.

The ground through here was softer. We began to have trouble walking. The mud pulled our shoes off, so we had to carry them. The raft was still a couple of hundred yards ahead and the going was slower and slower. We were up to our ankles. This stuff was less supportive than the fun mud, and it didn't seem to have the solid layer underneath—I tested, reaching down with one foot, something I soon regretted. Pretty soon we were up nearly to our knees, pulling ourselves along with our hands. "You know," I said to Fred, "I could see how an animal could get caught in this, and flounder and never get out."

Fred had been trained in the Marines that the way to negotiate quicksand was to get down flat on top of it and swim. But this wasn't quicksand, it was slow mud. The term "sinking sensation" took on a new meaning for me.

You had to push down hard to get any traction, but when you pushed down hard you got in deeper. And every time you pulled your hand or foot out, it was heavier with mud.

Nobody made conversation. We labored. The more I strained, the more mired I got, and the more I tried to be casual and take it slow, the more time the mud had to draw me down.

Crawling now, I thought back to the animals we were offered in the village of Santa Maria, a couple of days before.

EVERYWHERE WE WENT, kids tried to sell us pets—a monkey with a cord around its stomach that looked like it had been there all its life (that was Blanca—we took the cord off after we bought her and in time she escaped). An unfledged baby bird whose rudimentary wings the kids made flapping motions with. And, suddenly, some strange animal that ten or twelve kids were gathered around. They were smiling those fresh smiles, laughing innocently, and holding this animal that I couldn't quite see. . . .

The group spread at my approach and one child held this animal up toward me—*and another child pulled something out of its stomach.*

It was nightmarish. Whatever the thing from the stomach was, the kids were playing roughly with it, tucking it back in and then pulling it back out—the thing was a fetus, still connected umbilically to its evidently marsupial mother's pouch.

"What is *that?*" I said.

"It's a monkey," said Ney.

"No, it's some kind of marsupial."

"Rat," said Ney.

"It's a Indian rabbit," said Julia.

"It's got *short ears,*" I said.

"Squirrel. Indian squirrel."

I think it was a South American possum. Whatever it was, it was stuck where it didn't want to be. And so was the second animal we were offered there, the one that looked like a wookie in the face. It was a baby sloth. The kids who had it were tossing it around. Carol and John took it and cuddled it, but it seemed inconsolable. Set on the ground, it would reach . . . out . . . its . . . arm . . . in . . . an . . . agonizingly . . . slow . . . and . . . hopeless . . . sort . . . of . . . move . . . toward . . . advancement, while emitting an unearthly noise, a long, slow, high-pitched *eeeeeeee.*

We thought of adopting this sloth but what it needed was its mother, and Ney said, "The two things in the jungle that got the most diseases: the sloth and the turtle." Of course we had just bought a turtle that morning at Ney's urging. But nobody wanted to hear that *eeeeeeee* on the raft at night.

I'M NOT SAYING we were in as bad shape as that sloth when we were in the bad mud, but we were proceeding with great difficulty. It came to me that I might actually not make it to the raft. I was progressing about three inches every time I reached forward, and I couldn't get one knee clear without getting the other one so deep that I couldn't get it anywhere near clear. I was still ten yards from the raft and the mud was getting softer. I accepted a tow.

Fred made it out under his own steam by carrying two flotsam logs with him, putting them down in front of him, and pulling forward.

John and the boatmen slithered right on out and came back with a rope to haul the rest of us out one by one.

My rainpants were full of mud and I saw that the flashlight in my waistband had been sticking straight down, adding a lot of drag. But I still felt dismayed. When I was eleven some of the other boy scouts had to hang back toward the end of our fifty-mile bike trip and walk with me up the steepest hills, and I'd been determined ever since not to let something like that happen again. Heinz would probably have made it in without a tow if he hadn't been carrying two cameras. I would have made it if I'd had two weeks. Maybe.

I sat on the side of the raft getting ten pounds of mud off myself and thinking that this was a hard old jungle. I had swum with piranha, played with fire and army ants, drunk beer fermented with spit (I didn't tell you about that—Ney didn't tell me about the spit until after I drank it). But this mud . . .

The others took their tows serenely. "Honey," said Carol, waiting for Stephen as he was brought in face-first through the glop.

"I'm home," Stephen said.

Hannah, who had said "Bloody hell" when she got her foot wet above Chasuta, came scudding in like a body surfer, as if the mud were a stylish element.

Ney was last. John hooked him up to the towrope and then pushed his face down into the mud. Ney laughed, everybody laughed. After all was said and done, "What other guide . . . ?"

"When I saw you having trouble," Hannah told me, "I thought, 'This is serious.' " That helped my feelings some. It also reflected my sentiments exactly.

When we reached excursion's end in Iquitos—a city of two hundred thousand, the largest city in the jungle—we ascended the mud slope into town by twenty trembling precipitous feet of metal stairway, which was only tenuously connected at a point halfway up and was secured only on one side at the top. Then, at last, pavement. Firm footing.

"They can't build a pier here," Ney said. "Rainy season, the river comes right into town. It going to carry the best hotel away. Thass right. The river turn the town to mud."

MAN-EATING FISH are one thing. But if anybody tries to get you to go into a twenty-thousand-gallon tank full of Peruvian *mud* at Circus Circus, say no. And don't go a-benturing in the Amazon without a stout rope and son.

I MODEL FOR *GQ*

O n a scale of the ones to the nines, I am usually dressed to roughly the twos. In order to avoid giving offense at special occasions, I will go as far as the threes or fours. The only reason to move on up to snazzy, however, is to attract business or women. And the type of business or women you attract by dressing snazzy is the type that will expect you to dress snazzy all the time. I wouldn't want to live like that.

Another reason I am not natty is that I like to eat lying down sometimes. I also like to eat sitting up, standing and walking, but let's face it, you can't always be sitting up, standing or walking when you eat; sometimes you're going to be eating lying down. Or at least leaning back. And you spill stuff on your lapels. Or, let me put it this way: I do. And I'll bet so did Adolph Menjou, the notoriously spiffy Hollywood dresser who fell all over himself ratting on people during the McCarthy era. The difference is that he probably had hundreds of jackets. If he spattered *putanesca* sauce on one, out it went. I can't dress on that kind of basis. I have too much loyalty.

But maybe this is all a defense. Maybe I am *afraid* to look like those guys who wear clothes for a living in classy men's magazines. Maybe it's just *me* who refuses to believe that no man can be *so into* clothes. Maybe I just *imagine* that these men, instead of putting their pants on one leg at a time like everybody else, must put themselves on first. Or else melt themselves down and pour themselves in. Or . . .

A test of my integrity, then. Could I somehow pose for *Gentleman's Quarterly,* wearing *fashions,* and yet give people back home no grounds for exclaiming, "I hate to see this. Old Roy has gone off up North and taken to prancing around in Men's Clothing"?

To perform, however briefly, as a male model might be to abandon all hope of ever being inducted into the National Academy and Institute of Arts and Letters. But a man has to do what a man has to do. Other comedy writers who were approached by *GQ* for this shooting refused to put themselves on the line. It is not for me to judge them.

In the end, I worked with a chicken.

. . .

THE MORNING, IN photographer Walter Chin's studio, was devoted to group poses. Randy Cohen, Paul Rudnick, Billy Kimble and I—who carry on, in various ways, the comedico-literary tradition of Aristophanes, Dante and whoever (not one of us, I believe) wrote *Revenge of the Nerds*.

Right away, our hair got geeked up. I didn't see how I could object to a trim, because I had let myself get pretty bushy, partly in order to balance out a recent recrudescence of jowls. "You won't recognize yourself," our groomer told me. Our groomer was named Mel. But she was, I swear to God, a woman, and a very appealing one too, otherwise I would not have sat still while Mel reshaped my locks and swept them back with coconut oil in such a way that when I looked at myself in the mirror, in what may have been a reactionary light, what I saw was a fey Patrick Buchanan.

"Yes, fine," I said. "As long as no one else recognizes me either."

Furthermore, Rudnick and I consented to pose for one shot with our heads touching—something you would never have caught, say, Ring Lardner and George Kauffman dead doing. Hey, what am I, so insecure in my own sexuality that I won't pose with my head touching another man's in a tasteful and perfectly natural way?

Oh, my God.

Aside from that, all we had to do in the morning was stand there wearing fairly tweedy grey clothes, for the most part, and holding books.

I held Montaigne. Didn't just hold him, but read him appreciatively for, strangely enough, the first time. Montaigne and I met cute, you might say. Check out "On Cannibals":

"The first man who rode a horse [to where a certain tribe of cannibals lived], though he had had dealings with them on several other trips, so horrified them in this posture that they shot him dead with arrows before they could recognize him."

How often we see this in civilized life, as well: by the time people figure out who we were and why they shouldn't have been doing what they were doing to us, we are dead.

I lack the space, here, to share with you all that I learned about being a mannikin. Much of it is common sense: don't change socks too close to the lunch, that sort of thing.

"The clown shoes are here," Cohen and I overheard someone say. "Where's the rubber chicken?"

Cohen and I looked at each other. "I don't like the sound of it," said Cohen.

Cohen and I thought quickly. Two of us could stay and do our individual shots that afternoon. Cohen and I got dibs. Rudnick and Kimble agreed to come back the next day. As soon as they were out the door, Cohen spoke for both himself and me:

"Nothing wacky, please," he said. "I try to stay away from wacky. If some people wear a chicken on their shoulder, it's one thing. If I wear a chicken on my shoulder, people will say, 'Where's the irony?' "

Nobody had told us about any chicken, or any clown shoes. Let Rudnick and Kimble do those. I consented to pose with the burning typewriter, since it seemed very Jerry Lee Lewis, and Cohen said he would do the magic scarves.

"Work with the scarves?" he confided to me. "Yeah, okay—instead of the dog peeing on my leg or worse, me peeing on the dog's leg. . . . I feel manipulated."

The thing is, the whole crew was so nice. Easy for them, of course— being artists, they were all dressed in black. But when one of us didn't want to do something, *they* looked embarrassed. I can readily imagine a scenario in which torturers are trying to make me give up atomic secrets and I cry, "No matter what fiendish methods you come up with, you cannot force me to go against my principles and betray the vital defenses of my native land!"

And the torturers sort of flinch and blush and look at their feet, and mumble, "Gee, we're just . . ." And I begin to see things from their point of view, and . . .

Furthermore, it is hard to keep perspective when you are sitting there under lights as big as doors, and eight or ten artistically dressed people are frowning at you as if you are a madonna whose shoulders aren't quite square, and Mel keeps dashing up to *primp* you, quickly (more or less in the way your mother used to apply final touches to you before Sunday school, only Mel has a nicer touch), and then slipping away before you can work up the nerve to try primping her back.

And there I sat, in a leather jacket which, if I saw someone wearing it in the street, would make me wonder why on earth anyone would ever wear such a weird leather jacket. I had already done the burning typewriter. What was needed now, I was told, was "just a straight" pose. (Whatever that might mean to people who had been unable to understand my unbending resistance to the suggestion that I strike a graceful-wristed Vanna White kind of ta-daa pose next to the burning typewriter.)

The truth is that being asked to pose "straight" makes me feel uneasy. Once, years ago, when I was on a book publicity tour, an intense young newspaper photog looked through her lens at me for several seconds and then, without shooting, looked up with dissatisfaction. "I don't see anything," she said.

Trying not to look stricken (which might hurt her feelings), I asked whether she had left her lens cap on.

She ignored this suggestion. "I thought there'd be more *texture* there," she said. Without knowing *exactly* what she meant, I felt that I knew . . . what she meant. Why would anyone, immediate family members aside, want to take a picture of me just standing there sort of looking like myself?

Which is more or less how—except for hair and attire—I sat there in Walter Chin's studio looking. Walter Chin looked uninspired by the sight.

People squinted at me. Adjusted lights. Moved bits of me around. I tried to smile, but to smile for a photographer (though some of my best friends are photographers) is something that I can do no more wholeheartedly than I can pee for a doctor. You're not doing it for the pleasure and release, you're giving evidence to someone you don't know at all well.

Spontaneously, one of Chin's assistants had an idea. He started *throwing the chicken around behind me.* Chin's eyes brightened.

"It looks like the scene in *Eraserhead,*" Chin said. "The things coming through the air. The sperm and things."

"Give me the chicken," I said. *"At least I'll know where the chicken is."*

I know better, professionally, than to pose with a chicken. But I am incapable, personally, of saying, "I will *not* pose with a chicken!"

"Truly man is a marvelously vain, diverse and undulating object," wrote Montaigne. "It is hard to found any constant and uniform judgment on him."

DEMME:

=======A DAMN GOOD=======

KENNEL MAN

If you keep up with the uncategorizable-movie scene at all, you probably know that Jonathan Demme is the director of a heart-warming comedy (*Citizens Band*) that leads us to believe, for several delicious moments, that the hero has unwittingly been eating his dog; and another comedy about ordinary life (*Melvin and Howard*) in which two men called the Bait Brothers sing and dance in a single suit of clothes; and so on. But did you know that Demme is named for his lineal ancestor Jonathan Edwards, the great eighteenth-century American theologian who wrote *Sinners in the Hands of an Angry God*? Or that a pivotal role in Demme's development was played by grey-hound blood?

Demme is a chunky, eager-faced, affably new-wavish, very young-looking forty-four. He sits there in his athletic jacket with Japanese-English embroidery (EXCITING LEAGUE, UNITY LEAGUE CONQUEST TEAM 74-75, NORTH SHORE MAPLE VALLEY HIGHWAY) and a Jesse Jackson button on it, and tells me that he doesn't like being focused on, because a movie involves many people working together. And I take his point. So let's focus on me.

I am a cameo. My roughly twelve-second appearance (part of which time I am behind someone's head) in Demme's latest movie, *Married to the Mob,* places me in a long tradition that seems to include every nonactor Demme has ever known: his mother, his father, one of his brothers, his wife, two of his sisters-in-law, his father-in-law, himself, some of his high school buddies, most of his production staff and David Byrne's mother, to name a few. What is it like to direct your own mother? "On the first take I looked at her and thought, 'This is over the top,' and then I thought, 'This is *really* over the top,' and I said, 'Mom, just be yourself,' and she said [he does his mother waving her arms and shouting], 'I *am* being myself!'" Her name is Dodie. But enough about her.

Here I am in a corridor of the state courts building on Centre Street in New York, dressed more or less as myself, jostling and straining, trying to get the ear of a Mafia don, and an armed guard is shoving me, and I feel—oh, perhaps *radiant* isn't the word, but let's say *enhanced*, because I am part of this strange comedy whose director has been called the Preston Sturges of our time. Sturges may be my favorite director, but he is dead. Whereas Demme . . .

Sorry. Back to me. I play, as far as I am concerned, a pivotal role in *Married to the Mob*. In the credits I am identified as the Humane Reporter, as opposed to the Pushy Reporter and the Zany Reporter. I have a line:

"How are the feds treating you, Tony?"

I jostle and strain with real conviction, because my motivation is to stay on-camera as long as possible, and that means struggling as hard as I can to interview in a crowd. I shout my question at Dean Stockwell, who plays Tony "the Tiger" Russo, a kind of sympathetic murdering bastid. Then, if you look as closely as I can assure you I have, you can see me in the background smiling broadly at Tony's quips, which are not actually very funny except on a certain level. In fact there is an eerie, dreamlike quality to this scene I'm in, as far as I am concerned. Here I am in a darkened screening room watching what may well stand as my entire body of work as a screen actor pass before my eyes, and the whole thing is being dreamed by a character played by Dean Stockwell! (Whom I met, by the way, and he seemed perfectly nice.) So of course I'm laughing at his jokes. That's the way I figure it. Why else would a person with a sound sense of humor laugh in such a nakedly exposed way (if you're looking close enough) at quips that aren't funny? It's because I have an intuitive grasp of dream-scene logic. Either that or I will do anything to please anyone with whom I am associated cinematically in any capacity.

There is another reason why the scene holds an eerie, dreamlike quality for me (and this is why I call my role pivotal): my entire reaction to this movie turns on the thought, "How can this be a real movie if I'm in it?"

So let us, with real reluctance on my part, focus on someone else. Michelle Pfeiffer. In *Married to the Mob* she plays the central character, Angela DeMarco. Angela has been suffering role strain as the wife of a mobster, and now that her husband has been rubbed out she tries to escape the clutches of the "family," particularly Godfather Tony.

One of the great things about Demme's movies is how the women in them glow. Mary Steenburgen in *Melvin and Howard*, Melanie Griffith in *Something Wild*, Candy Clark in *Citizens Band* (just to mention principals) have a redoubtable, quirky-to-kinky, inner-directed dewiness that to be sure derives from themselves but is also distinctively Demmean.

How can I justify that adjective, *Demmean*? Without focusing on Demme. Well, I sat in a booth at Sigma Sound in New York and watched as composer David Byrne, music supervisor Gary Goetzman and sound mixer Chris Newman laid music under a scene in which Pfeiffer says to Matthew Modine:

"My husband useta work for Tony Russo. And he was iced. And ever since, Tony's been tryna screw me."

On the page, not so luminous. But I viewed that scene eight or ten times on a monitor, back and forth, and every time it was savory. It was like reading over and over a particularly decorous and sensuous passage from "The Eve of St. Agnes" by Keats. Angela's declaration causes Modine to fall in love—which is understandable but awkward, because what she doesn't realize is that he is an FBI agent out to get Tony through her. ("I've misjudged you," he says, and that means one poignant thing to him but quite another to her—Demme's movies are full of people leading incongruous double lives yet fruitfully coexisting.) Modine's partner (played by Oliver Platt, who looks a little like Demme to me, but Demme doesn't see it) looks bemusedly semismitten himself, although he is only eavesdropping on their conversation electronically and can't see her lips. Never before on screen, I venture to state, has a woman looked and sounded so undesigningly exquisite saying "iced," as in offed, in a Long Island Italian accent. Demme's movies are full of moments that lift me slightly off the ground.

So where does that leave us? Except for what I've read here and there, I don't know what a director does. I've watched John Huston, Robert Altman, Mike Nichols and Demme direct, and they all seemed interchangeably unobtrusive. The only direction Demme gave me personally, aside from encouragement to be loud, was after the run-through, in which I got shoved out of the shot. "If you want to fall back like that again," he said, "it might be good." I nodded but was not about to comply.

Mark Burns and Barry Strugatz wrote Pfeiffer's lines, and she delivered them, and Modine reacted to them winningly, and Richard Ericson was her dialect coach, and Tak Fujimoto lit and shot her, and Craig McKay was the editor, and Ed Saxon and Kenneth Utt produced, and Orion came up with the project to begin with, and there are so many others I could name. All I can tell you about the Demme touch, as such, is that his demeanor, on and off the set, is cheerfully invigorating. I've spent time with him at infrequent intervals over the last eight or ten years, and the only time I've seen him looking anxious was when I laid on him my theory of him as culture hero.

So I withdraw my theory. Here it is:

In Demme's four most Demmean features—*Citizens Band, Melvin and Howard, Something Wild* and now *Married to the Mob*—a fresh-faced, apparently too-nice-for-his-own-good young man (played by Paul LeMat, Paul LeMat, Jeff Daniels and Modine) runs up against various corrupting aspects of American life and manages courageously (in three of the four cases, by kicking ass) to justify his essential sweetness. I put it to Demme that this was also the story of Demme as filmmaker—except that the jury is still out on his justification, because (the curse of low tastes and capitalism) none of his features has been a big commercial success. As I say, he didn't go for the concept. "All those movies—I get hired to make them," he said.

But we have got to have some kind of theme here. Demme's movies do. "Can't face your own brother? You got something to say to me, say it to my face," says Paul LeMat to his brother in *Citizens Band.* Not so heavy, or else too heavy, on the page, but in the movie it nicely plaits various plot and subplot strands along with the obvious one that LeMat has just caught his brother out as the ominous CB voice, handle "Blood," that has been threatening him.

You may be wondering about the greyhound blood.

First, a little exposition. Demme and his wife, painter Joanne Howard, and their baby daughter, Ramona, live in a sun-drenched NoHo loft decorated with dozens of Haitian and Latin American folk paintings and some of Joanne's: a sinuous dark suggestion of landscape that is actually more of an *S* with a real snakeskin impastoed in; an airliner with dreams of wings and angels arising from it. In moviemaking, Demme says, "different levels of attention come into play. One of them is the adolescent who enjoys a good gunfight and wants to go for popcorn if the kiss goes on too long—I feel my heart sink if the characters settle into a conversation." So it is not entirely my fault if this article jumps around. While laying out bagels and lox, playing with the baby, using the phone, taking a snapshot of the baby and me, showing off paintings and setting off to see a friend's sculpture, Demme reveals that he grew up on Long Island and in Miami loving movies but never expecting to make them.

"I don't know what it is, about the family structure or what, that makes a kid get so hooked on movies. When I was twelve or thirteen I'd go alone on the bus or train to see movies all over Long Island. I'd cut out ads—I had stacks of movie ads. Go down in the basement of apartment buildings to cut out ads from great stacks of newspapers with that awful smell they have when they've been down in the cellar too long.

"The first time I saw a TV, I remember standing there, a six-year-old in a cowboy hat, watching a shoot-out with Hopalong Cassidy—one of those fights in the rocks. Then the cute older girl next door took me to see *Treasure Island* with Robert Newton—'arrrh, me hearty.' There were these great pictures—*Mighty Joe Young, Yankee Doodle Dandy*—on television, the Million Dollar Movie, the same movie repeated all week. But it never crossed my mind that you could *do* that. I wanted to *watch* movies. Never thought I'd be involved in the process. Why would I want to be? Just go see 'em is the best!"

When the family moved to Miami, his parents would take him to an art theater—*Black Orpheus* stands out—and he enjoyed that fare as well as the popular. "Me and my friends used to drink a lot of beer and go to the drive-in. Sometimes with dates, sometimes without 'em. My friend Buzz Kilman—he's the Ruthless Sniper in *Married to the Mob*—he's now a radio personality in Chicago. He and I were in the same high school fraternity, Deucalion. He was president and I was vice-president. We were both going steady, with Linda and Becky. New Year's Eve we took them to the Miracle Theatre on the Miracle Mile at 10:45 to see *Father Goose* because that way we could stay for the midnight premiere of *Goodbye Charlie.* Our girlfriends were pissed, and they let us know it, and we didn't give a shit. They had their little dresses that everybody gets for New Year's Eve—had their hair done, these incredible triple bubble flips . . ."

"And they weren't even at a theater they could make out in," says Joanne.

"Right. It wasn't a drive-in! Buzz and I thought we were making a sacrifice because we couldn't bring any beer in."

Still, movies weren't a *career* obsession. Demme intended to be a veterinarian. He had a job as a vet's assistant. And he found out why this vet charged nothing for putting greyhounds to sleep—greyhounds who didn't pan out as racers or breeders.

Greyhound blood is the richest of dog bloods. Only greyhound blood suits any breed of dog in transfusion. So greyhound blood was worth seventy-five dollars a pint. Before destroying an unwanted greyhound, this vet would bleed him for a few days.

And Demme thought, "Well, gosh, I want to be a vet. Maybe I'm not cut out for it. But these dogs are going to die anyway, and the blood will help other dogs. . . ." So he would grit his teeth and bring the doomed greyhounds up from the kennels to be bled.

Then little Jojo arrived. The prettiest, wiggliest little greyhound Demme had ever seen—a point he made to the vet.

A gleam came into the vet's eye. "You're not supposed to get emotionally involved with the animals," the vet said. *"Goooo* get lit-tle Jojo."

And Demme did. And watched little Jojo be bled. And decided he couldn't let it happen again. "I called up a guy who lived on a farm and said, 'Do you want the best dog you'll ever have?' and he said, 'Sure,' and I got little Jojo and took her to him.

"And the next day the vet looked at me and said, 'Goooo get lit-tle Jojo.' He was such a prick. I mean, he was a nice guy, but he was being such a prick. And I said, 'I can't get little Jojo.'

"And he said, 'You have to get little Jojo. You'll never be a vet if you . . .'

"And I said, 'No, you don't understand, I can't get little Jojo because she's gone. I took her somewhere where you'll never find her.'

"And he said, 'Not only are you fired, right now, and you'll never be a vet, but if you don't get that dog back to me tomorrow I'll have you arrested.'

"And I walked out saying, bleeding heart, 'Well fugyoo then, just call the cops, then,' and went home.

"After a few days he called up and said I could forget about being taken into his practice, but he'd give me my job back. 'You'll never be a vet,' he said, 'but you can be a damn good kennel man.'

"That had a great effect, seeing what a business veterinary medicine was. It wasn't about saving little animals, it was about making a lot of money."

Let's face it. People have said the same thing about the movie industry. But Demme says, "I still feel on a certain level how amazing it is to me to be a moviemaker."

It came about in this way. He couldn't learn chemistry at the University of Florida. "Did you ever just block on a subject, and not get it?" My theory is that every time he looked at a beaker he thought of little Jojo, but at any rate he washed out of pre-vet. He had been reviewing movies for the campus paper and the *Coral Gables Times-Guide.* Through his father, who was in hotel and airline publicity, he met the mogul Joseph E. Levine, who gave him a job in movie publicity. Pauline Kael met him during this stage of his career. "He had a mustache then. Neither of us had any idea I was meeting a budding filmmaker," she says. But within a few years he had met the eminent B-movie producer-director Roger Corman, who has a history of helping young filmmakers bud before they expect it. By 1974 Demme was the auteur of *Caged Heat.*

After that things got rockier. His first effort after he outgrew the Corman stable was *Citizens Band,* which got great reviews but made no money under that title or when it was rereleased as *Handle with Care. Melvin and Howard* came out in 1980. It was chosen as the year's best film by the National Society of Film Critics, and Demme was named best director by the New York Film Critics. The movie didn't make money.

I got to know Demme around this time. He wanted me to do a script with him, and I was eager, and I did learn about one thing a not-yet-bankable director spends a lot of time doing: trying to get something going. Here was a guy who had twice found indigenous magic in small-time America, and many were the sluggish, oft-passed-on scripts and weird novels that he hustled to dredge a project out of. But the star or the producer or some other element always fell through, which is to say the money was never there—until *Swing Shift* came along. I had a chance to do the third or fourth rewrite of that script. "I think we're going to fall in love and get married," the producer said. "We're going to kick ass!" said Demme. But then somebody offered me a chance to write an original script, and Demme unselfishly advised me to do that instead.

Swing Shift was to be Demme's commercial breakthrough. Goldie Hawn, the first big name he'd worked with, was the star and executive producer. Pauline Kael, who has seen the print that Demme and editor McKay put together, says it is terrific and that it also makes Hawn look much better than the version that was released, which was reworked by other hands because Demme refused to go along with the changes Hawn demanded. *Swing Shift* did not advance anyone's career.

Demme doesn't like to talk about the *Swing Shift* struggle. "It was emotionally and psychologically very exhausting—but that wasn't about the horror of what can happen to you in the movie business, or the horror of a director having his movie taken away from him, though that was horrible. It was about being in sustained conflict with essentially decent people. Nobody giving in. It didn't sour me on anything except conflict. It didn't sour me on Hollywood, which is a state of mind anyway. It just kicked the shit out of me for a while."

He kept control of his next feature, *Something Wild,* which is rife with surprise. I'm not going to spoil it for you; rent it on video. Let me just say that Demme recalls realizing what a director could do when, in college, he saw *Shoot the Piano Player,* "and gangsters are interrogating Charles Aznavour, and he says, 'If I'm lying, may my mother drop dead.' And Truffaut cuts to a shot of an old lady collapsing! Such a rule break, such a preposterous thing in the middle! I thought, 'That's a real director! That's a crazy director!' " *Something Wild* is much more surprising than that. It is as funny and Americana-packed as Demme's other features and is also scarier than *Fatal Attraction,* without being sleazily manipulative like *Fatal Attraction.* Large audiences went for *Fatal Attraction* but not for *Something Wild.*

There have been many neoattempts at screwball comedy and film noir lately, and some of them have been popular successes. Demme managed to get both genres dead-on and enriching each other in the same movie, and people hung back. *Offbeat* is a word that is often applied to his movies. Offbeat in the Eighties means being serious about more things than business.

Demme is cochairman of Filmmakers United Against Apartheid. His Americanascape makes a demographically apt, cinematically overdue point of including numbers of friendly, self-sufficient nonwhite persons. He plans to revisit Haiti soon to make a second political-documentary-you-can-dance-to (the first, *Haiti Dreams of Democracy,* appeared on cable this year), in which folk musicians deride the thugs who run their country. He is earnest about social fabrics and about how movies affect them.

"I think it's obscene to show death as an orgiastic moment in life," Demme says. "Surely this must be one of the things that make kids pick up a real gun to capture the thrilling moment. *Something Wild* disturbed people because it tried to be loyal to the idea of showing how terrifying it is to get in a long fight. People got emotionally disturbed. That disturbed me. I don't want to upset people in their life.

"I never wanted *Married to the Mob* to cross the line into being a disheartening circumstance for anybody." So its violence is stylized, bloodless, zany.

Demme calls it "escapist" and "commercial," but he is taking the risk again that audiences will say, "What kind of movie is this, anyway? A kind of postfeminist bedroom farce in which eleven people are shot to death?"

One of the reasons Preston Sturges died a flop is that his movies became more interesting and Sturgesean than immediate mass audiences wanted them to be. But Sturges also made a self-destructive point of defying the soulless moneymen, and he wasted his capital.

"I'd love to have made some of Preston Sturges's movies, but I don't want to *be* Preston Sturges," Demme says with feeling.

"Did you ever see *The Legend of Lylah Clare*? Peter Finch plays a caricature of a serious director, and Ernest Borgnine is a caricature of a studio head. There's this great scene, where Borgnine says to Finch, 'If it wasn't for guys like me, guys like you would be making home movies for an audience of one.' And that's *true*.

"The hardest thing about making a movie is getting a good script. It's hard to write a good script. I have tried and failed. *Something Wild* is all in Max Frye's script. Getting a good script that looks like a worthy investment for executives of corporations who in order to remain in their jobs have to realize a significant profit. You can always make the really cheap offbeat thing, get your offbeat fun in. On the other hand, if you find a commercial script like *Married to the Mob*—jump in with full fuel."

But how long can his fuel last if he doesn't produce a major hit?

It seems plain to me, as Humane Reporter, that Demme is up to higher comedy than people are prepared for nowadays—and yet it's comedy that has the straightforward common touch of a small-town newspaper column.

"Jonathan Demme is our most direct contact to the avant-garde," said *The New York Times* after his full-bodied, no-dialogue Talking Heads concert film, *Stop Making Sense*. But I can't imagine *anyone*, however hip or unhip, not responding to the climactic scene of *Citizens Band*, in which all the characters, hitherto alienated one from the other, are brought into heterogeneous concord in the woods, in a secular heaven of no-fault bigamy (you have to be there), found cattle, and misty end-of-the-rain light.

I always thought of Jonathan Edwards as a fire-and-brimstone Calvinist, but after I learned that Demme was Edwards's descendant I looked him up and found that he often spoke of sweetness (an "inward sweetness," an "awful sweetness") and light. Here's a passage with a moviemaking application: "What an infinite number of . . . beauties is there in that one thing, the light, and how complicated a harmony and proportion is it probable belongs to it." And here's something that fits Demme's movies in particular: "The beauty of the world consists wholly of sweet mutual consents."

Nothing is forced in Demme's movies, and yet points are made. There's a moment in *Married to the Mob* when the Pfeiffer character's little boy, whom she's been trying to raise decently in murderous circles, shoots at his happy dog with a laser-tag gun the godfather gave him, causing a laser-tag target on the dog's head to beep. The dog whimpers and runs. Pfeiffer and the viewer cringe, and perspective is lent to all the bizarrely affectless real-bullet mayhem in this and other movies.

("You mean I have to kill them?" Matthew Modine asked Demme before his big shoot-out scene, and Demme said, "You didn't read the script?" But Demme says he's "nervous that that scene might've pussyfooted its way into 'It's easy and fun to shoot mobsters.'" He says he wanted us to feel sorry that all those characters die.)

But even humane people got to pay the rent. Pfeiffer holds her own because she doesn't care about luxury and is a good worker. Demme believes he can hold his "as long as I do real professional work, and it shows on the screen—it doesn't look like a lazy person's done it." And he eschews heroics. He says he's happy in his working arrangement with Orion. "I have as much control as anybody who's been around as long as I have. Creative control through two cuts and two previews. After that, if a studio wants changes, you have to find a way to make what you want to do *work*. You have to make a *case* for it."

In *Something Wild* a Florida artist named Jim Roche had a cameo role, dispensing Pepto-Bismol to the Jeff Daniels character. (Demme became friendly with Roche after mistaking his studio for a first-rate junk shop.) Roche came up with an ad lib. I'm a *writer*, and I didn't try to ad-lib in my cameo, but never mind. This ad lib worked so well that Daniels decided to repeat it toward the end of the movie—after, as Demme says, "he's seen violence in an intense form and walked away from it."

The ad lib is, "Remember, it's better to be a live dog than a dead lion."

Hey, my man saved little Jojo, didn't he?

"I'm never sure what people make of these thematic lines," Demme says.

YOU DON'T SAY

"MUSH"

The dogs liked it.

That is one of the two main things I have always wondered about dogsledding. The other night I saw a Broadway musical in which a dog was featured, and I don't think the dog liked it. In fact I think the dog minded it. It was indoors, and the dog didn't have enough to do. When it came time to take bows, the dog stuck his head in from the wings, looked around, and withdrew. But the dogs I recently went dogsledding with in the Green Mountain National Forest, near Middlebury, Vermont, had nearly as good a time as I did, I believe.

I have never felt entirely comfortable being borne along by literal horsepower. Horses never make me feel that they really want to take me anywhere. Oh, sometimes it is all right as long as I am behind the horse, or on his back, but when I come around front and try to establish eye-to-eye solidarity, the horse always looks at me as if he'd never seen me before.

And of course cats are out of the question.

But sledding with eight dogs is something I recommend. Ed Blechner, who grew up in Brooklyn reading adventure stories and went on to become an instructor for Outward Bound, now runs Konari Outfitters, Ltd., of Addison, Vermont. He sells "quality working-dog equipment, accessories, and winter gear" by mail order, and he also takes people out on day-long or overnight dogsledding trips.

The full-blown camping excursions entail a good deal of brisk-paced cross-country skiing (the equipment rides on the sled), and the brisker I get on cross-country skis the more I tend to fall on my behind, something I don't like to do when dogs are watching. Furthermore, although I have survived quite a few New England winters in my time, I confess to being a bit of a weenie when it comes to serious frigidity. The prospect of spending the night in a tent when the temperature is below zero does not make my mouth water. In fact it makes the inside of my nose freeze up. So I took the day trip. But I got the clear impression that the dogs would have thought more of me if I had kept them out all weekend, so I wish I had.

"Please note," says Blechner's catalog, "that all of our trips are participatory in nature—*we do not* (except in emergencies) put you in the sled and drive you around." Blechner said: "That would be boring for the dogs, boring for me, boring for the person riding in the sled." The dogs don't get off on hauling tourists up and down a trail where they have already smelled everything, Blechner explained, "but they're born with a willingness to pull. As long as you make it fun for them, they don't like to be left behind."

Blechner has twelve dogs in all. Eight congenial ones can make a team. I regret to say that the dog Blechner credits with the most personality also has such intense caninity that he was left home in the kennel. He's an Alaskan malamute named Rainy. He looked like such a hell of a dog in the picture I saw of him as a pup that I yearn to be his Jack London. But he is so up-front about being top dog that he doesn't get along with some of the others.

"I don't care if you have a little Pomeranian in a New York apartment. That dog looks at you as if you were a member of a pack," said Blechner. "And these dogs are descended from wolves. In every wolf pack there's an alpha male and an alpha female that dominate. I know a couple who had a female wolf in their family. She thought she was the alpha female and she and the husband were going to be leaders. You can imagine his wife had a little trouble with that situation.

"I picked Rainy from a litter. He was sitting there leaning back with his legs out straight: I knew what I was getting into. He will challenge you psychologically. And these dogs will scrap just like siblings. It's no fun trying to break it up."

As it happens, I like breaking up dogfights. It brings out my middle-man instincts. But my hands were full just trying to drive these dogs, though they were in good spirits and Blechner was jogging along ready to take over.

Four pairs were harnessed along braided polyethylene gangline. At right lead dog we had Janda, a six-year-old white Samoyed weighing about sixty pounds. She's so smart that you have to watch her or she'll decide for herself when it's time to turn. Next to her, and almost as smart, was Stormy, an off-white Siberian husky, six years old, seventy pounds. In Rainy's absence the alpha male might be Stormy or it might be Drifter, who was conveniently located four dogs back.

Behind the lead dogs were Tubby and Maple. Tubby, who is actually almost whippet-lean except through his barrel chest, tends to jump straight up in the air in the eagerness of his pulling. He's a fifty-five-pound gray-and-white Siberian husky. Maple, a seventy-five-pound malamute, is Rainy's niece, only one year old. "Maple didn't work well the last few times next to Hamlet," Blechner said. "Hamlet's kind of flaky. Tubby's a little more experienced. These dogs learn from each other the way kids do from an older sister or brother. But Tubby's not used to dealing with the public." Alongside Tubby, Maple was easier to keep in line. And after a day next to Maple, Tubby became a bit less of a private dog, at least with regard to having his ears scratched. Maple is excellent at dealing with the public: The first time I hunkered down to pet her during a break she crawled up into my arms.

In the least responsible positions, third row back, were Panda and Hamlet. Panda is a fifty-five-pound, four-year-old, red-and-white Siberian husky whose ankles toe in, giving her a rolling gait, which means she may not have much of a sledding future, but she is as nice a dog as you'd ever want to meet, if you hadn't already met Maple. Hamlet, a three-year-old, black-and-white Siberian husky, began to soliloquize whenever we stopped moving.

And closest to the sled were the wheel dogs: Drifter, a five-year-old, black-and-white Siberian husky who is Panda's father but doesn't know it, and Thule, an Alaskan husky, five years old, fifty-five pounds. Firmly but nonviolently, Drifter makes it clear to Thule that he does not like to be crowded. Don't get down close to Thule, whether you're a dog or a person, unless you like to be licked a lot.

The sled is eight feet long, made of bent ash and rawhide on metal runners. It was built by a man who went on expeditions with Admiral Byrd. Working Eskimos, trappers and explorers used this kind of sled before snowmobiles came along. It weighs fifty-five pounds and can carry up to seven hundred pounds of cargo. A working sledder can't afford to be part of the load himself, so uphill he runs along behind, on the flats he pedals with one foot like a kid riding a scooter, and downhill he rides with both feet on the runners.

There are no reins. You hold on to handlebars, and you keep the lines taut by riding the foot brake just enough. You holler "Gee" to signal Janda to start them turning right and "Haw" for left. To stop them you holler "Whoa," but you also have to jam on the brake—which digs down beneath the snow and makes a terrible grating noise on the frozen ground—with plenty of force, because the dogs don't like to stop.

Starting them is easy. As soon as they hear you let off the brake, they're going. I had to keep reminding myself to let it off inaudibly so I could have the pleasure of hollering the go signal.

Which isn't "Mush." That's the second of the two main things I always wondered about dogsledding. Somehow hollering "Mush" has never appealed to me, and I was pleased to know that what you say is "Hike." Or "Let's go." "Mush" is a corruption of the French Canadian *marche,* which is no longer au courant, according to Blechner: "Even though dog drivers are called mushers, no one says 'Mush.' "

"Hike" is what we used to say back home to start a football play, and it made me feel good to say it to these fine dogs. It made them feel good to hear it. And running along behind them was the only way in the world I was going to stay warm. What with the wind-chill factor entailed in rushing along through a day that was unseasonably bitter even for Vermont in January (over snow that was only a couple of inches deep and didn't bedeck the treetops, so that the hillsides from a distance looked like they needed a shave), we were talking subzero conditions.

I wore three layers of pants and shirts, a big hooded down coat, bulky leather-and-rubber boots with thick felt liners and two pairs of heavy wool socks, a polypropylene cap and wool scarf under my hood, and leather gloves with knit liners. But whenever we stopped for a rest my fingers and toes started complaining.

And I told my fingers and toes to shut up.

And Hamlet was whining and moaning and Maple was looking back at me grinning and "Hike!" we were off again bucketing along, the dogs yelping and trotting and I running and pedaling and hopping on and hopping off. The dogs and I all liked it. Now I would like to quote a passage from Blechner's catalog that suggests what it would have been like if we'd spent the night together:

". . . a night in the middle of January with a full moon can sometimes be cold enough to make your pulse freeze and bright enough to thread a needle by. The dogs had settled in for the night, strung out on their picket line, each forming a small crater in the snow. They were as quiet as the night itself . . .

"It wasn't long before I first heard Janda's bark. . . . It wasn't a bark, bark, bark sound but more of a bark, pause, bark, pause. When Janda barks like that, it usually means there is some wild animal . . .

"It was about a minute before the sound erupted. . . . Its closeness startled me—a high-pitched yelp and wail, the unmistakable howl of the Eastern coyote. It didn't take Janda long to get the whole crew involved. I held my breath as the . . . dogs and their wild brother sang in a howling serenade."

Do you get that with snowmobiles?

Here is the way I figure it would be with the coyote and the dogs and me.

"Yarp. Aroooooooooooo." (High-pitched yelp and wail.)

Janda joins in, with Stormy and Drifter leaping to be next, and Hamlet with his more complicated wail, which might be interpreted as "Awooo, or not awoo . . . What a piece of work is dog, in instinct howwwwooooooooooooooo."

And Maple. Maple's call I believe would be a bit like that song in *The World of Suzie Wong,* "I Enjoy Being a Girl," only more contemporary and growlier.

You don't sleep with the dogs. They nestle into snowhollows, chained up. If they aren't chained, Blechner says, "they get into trouble—in human terms. Not what a dog would call trouble."

I go outside to join them, and some of them would clearly prefer that I had stayed with my own kind, but Maple gives me an encouraging look, and I do my own ululation, developed over the years:

"Warf. Warf. Warf. Waroooooooooo."

And there is a pause.

And then, from the coyote, a kind of *"What* in the . . . ?" yelp.

And from Maple. "Human. But he's got some dog in him."

YO YO YO,
ROWA UH
ROWA, HRU HRU

One raccoon will go through a watermelon patch taking just one plug out of every melon, as slick as a man would with a knife. Or a coon will reach through chicken wire and somehow bring just about all of an unwary hen out through that small hole. A twenty-pound coon, boar or sow can whip one good dog or two halfway decent ones.

Still, even though five or six dogs tearing into a coon in the glow of their owners' hunting lights in the night woods do make a glorious tangle of color—redbone, bluetick, black and tan, brown-and-black-and-white treeing Walker and various brindles such as English and Plott—the killing of a coon by dogs is one of the uglier, not to mention least equitable, sporting scenes. The coon makes crazed hissing noises and the dogs seem to despise it. The justification given by coon hunters—all over the South, Southwest, Midwest and as far northeast as upstate New York—is this: if the dogs don't get to fight a coon every now and then they will lose interest in the sport. The point of most coon hunting, these days, is not killing coons.

It is the music. And the feeling of being close to animals.

Not closeness to the coon so much, though many coon hunters take pride in their ability to climb any tree a coon can.

"Bob finally made it to the swaying top," reports Nick Sisley of Apollo, Pennsylvania, in *American Cooner* magazine, "and after some poking was able to knock out the coon—alive. It hit the ground and four dogs piled in. Men were grabbing dogs, and dogs were biting anything that looked like fur. Woe the fellows with a little hair on the back of their hands."

And then there is the musical aspect. Kelly Bragg of Hinton, West Virginia, advertising in *American Cooner* some pups sired by his dog Blue III, writes, "I would rather hear Blue III open at night than to hear Tennessee Ernie sing 'Peace in the Valley.' "

To "open," it should be explained, is to begin "bawling" or "giving out that mountain music." And that music not only charms, it communicates: ". . . for when Blue III opens," continues Kelly Bragg, "he is moving on, and a coon is going to climb."

That is something: to catch the exact drift of a dog way off in the distance, maybe two or three miles, in the dark, in wild country, following its instincts and training through thick cover, running as hard as it can. A good many men go coon hunting three or four or five nights a week, sometimes all night long, in good weather and bad, year-round. "In 1964 me and my wife got into it about coon hunting," says John L. Smith of Garland, Texas, a dry-wall contractor and father of four. "She got mad and said, 'All right, you just go on and hunt, then!' 'Well, that's good,' I said. I hunted forty-two nights in a row, and she never said anything more about it."

Neither coon meat nor coonskins are of much economic value today, and many inveterate coon hunters profess never to have tasted coon. Even most of those who prize the meat highly—barbecued or baked with collards and sweet potatoes—look down on the kind of dog that is best for a meat hunt.

Such a dog is known as a silent or semisilent cooner. Low-bred, maybe three-fourths cur, the silent or semisilent dog sneaks up on a coon with little warning and is therefore more likely to make it settle for a low tree. The dog will then be held back while the hunter shoots and retrieves the coon. Not much pleasure to that.

For the pleasure hunt, a few friends go out in the woods at nightfall with their dogs, turn them loose, build a fire and sit down on a log to tell stories and listen for the dogs to tune up. It is best if the dogs strike the trail of a strong, wily and experienced coon that will lead a long and melodious chase.

Melodious because as soon as the dogs pick up the scent they begin to bawl, and they continue to bawl—"Aooo, aooo," each dog in its own distinctive tone—until the coon is treed. The hunters know when the dogs are "on tree," because the dogs so signify by changing the music. Ideally a dog will "chop" on tree: a brisk, tenacious "Yo yo yo . . . yo yo yo," or "Rowa rowa rowa uh rowa rowa uh rowa," or "Hru hru hru . . . hru hru . . . hru hru hru." The pattern varies.

"Bawl on track, chop on tree is your perfect dog," says T. K. Chilcoat of Ashdown, Arkansas, who is president of the Saline River Coon Hunting Association. "But some dogs may bawl on tree. If I had a good coon dog and he meowed at the tree like a cat, and I could hear him, it'd be fine with me."

When the coon is treed, it is time for the pleasure hunters to get off the log, douse the fire, button up their heavy coveralls and strike out through the brush, brambles, creeks, bogs or even rivers between them and the tree. The hunters locate the coon by making coon-squall noises while shining lights up into the tree. Coons are smart, and will scrunch up in the crotch of a limb and even cover their eyes with their paws, but unless the leaves are too heavy or it is an old den tree—a hollow tree inside which coons live or hide—the coon's eyes will eventually shine in the light.

Then the coon may be shot, or one of the hunters may shinny up and shake it down for the dogs. But if the coon has run a good race it may be granted a reprieve and the dogs will be pulled off and led away to strike another trail. For it is pleasurable just sitting on the log and saying, "There goes old Brumby," or "There goes old June," and telling about the time an old rough coon ran for four hours, perhaps back and forth through the corn when the roasting ears were just coming out, or up and down a railroad draw as the hunters sat listening, the coon passing near enough that they could hear the patter of its feet.

A business hunt brings people and animals together on only slightly different terms. The first step is for the owner of a distinguished dog to place an ad in *American Cooner.* There will be a picture of the owner holding up the tail of a stiffly posed redbone, and another picture of the same dog barking its head off at the base of a tree. The text might run something like this:

"AT STUD. Elvidge's Red Marvel. I have owned this hound just one year and have the names and addresses of 94 men that have bred their females to him. Boys, there must be a reason. Marvel is a beautifully made hound; tight cat feet, big-headed with long, wraparound cars and the most beautiful redbone coat you will ever see. His daddy was Louisiana Bugle and his mother was Far Cry Ann.

"Red Marvel has been straight on coon from a pup up. He is good-natured, a gritty kill dog, and will take any water a coon will cross. Boys, this Marvel dog has a tenor bawl that will make the little hairs stand up on the back of your neck. He is not mean or fussy in any way and he trees with a machine-gun chop that will drown out the average dog.

"I may sound enthusiastic about this young hound and I am. Come on down and I will hunt with you any night except Sunday until you are satisfied Marvel is all I say. If Marvel don't show you coon eyes, then I will buy your gas.

"RED MARVEL'S STUD FEE IS $125.

"I want to say that Wayne Sudduth and his brother Worley were down here hunting last month with their dogs Red Girl and Rose, and

I have never met any two finer sportsmen. Wayne, you and Worley are always welcome at my house to hunt or visit.

"A.O. ELVIDGE, Rt. 1, Box 5, Furnis, Tenn."

In response to the invitation in such an ad, a man from maybe a couple of hundred miles away will drive down with his gyp (the standard coon-hunting term for a female dog; bitch is no word to use around ladies), and the two men and the two dogs will go out hunting. If the gyp's owner likes what he sees, his hound will show up at the house of the stud's owner, in a crate, the next time she is in heat.

Some good coon hounds get to be worth a lot of money. For example, Danny Boy, a treeing Walker owned by J. P. Tyree of Lewisburg, Tennessee, which in 1971 became the first dog ever to win both the American Coon Hunters Association and the United Kennel Club world hunts in one year. Tyree says he has turned down an offer of ten thousand dollars for him.

The ACHA world hunt (which has been held recently in such places as Oblong, Illinois, and Van Wert, Ohio) attracts some three hundred entries, lasts for five nights and rewards the first-place dog's owner with what may be the most imposing trophy in sports: a seven-foot structure, four tiers of bronze and walnut supported by ten columns of the same materials, topped off by a bronze globe from which sprouts a bronze tree on which a bronze dog is treeing a bronze coon.

Other competition hunts are more modest in scale. The duration is only one or two nights, maybe fifty or sixty dogs are entered, and the trophies are no more than waist-high. A local coon-hunting association places an ad in *American Cooner*, "Nite Hunt and Bench Show," on some forthcoming Saturday or Friday and Saturday. Everyone invited, dinner on the grounds, plenty of trophies, drinking forbidden.

The assembly point is some community meetinghouse. In Spanish Fort, Texas, at the very end of a dirt road on the Oklahoma border due north of Nocona, it is a renovated ninety-seven-year-old building owned by Virgil Hutson, the Spanish Fort Coon Hunters Association president, who uses it as a clubhouse and a store for the sale of coon-hunting sundries: "Dog Bloom VM250, The Supreme Conditioner"; "Cooneye Shiner Light Fits Cap Bill or Belt"; "Coon Drag Stick"; "Carhartt Insulated Coveralls"; "Brown Canvas Hats, Jones Style with Coon Face on Front"; "Bandy Tri-Wormer."

The host club's wives open the kitchen for a two-day hunt on Friday morning and keep it open—serving chili, eggs, sausage, steaks and french fries without ceasing—straight through into Sunday afternoon.

Pickup trucks, station wagons and campers carrying caged dogs start arriving Friday morning.

The crowd of hunters and dog traders and onlookers grows into the afternoon. Included are contractors, janitors, roustabouts, carpenters, college students, farmers, high school kids with peace symbols on their clothes, millworkers, car dealers and what have you. One or two hunters may be black. The arrivals are likely to represent three or four states, and one or two may have come from four hundred miles away.

There is some idle introductory joshing, but most of the talk concerns which breed of dog is the best. Say the location is Dierks, Arkansas, the piney-woods headquarters of the Saline River club. T. K. Chilcoat is liable to come over to where past president Dale Thomas is talking to someone and say, "Only thing Dale'll lie to you about is a spotted dog." (That is, a treeing Walker.) "Then, too," Chilcoat goes on, "that is about all he'll talk to you about."

This does not discourage Thomas: "A black and tan is loose-eared. A Walker's ears're growed onto his head better."

"I don't know whether Walkers tree coon better or not," adds another Walker man. "I know they do it more often."

Despite the prevailing tone of bland objectivity, such arguments may grow heated. But they do not reflect directly on a particular man's dog.

"Evra man is proud of his dog," points out Chilcoat.

"That's right," says Thomas. "You don't run a man's dog down. You might as well say, 'Your baby's ugly.' "

The preliminaries to a competition hunt used to include coon-on-a-log, coon-in-the-hole and the waltzing keg. In these events a coon is put, respectively, on a log floating in water, in a hole whose opening is just the size of a dog's head, or in a keg suspended in the air on ropes. Then all the entered dogs are turned loose on it. The dog that seizes, holds and removes the coon wins. Especially in the hole, the coon has the initial advantage, but this hardly makes up for its chances in the long run, and Humane Society pressure has forced such activities out of UKC-licensed hunts.

The rule now is that there can be no direct contact between dog and coon in a preliminary event. This leaves room for water races and treeing contests. In a water race, a coon is towed across a pond in a Styrofoam boat suspended from a cable, and the dogs, divided into heats, swim after it. A redbone of T. K. Chilcoat's once jumped into the wrong heat and finished creditably even though it got a late start and had to tow the big piece of pulpwood it was tied to. The swimming dogs in the pond and the tied-up dogs around it are all bawling; dogs are getting loose, jumping in, splashing, dragging little girls into the water; the little girls are yelling, "Stop! Daddy, come catch your dog!" And Daddy is yelling, "I told you to hold that dog."

A treeing contest is also tumultuous. A caged coon is set up atop a sapling or pole. All the dogs in the contest are given a good look at it. They bark and lunge at the pole and sometimes get loose and ascend it about halfway. Maybe the cage hasn't been pulled up to the top and one dog is able to grab it with its teeth. The treeing-contest officials pull the cage up to shake the dog off but it hangs on until it is four feet off the ground and even then it has to be pried off. Then one dog at a time is loosed to show off its tree form. In most contests the winner is determined purely by the number of times it barks—a hundred chops in a minute is good.

Now comes the bench show, in which dogs are judged solely on their looks. But looking good and hunting good are known to be two different things. It is when dark is falling, and men start saying things like "This old dog can't find enough woods to hunt in," that the real action develops.

The entries hunt in casts of four dogs, which hunt together for three hours, with a local man along as guide and scorekeeper. That's right. A man carrying an official scorecard. Coon hunting has been refined to that point. Scoring high requires close teamwork between dog and handler. As Everette Endsley, who handles Danny Boy for J. P. Tyree, puts it, "You got to really call like your dog is doing. And he's got to really be doing it, too." The reason Danny Boy is the incumbent best coon dog in the world, says Endsley, is that he is a good honest dog. "If he smells a coon he'll bark. If he don't he won't. If the coon runs off through yonder he'll run off through yonder after him. He won't fool around."

The testing of such honesty gets underway as follows: the different casts fan out over, say, a forty-mile radius. It takes a few hours to get gear and dogs together and drive over dirt roads to an isolated spot. The dogs in a given cast are turned loose.

As soon as Danny Boy bawls once, Everette Endsley will call "Strike Dan," but a less distinguished dog handler will probably want to wait for the second bawl to make sure. At any rate, the first man to say "Strike my dog" is accorded a hundred points on the scorecard. The second striker gets seventy-five, the third fifty, the fourth twenty-five.

A problem that may arise here is that two men may strike the same dog. Since every man is supposed to know his own dog's voice like he knows his wife's, this is ticklish. Ten or fifteen years ago, "when coon hunting had a rough name," as one hunter puts it, two men claiming the same bawl might have fought. But today one man will make a semigracious concession. "If another man jumps in on my dog," says Everette Endsley, "that's his chance to take. If he can call my dog better than I can then he's welcome to it." But you know Everette won't like it.

After the striking comes the treeing. The handlers head out in the direction of the bawling dogs. Along the way they speculate on the type of coon they are dealing with. "He been crawfishing up and down that creek," one may say, "and they running back and forth following that feeding trail." Or, "They got an old ridge coon goin'. Them ridge coon're long-legged coons. He'll run like a deer."

Maybe one dog still hasn't opened. "Gerald, where's your dog?" somebody may say.

"I guess he fell in a well," says Gerald, listening.

"He might not like that coon, you reckon?"

"He might not," says Gerald. "If he does, he'll let you know."

There is no telling where the coon's trail may lead. "A dog running a coon would be no race at all right out on the highway," points out Everette's cousin John Henry Endsley, who won the World Hunt in 1964 with Sailor Jr. "I can outrun a coon myself. But a coon can get through a fence where a dog has to slow down. A coon can run up the side of a tree and a dog has to stop and check to see whether he stayed up or jumped down and ran on. A coon can make the walking rough."

Then some dog may begin to chop and its handler will say, "I'm gonna hafta tree old Rebel." Or old Rowdy, or old Girl. The first man to call tree gets a hundred points on the card, and so on, just as in striking.

Usually all four dogs will be found together at the bottom of a mighty oak, chopping and jumping up and down and chewing on the bark. The question is, is there a coon in that tree?

If coon eyes shine, well and good. All the points on the card count plus. But the coon may be up inside the tree. In that case, if the hole in the tree is low down, the hunters may get down on their hands and knees, after pushing the dogs away with some difficulty, and peer up inside with a flashlight, or poke up with a stick. This is a good time for stories about the man who started messing around in a tree like that and a whole hive of bees took off up his shirtsleeves, or the time someone shot a coon out by disassembling a .22 rifle, reassembling it inside a hollow tree with the muzzle up, and pulling the trigger. But many a cavernous or heavy-leafed tree refuses to yield a glimpse of a coon. In this case no dog makes points.

Then again sometimes a tree's limbs are all visible, its trunk is solid and there is no coon anywhere. This means the coon has jumped down, maybe from fifty feet up, and slipped away. The dogs are chopping at a "slick tree." Or, even worse, they may have scared up something other than a coon—a bobcat, a possum or a housecat. If a dog trees "trash" or comes up with a slick tree, it is a "minus dog." Its points all stand, but as a deficit.

In the space of three hours there may be four or five more trees to recoup on, but minus points are not good for a coon hunter's spirits. After a slick tree the talk may well be of bygone dogs that were better. Ben Childress of Fairfield, Texas, tells of Sugarfoot, a redbone grand champion who was still hunting at the age of nineteen. "Sugarfoot had a choking chop, from deep down in his chest," says Childress. Then, while negotiating a creekbed, he lets his own voice go soft saying, "It was just an outstanding privilege to go out in the woods with that dog."

It is at this point that the limits of a competition hunt become evident. Just walking through the woods reminiscing and hoping the next tree won't be slick or trashy is too passive. The compensations are trophies and points toward champion and grand champion status if your dog is one of the top ten in points for the whole hunt.

All the fun is over for the dog, which is led off to pose for pictures— its toenails scratching uneasily on the clubhouse floor—and doesn't get to kill any coons. And the man has run up against section fifteen of the official honor rules: "No shouting encouragement to the dogs."

That is what's missing. That is why there is no recourse for a competition hunter but nostalgia when his dog is not doing its job.

But it may be that while all the official plussing and minusing is going on around the countryside a man swings into the hunt head-quarters who isn't entered but is looking to stir up a pleasure hunt. Let us say that, unlike any of the competitors, he has had a little something to drink. This is a man who before the night is over is going to be shouting encouragement to his dog.

Call this man Troy. The dog he brings in looks as if it needs encouragement, or even a doctor.

"See," explains Troy, "his hair's right. But his flesh ain't right. But my flesh ain't right either." He grins at this. Troy is short, gristly and loose jointed. His overalls hang loose around his next inner layer of clothes. He is feeling good, and in spite of appearances he is proud of his dog.

"He ain't too good to look at," Troy concedes. "But I tell you what, dear dad, when I turn him loose you won't be looking at him anymore.

He'll strike as soon as he smells. He ain't a pretty dog, but a pretty dog don't tree *coon*. I ain't a pretty boy, either, Mr. Man, but a pretty boy don't have *that*."

Troy holds up his right forefinger, which is half missing.

"That ain't from saying good morning, dear dad, that's from grabbing *coon*. Feel that dog's ears. They're chewed, Mr. Man, and that's birdshot stuck in 'em. That is a dog there that's been hunted. Now feel my ears."

Nobody does, but one bystander who is staring at Troy's dog goes so far as to say, "They ain't supposed to be pretty to run coon. They look kinda woolly when they run coon."

"I don't give a damn what they run," says Troy with obscure logic, "from a mare mule to the Queen of Sheba—that black and tan, when I strike him he'll be trailing coon, dear dad, and when I tree him he'll be on the tree. And in one hour or two months or the next morning, when we go back, Mr. Man, he'll have his toenails jabbed into that tree."

So Troy gets up a hunt, with a man who has a dog that digs out so fast after coon, he maintains, that you better not put it down on a gravel road or it will knock the windshield out of your truck.

On the way to the woods in the pickup, Troy mentions a few of the wild and bloody fistfights he has been in with people. "I ain't never met a man I was scared of," he says in conclusion. "But I have met a few I wish to hell I had been scared of." When someone asks him if his dog is really as good as he claims, Troy says this: "My daddy told me, 'Son, I got one ol' boy I could never tell nothing about, whether he was lying or not,' and that was me. He sure couldn't whip it out of me. 'Cause he tried that, a plenty of times."

And then Troy is out in the woods with his dog out farther, and the dog isn't opening yet, and still isn't, and here is what Troy says when he is encouraging his so far silent, distant dog:

"Lemme hearrrrr ya holler." And, "Talk toooo 'im." And, "Get them coooooon."

Troy is not just saying these things, he is bawling them, and he is in good voice. Also he moves well in the woods or the underbrush, he is noted as a climber, he fights bigger men ferociously. Troy might be too inclined toward inscrutability to be a top honest coon dog, but he would be an interesting one, and in still another life he would make a fine rough coon.

YET ANOTHER
════════════TRUE STUDY════════════
OF MANKIND

In Meeteese, Wyoming, researchers studying the world's only known colony of black-footed ferrets will do a study to find out if current studies are disturbing the species. **—USA TODAY**

"D'you think we're *disturbing* these ferrets?"

"Mmm, it's a question that merits
A study. Let's get it funded."

"But what if it undid
All we have learned up to now?"

"I don't see how.
I mean they look all right to me.
How undisturbed can a ferret be?"

"But what if we came to determine—
There, look at that one."

                    "That one's an ermine."

"Oh. But what if we ferreted out
A factor that made us doubt
That ferrets, while we're seeing them,
Are ever ferrets being them-
Selves?"

            "Oh, we know about that."

                              "We do,

Do we? And they do too?"

"Who?"

        "The *ferrets*. The *ferrets*.

Sometimes, with you, I swear, it's—"

"No. Ferrets who knew what
We know would not
Be ferrets, as we know them."

"Why don't we put them in cages and *grow* them?"

"Wouldn't be the same."

               "Well, neither is this."

"Exactly our hypothesis.
We'll draft an act of science,
Demonstrate ferrets' compliance,
And name it after us:
The Mirabeau-Lapidus—"

"Or Lapidus-Mirabeau."

               "No,

The last one was Lapidus-Mirabeau."

"Which one?"

               "The one this next one refutes."

"*What?* The last one was *newts.*"

"The Mirabeau-Lapidus Rule of Vexation."

"All right, *you* fill out the application."

"Don't be a child."

"You are driving me wild."

ON SCIENCE

If doctors know a disease so well,
How come they never catch it?
They're the ones who always tell
You when you itch don't scratch it.

HYENAS FEEL
══════GOOD ABOUT══════
THEMSELVES

My assumption had always been that hyenas skulk because they feel lowly, but after observing hyenas in the East African bush, I am inclined to believe that mother hyenas say to their young, "How many times have I told you? Stop holding your head up!" A hyena's laugh sounds like the whoop of an old boy who's just heard a good one. It isn't hard to imagine one hyena nudging another when a real jaw-dragger goes by and saying, "Look at that sumbitch skulk!"

That impression may be colored by my own ethnic background. But such as my impressions of wild East African animals are, I want to get them down, because the animals may be on the way out. At least all of them that can't share space with crops and buses.

The cheetah, in my experience, is typically surrounded by nine or ten Land Rovers and vans. From these vehicles people take photographs and ask loudly, "WHAT DO THEY MAINLY EAT?" At the moment the cheetah and her cubs are eating some form of antelope. Which form is a matter of audible disagreement among the vehicles' various guides.

"Do we need a constant comment'ry on the disemboweling of poor little whatsit?" asks one of the tourists. One of the guides is commenting so loudly that a serious camera user in another vehicle shouts, "Shut up, man!" The guide takes umbrage and begins to yell, "Who are you? Who are you?" The guide in the vehicle with the shouting photographer begins reasoning in Swahili with the offended guide, but the latter yells, "I will talk! It is a free country!" The cheetahs give no indication that they notice, but you think they must.

Our guide, Richard, of Little Governor's Camp on the Masai Mara in Kenya, quietly observes things that the other guides don't. "It is a Thomson's gazelle baby," he says of the cheetahs' meal. "There is its father." Up on a rise fifty yards away, the father is staring at the devouring of the son. Once the father stamps his foot, which is too small to help. Over the rise are another male and two females, one of which is the prey's mother. She is staring into space.

We drive on and see a young impala off to itself. A baboon is sitting patiently between it and the herd. "The baboon will eat the baby," Richard says. "There is the baby's parents. They know where the baby is. It was asleep. But they do not know the baboon is there. He is clever. He waits till the baby is used to him. It will take about one hour."

For a while we manage to be the only car parked next to a pair of sleeping lions, waiting for them to mate. A pair of lions will keep company for a week and have sex every twenty minutes or so, day and night, for that period. The male of this pair wakes up, licks the female for a few moments and then mounts her. She growls. He lies back down acting as if doesn't matter to him, he just thought she wanted to. It doesn't seem to occur to him that our presence may have something to do with her attitude.

We watch another lion eating a fresh warthog's head. The roar of a lion is like a stone rolling away from a tomb. You've heard of a whiskey baritone. A lion's roar is warthog-head bass.

That night at dinner a woman cries in exasperation, "We did not see one copulating lion!"

You know how New York has pigeons? That's how Kampala, the capital of Uganda, has marabou storks. Stiff-backed, five-foot-long birds resembling public officials, baldheaded except for straggly fuzz, they stalk or glide through the midtown area, eating garbage and perching on used and disused buildings. Urban marabou may be the African fauna of the future. Scavenger birds, and goats no doubt, and here and there a rogue hippo such as the one that "emerged from a sewage pond and attacked a bicyclist on the outskirts of Nairobi," according to *The New York Times,* just before I traveled to East Africa to see wild game before it's gone.

Here, far from the zoo, the hippo is a purple animal with big soulful eyes. Around the eyes and on the underside, pink. The tail looks like a nose with a stringy mustache under it. Hippos in the wild usually have scarred backs from fighting among themselves, biting each other. They can come up under a small boat and flip it.

"I see no hope for it, really," says an old white Kenyan hunter, "it" being Kenya as a place to behold fabulous beasts. Of course there is aways the chance that he meant a place, *run by white Kenyans,* to behold fabulous beasts. White Kenyans have a deep emotional investment in their sense of Kenya as paradise lost.

Tourism is Kenya's number-one industry. Tourism means coming to see the animals. And the minister in charge of protecting the game is no longer the one who escorted nine Arab sheikhs on a shooting spree—two hundred animals they bagged, including lion and water buffalo and cheetah—in a game preserve a few years ago. So there may be room for optimism. The trouble is, there's less and less room for the game.

The main reason that the youth of today may be the last generation to see free-ranging lions is the African youth of today. The infant mortality rate in Kenya is no longer 50 percent, thanks to modern medicine. Even with the AIDS epidemic, adults live longer too. And birth control is unpopular. Kenya's population is the fastest-growing in the world. It needs more and more arable land—the already limited supply of which is being shrunk by drought—to grow crops and raise cows on, which leaves less and less land for the king of the jungle and so on.

On the other hand, a modern young Ugandan, a journalist of Kampala (one of whose slim newspapers, *The Evening Times,* comes out quarterly), told me he had managed to get through his coming-of-age lion hunt without reducing the lion population. He and his friends had one surrounded, late at night, and were closing the circle, *hoomba, hoomba,* with their spears raised. He was feeling, I gather, like an American Little Leaguer who prays the batter won't hit the ball to him, when he felt more than heard an enormous uncoiling whoosh go right past him in the pitch dark.

"I didn't say anything," he said. "I continued to move in, spear up, *hoomba, hoomba,* as did the others. I believe that in this period many lions may vanish mysteriously from hunters in that way."

ZEBRAS LOOK so zebraic! I don't know, you'd think they might feel too boldly patterned. You wouldn't think they'd all feel up to it all of the time. You'd think an occasional one would be gray all over. But no. There they are, herds of them, walking around outdoors, just as zebra-striped as you please. They bray, or honk—a quick harsh hee-haw-heehaw that sounds almost like a bark—when they're deciding to move to a different grazing spot and spreading the word.

Game is of course a speciesist term. Being a water buffalo is not a game to the water buffalo. Not a business either, more a way of life. Bit of cheek, really, calling oneself a big-game hunter or even referring to the taste of a fellow animal as gamy. But consciousness-raising along those lines won't help much. In most parts of Africa today hunting is illegal, and the poachers who kill rhinos and elephants for their horns and tusks, or the odd giraffe or hippo for its meat (the former is said to taste like beef or horse, the latter like pork), are not patronizingly sporty.

I picture the mongoose killing a snake. But according to my observations from a Land Rover, mongoose parents are so preoccupied with keeping their offspring safe from predatory birds that you wonder where they find time for snaking. The mongoose family is living in a termite mound (having eaten the termites), which has ten or twelve tunnels and exits. Mongoose babies are popping out of first one hole, then another—squeezing out past their parents even—and the parents are rushing out, grabbing the babies in their mouths and bringing them back, and the babies are popping out again. "I've seen it in a nature film," says a Land Rover passenger. "But I never dreamed it was actually *there.*"

THE BRIGHT RED soil and lush green fronds alongside a Ugandan highway suggest the fantasy junglescapes of Henry Rousseau. And right out on the road itself in the middle of nowhere are stately deep-black women in bright, many-colored dresses holding huge fish out at arm's length for sale; and a wedding procession on bicycles, the bride on the back of one of the bikes; and baboons sitting out in the middle of the road looking like they're waiting for someone to mug; and a funeral party in suits and ties in the back of a pickup; and a man walking along with six jerrycans of water, three handles in each hand; and at least twenty fuel trucks, heading somewhere, for every gallon of gas available for sale in the service stations.

The highway's very surface is of great interest. It was customary for contractors to charge the government, say, eight million shillings for road repair, kick three million back to selected government officials, keep four million, and spend one million for the repair—until it occurred to someone, why kill the goose that laid the golden egg? Do the deal, sure. But why fix the road? That way you can begin new repair contract negotiations immediately.

In some spots the road actually has been resurfaced lately, and tree limbs have been put down to keep people from driving on it till it dries, but people are driving on it anyway, and women are picking up bits of driven-over limb for firewood. A far more typical stretch of Ugandan highway, however, is roughly 55 percent pothole. Many craters are big enough for several baboons to bathe in after a sudden driving shower. Riding in a rebuilt '76 Nissan with no brakelights that is weaving around these potholes at seventy-five miles an hour through drifts of exhaust and clouds of dust or plumes of red water—now both the car you are in and the car bearing down on you are on one side of the road, now both on the other—makes it hard to worry about threats to any species other than oneself.

A GIRAFFE RUNNING—that neck pumping loftily along over cantering legs—is like several animals at once, but highly coordinated. A giraffe has tremendous eyelashes—talk about looking down on tourists superciliously! An old elephant looks like two men in an elephant suit that is far too big. A baby elephant looks cuter from a distance; up close it is already wrinkled, and you realize that what makes an elephant's visage is the ears and tusks—the rest is saurian and chinless. But when it all is said and done, a baby elephant at any range is awfully cute. We saw one that had no tail. "A hyena eat it off," our guide, Richard, said. "When it was little. There will be problems. With the flies."

THE ONLY ANIMAL in East Africa whose eyes I looked into was a lesser kudu. Before it looked away, we had this unspoken talk:

"I am a kudu.
And what is it you do?"

"Write."

"Quite."

HOW TO STRUGGLE

When I was twelve, I would wake up in a cold sweat. Because of the rumors.

"In high school," it was whispered, "you have to do everything in pen and ink. And you *can't cross out.*"

Which meant I was dead. If I couldn't erase or cross out, I would have to turn in papers whose every other word was wrong. And if by some chance I mastered high-school conditions well enough to get into college, what would be demanded of me there? Typing probably. Thousands of words a minute, about philosophical thoughts and in foreign languages, right off letter-perfect.

It turned out the rumors were exaggerated. You could cross out sometimes, and when you couldn't there were ink erasers. *Aaaaargh.* When I think of all the hours I spent scrubbing little holes in my paper and brushing away eraser detritus!

And later there was Ko-Rec-Type, which I always put in backward. And corraseable bond. Greasy smudgy pages you might as well have wrapped your sandwich in.

Those were the days—when there was no way to forget that writing is a struggle. Now on my computer the words flow like gravy and come out as if engraved. It's like finger-painting, only tidy.

Flaubert wrote with a pen. "Sometimes I wonder why my arms don't fall off my body from fatigue, and why my brain doesn't turn to porridge," he said in a letter to his mistress. "I love my work with a frenetic and perverse love, as the ascetic loves the hairshirt which scrapes his belly. Sometimes, when I find myself empty, when the words refuse to come, when, after scrawling pages on end, I discover that I have not written a single sentence, I fall on my couch and lie there dazed in a private swamp of misery."

That was writing. *Le mot juste* was what Flaubert was after. What we see so often today is *le mot facile.* And you know what Richard Brinsley Sheridan said (excuse me for a moment while I scroll down and pick it up from my notes, tum-te-tum):

"Easy writing's curst hard reading."

What I have written here so far looks pretty. But on this machine it would look that way if it were gibberish. As it happens I have changed every sentence, except Flaubert's and Sheridan's, several times, perhaps not often enough. If I were working on my old manual Royal, I would be looking at the remains of a chicken's breakfast by now. Anything this pretty, in the old days, I would have known was awful.

So here are a few things I do to convince myself that I am still actually writing:

■ Twiddle-twiddle away at my softly clicky keyboard for a while, making twiddly adjustments all along—and then print what I have twiddled. Glare at the printout and snarl and curse and scribble almost illegibly all over it with a ballpoint pen. Go back to the machine and enter the scribbles. Repeat this procedure until I hate the very meaning of every word I know.

■ Think teeth. The pleasure of writing—the prospect so savory, the execution so strained—is comparable, I have always felt, to that of eating a juicy steak with bad molars. To put it another way, writing is like pulling teeth, which is why mine so often reads like the work of a dentist.

■ Wake up in a cold sweat.

WE FEED,
WE LIONS

In Central Park one sunny afternoon, a perhaps apocryphal small girl came up to Mark Twain and asked if he would take a walk with her. Touched, the eminent author bowed to his little fan's smiling parents and set off with her on a long and richly conversational stroll. In conclusion he gave the child a nickel and observed, "Now you can tell all your friends that you have walked with Mark Twain."

She burst into tears.

"Come now," he said fondly. "Perhaps we shall meet again."

She was inconsolable. He appealed to the mother, who was no longer smiling.

"We told her," she said stiffly, "that you were Buffalo Bill."

Recognition is seldom quite what it seems. And yet, it's something. This month Cynthia Ozick, Philip Roth, Ved Mehta, Susan Sontag, Dr. Seuss, 191 other important writers and I will be the honorees (we don't have to pay) of a fund-raising gala, at and for the New York Public Library, called A Decade of Literary Lions. I was first leoed back in 1987, at the seventh of the annual Literary Lions dinners that began in 1981. Twenty or so new lions have been named each year. I made it five years after Henry Kissinger but one year before Alfred Kazin and two years before Edward Albee, but who's counting?

You can bet I will be there this year, with bells on. Not literally. But if the invitation specified bells I would rustle some up. Writers may scorn fame, fortune or (though I haven't heard anyone do so lately) the bitch goddess Success, pardon the expression. But *recognition* is another story.

Some years ago I met a well-known editor who had assisted John Updike in selecting stories for an anthology. The first thing she said to me was, *"I* wanted to include your story about fishing for chickens."

"Well," I said.

"But Updike wouldn't go for it."

"Well," I said.

"I *love* that story, but Updike kept saying it was slight. The more we argued, the more definite he became. He came around on every other story I tried to talk him into, but for some reason, not on yours. He finally said he didn't even think it was *funny.* I just wanted you to know I fought for you."

"Well," I said.

The truth is I have never written any story about fishing for chickens.

Or with chickens. Or in spite of chickens. Never any story whatsoever involving both chickens and fishing.

In a way, then, it is consoling to know that Norman Mailer, Ruth Prawer Jhabvala, Henry Steele Commager, Lady Antonia Fraser, Dr. Seuss and I are inferrably among the 198 most prominent writers over the last decade in America (or no: in English) who can afford evening wear; and Updike isn't. I don't know why, but he's not on the list. It is probably just as well. Say I introduced myself, one lion to another, and happened to mention, perhaps too quickly, "I never wrote anything about fishing for chickens." What would his response be? What would anybody's?

"Ah"?

Perhaps Updike opposes tuxes. I rent mine. If you buy formal wear you feel you ought to amortize it, and the next thing you know you have taken up society.

Delta Burke's wedding aside, the 1987 Literary Lions dinner was probably the fanciest occasion I have ever attended. Well, I recall an affair in Washington celebrating the hundredth anniversary of baseball, back during the Nixon administration, at which I saw Satchel Paige chatting with Melvin Laird. Melvin Laird was hot then. But that wasn't black tie, and it was during a period when ballplayers tended to wear pale blue suits with pale blue vests and pale blue shoes. In my experience baseball galas can't touch literary ones for style.

The first segment was cocktails: some 250 people, each with his or her own high sheen, drinking moderately (except for me) and greeting each other and being photographed. Guests included Jacqueline Kennedy Onassis and (I read the next day in *The New York Times*) Oscar de la Renta. I wouldn't know Oscar de la Renta if he said boo to me on the street, personally, but it will perhaps convey the tone of the crowd if I say that I would not have been at all surprised to learn that all the people in the room whom I didn't recognize were in fact either de la Rentas or wearing them.

I was drinking immoderately. Maybe it was retro of me, but in those days I was still proceeding under the assumption that part of being a writer is having a lot to drink whenever there is a lot to drink.

So I don't remember a great deal except that I was given a gold lion to wear on a red ribbon around my neck; at dinner I was asked "What is your new book about, how is it doing, what is your next book about and how is it going?" by people who had paid up to a thousand dollars each for the privilege (my answers to these questions were worth about fifty cents apiece, but I repeated them often); I mortified Robert Stone and myself by telling him how much I admired his work; and after dinner we adjourned to a room with a glass-domed ceiling and listened to Estelle Parsons read Longfellow. I swear it was Longfellow. Unless there is another poet who used the line "Dust thou art to dust returneth."

The key to a successful gala is getting yourself invited to the party afterward. A bunch of us went to Drue Heinz's house where I drank and ate so well that every night for several weeks afterward I had to fight off the urge to go hang around her front door in the hopes that another bunch of writers would be showing up there and I could slip in with them and get some more of that paté and cognac. There I mortified Raymond Carver and myself by telling him how much I admired his work.

I had a good time. But except when I was being mortifying, I felt more like a penguin than a lion. I wish awards had been handed out to the authors who had come from furthest away, had had the most and fewest marriages, and had been published in the most different magazines. I feel that I would have been a strong contender in the last category.

I wish the occasion had been more *actively* literary. At least one serious kiss or glancing fistfight. Impromptu speeches by the authors themselves (perhaps between stanzas of Longfellow). And, for those lions and patrons still standing, a party after the party: a wee-hours excursion back to the library and into the stacks to look at our books there; someone mistaking me for Willie Nelson so I could have an excuse to sing; cries of "Let's call Updike!"; the library raided because of neighbors' complaints about noise and carrying-on; staunch if largely verbal resistance to the police; and finally, along about dawn, the release of readers and writers—less soigné but better acquainted—into the streets on our own recognizance.

Maybe in the Nineties.

LIT

DEMYSTIFIED

QUICKLY

Though metaphysical, John Donne
Was not above a bit of fun.
Even being an Anglican priest
Did not to him mean *toujours triste*.
He touched with grace on matters fleshly,
And found God didn't mind espeshly.

■ ■ ■

The never-to-be-forgotten
Christian spokesman Cotton
Mather's father's name was Increase.
Both let human sin crease

Their brows impressively,
The better to practice ministry
(Puritan), in which craft
Cotton walloped witchcraft.

But those poor crones in Salem—
Cot did not in person whale 'em.
Preaching is one thing, judging another.
(None of them was Mather's mother.)

■ ■ ■

Dean Jonathan Swift
Seemed constantly miffed.
He never found it futile
To badger men for being brutal.
Savage indignation tore his breast.
He never cracked a smile, except in jest.

■ ■ ■

Blake's father was a hosier.
So's yer
Old man. At least, suppose yer

Father *were* a hosier. Dealt in hose.
Just suppose.
Would it make you be a poet?
I don't know—it
Might be one of those formative shocks,
To learn your father dealt in socks.

■ ■ ■

If Nineteenth-Century U.S. Lit
Has few embraceable men in it,
It's not the fault
Of Whitman, Walt.

■ ■ ■

"The Dead," by Joyce, which John
Huston based a movie on,
Answers gravely what
A woman wants: not whom she's got,
But someone worthier
Who died in youth for want of her.

■ ■ ■

Summoned by someone from Mississippi,
The Poetry Muse's response was snippy:
"Dear Mr. William Faulkner,
I go for neither highflown talk nor
Dialect nor melodrama.
Yours very sincerely, comma,
The Muse of Poetry. P.S.
Who gave you my address?"

The Novel Muse leapt at his offer;

Which is why we have Yoknapatawpha.

■ ■ ■

"Swansea girls!" said Swansea mamas,
"Stay away from Dylan Thomas.
    'Green raging am I
    In the death of God's thigh'
Is his idea of showing promise."

■ ■ ■

Edna St. Vincent Millay
Had more than a little to say,

But less than a lot.
And as for F. Scott
Fitzgerald, he died in L.A.

■ ■ ■

Kids past the age of twelve'll
Pooh-pooh Cooper, Poe and Melville
Nowadays. The only thing
They want to read is Stephen King,

Who dashes—in the space of months—
Off a creepy novel—once
He had a new one out in weeks—
Whose every floor and sentence creaks.

HARPER'S BAZAAR

ASKED ME

TO WRITE A REVIEW

OF MY LAST COLLECTION WHICH I AM NOW REPRINTING IN THIS ONE, SO SUE ME

So you fancy tales of adventure in Bloomingdale's ("Why I Smell Like This") and Peru ("O Lost!")? Do you wonder whether a normal person *could* spend twenty-five hundred dollars a day for room service, like Elizabeth Taylor ("I Just Want What Liz Always Has")? Do you relish ethnic poignancies that touch the heart of us all ("I Don't Eat Dirt Personally")? Then the book for you is *Now, Where Were We?*, by—oh, this is awkward.

To be candid, I don't feel entirely comfortable reviewing my own book *(Now, Where Were We?)*. There is my critical impeccability to protect. I would prefer to give my book *(Now, Where Were We?)* a blurb.

One gives other people wonderful, selfless blurbs. Did you see "I put it down once, to wipe off the sweat"? That was my blurb. For someone else's book. In return, one receives distant (yet not outlying) subblurbs. "I guess I owe Blount a favor and he is okay in my book, and speaking of *my* book . . ."—that sort of thing.

If one were asked to give oneself a blurb, one might say that *Now, Where Were We?* is a book that one would never, ever want to put down.

But this must be a *review*. Let it be, then, a "selling" review. One that can be quoted from in the adds. Has "pure gold . . . *hotcha!* . . . sheer magic" been overworked? "The most compelling book ever written, by far!"—*Harper's Bazaar*. "Not since the Bible has a collection so . . ."

Yes, *Now, Where Were We?* is a collection. So, as I have pointed out many times, is the Bible. Does that mean you can assume, when you see the Bible in a store, that you have probably already read most of it somewhere else? Perhaps. But how can you justify that assumption with regard to *Now, Where Were We?* Two of the pieces in this book have never appeared anywhere before, for reasons we needn't go into, and the others first appeared in publications ranging from *Antaeus* to *USA Today*.

I often wonder what reviewers mean exactly, when they say "ranging from . . . to. . . ." Once I contributed to a book about fishing which, as one reviewer put it, included "writers ranging from Ernest Hemingway to" me. Did that mean "from Ernest Hemingway all the way down to" me? I like to think not. At any rate "from *Antaeus* to *USA Today*" is an alphabetical range. In between come not only *The Atlantic, Esquire* and *The New York Times*—which, okay, maybe you have read every issue of those for the last few years—but also *Atlanta Weekly, Food and Wine,* the *San Francisco Examiner* ("Why Not a National Sodomy Day?"), *Southern* and *Think.* Get around to all those regularly, do you? And several other fine publications.

Now, where were we? In *Now, Where Were We?*—whose subtitle is *Getting Back to Basic Truths That We Have Lost Sight of Through No Fault of My Own* (included is my acceptance speech to the Democratic Nominating Convention, which the course of history prevented me from making)—we learn what my late father (who was prominent in savings and loan), Paul Valery and I have in common. In the book *(Now, Where Were We?),* we learn it. We don't learn it in this review. It is not the reviewer's place to give things away.

I'd feel silly *quoting* from my own book, wouldn't I?

"I grew up in the South. I can do the traipse, I can do the gallivant, I can do the lollygag, and I can do the slow lope. I can hotfoot it, I can waltz right in and waltz right out, or I can just be poking or dragging or plowing along. As a youngster I skedaddled. I believe that if called upon, for the sake of some all-in-good-fun theatrical, I could sashay. But I know that these gaits have their places, and on the other hand there is New York walking."

To walk in New York, as I go on to say in *Now, Where Were We?,* is "to cut through three nuns, two dogs being intimate against their walkers' wills, a blind man, a fender-bender and a multilingual fistfight without missing a beat or making *any* kind of contact with *any*body and then to take an intersection of Broadway and a major cross street in stride—diagonally against both lights—while someone is coming from the other direction pursued by transit police and a bus is trying to turn left in your face."

In fact, while quoting that second passage, I have improved it. I urge you to buy *Now, Where Were We?* (Villard Books, $17.95) and compare the original text.* It splits an infinitive. It also misses a beat.

See, I knew this would happen. I have gone for the jugular.

---

*Fixed in the paperback (Ballantine, $8.95).

THE WAY
═══════MAMA TELLS═══════
IT

Hairld! *Guess who's here to visit? It's Aileen!*
I was telling Lylah Battle about Mary Alec Poole—you know how Mary Alec is, she makes her children all go out the door in the morning in the order of height? Well, age.

Hairld! We're in the den. Come see Aileen!

And I looked over at Mama and I said, "Mama, what are you doing?"

"Nothing," Mama said. Like a child.

Hair-ullld!

And, Aileen, she was taking notes!

She didn't want to let me see them. I said, "Now Mama, I have a right to see that," and she said, "Why?"

I said, "Honestly, Mama!" I believe if she could get up from a chair quick as she used to, I believe she would actually have run off into the next room. I went over there and made her show me what she'd written down.

Hairld! It's Aileen. You know Aileen. Aileen Loach! Hairld!

She had written—scribbled, you know, but I know Mama's writing, it's the first writing I ever saw. She doesn't cross her *t*'s. Never has crossed her *t*'s, and never will. It's a wonder I cross mine. She had written: "I thought *I* was bad because I alphabetize my spices."

I said, "Mama, I didn't say that."

"What is your trouble with it, then?" she said. That's the way she talks now. Either gets it from the children, or television. And the *tone* she uses! She's gotten right snippy. I mean, you know Mama, she would always come out with the strangest things, but it's bad enough to talk to children the way they are, without your mother getting just as snippy, or I believe worse. And there's nothing you can do to your mother.

Hairld! Where are you?

You know how it started. Aileen! You don't know about this? I know you know about it, you just don't want to say you know about it because you know how torn up I am that everybody in the *world* knows about it.

Well, you're sweet. I think you're just *being* sweet, but you're sweet to be that way. I know I can tell you things, Aileen. Because you have got good sense about what to repeat. That is exactly what Mama has lost every least speck of. I lie awake at night, worrying. What has Mama told today? What is she getting ready to tell? To an *audience.*

Hair . . . uld! Aileen and me are in the den!

That's what I'm telling you. Aileen, you just don't *know.* It's . . . I don't know. Mama is so *quiet* at home, can't get a word out of her. I wouldn't mind a little adult conversation from her. She's as bad as Hairld.

Hair-ullld!

Mama could be company to me. But no, she sits there saving it up.

Of course, I know, you know, she got down so low when Lily died. That cat and her got to the point they were almost the same person. They'd rock and watch television, rock and watch television, Mama and that cat. Lily would not sit on anyone else to save her life, just Mama. But every now and then she would go out and get little birds and chipmunks and things—

What? No, *Lily* would. Honestly, Aileen, you're as bad as Hairld. *Hairld!*

Hairld has decided to be Hairld tonight, I'm afraid.

And what the *vet* believes is that she got ahold of a mouse or a bird or something that had died from getting ahold of something. Mama said Lily wouldn't get ahold of anything that wasn't moving. But the vet said well, it might have been some little animal that had *just* got ahold of something. Mama would never accept that explanation. Just would not accept it.

Hairld!

He can hear me.

You can hear me, Hairld!

Anyhoo, Lily came in and tried to throw up—when that cat couldn't throw up, you knew she wasn't herself. And died. And Mama was left—well, I know it *was* hard on her, but. She sat there on that rocker and said, "I haven't got anything to hold."

I said, "Hold the children, Mama."

She said, "They hurt my lap."

Well, I know they do squirm. "But Mama," I said—

Hairrrrld!

She didn't seem to have any heart for TV anymore. She wouldn't even want to get up in the morning, you'd have to send the children in there right after breakfast when they had jelly all over them. Even that didn't get her up one morning, I had to let them go out and play in the pouring rain and then run jump in bed with Mama wet as little drowned rats.

So I told Hairld to take her down to the senior center. Maybe I was wrong. But I thought maybe they'd teach her to crochet. I said to Mama the other day, I said, "Mama, why don't you *crochet?*" Other people's mamas crochet—or dried arrangements. But no.

Mama took a course in story-telling.

That's what I'm telling you, that's what the *problem*'s been. *Hairld! Hairld!*

She goes to festivals. They have *festivals* in it. All over the state. She wears an old-timey hat. And she tells stories.

And Mama doesn't tell stories about princesses and bears. No. Not Mama. She tells stories about *us.* Yes.

She wins *awards.*

She was in the paper about it. You didn't see it? Well, it was the Spartanburg paper. Somebody sent it to us. Aileen, I opened that paper up and I said, "Oh, my Lord." They quoted her stories in the paper. Stories about me and Harold, stories about the children—*and,* stories about nearly everybody we know.

And there just doesn't seem to be any stopping her. People come by and pick her up and drive her to these festivals. She's so popular. I guess she is. I could be popular too if I told everything I knew, but I wouldn't have any friends left.

Hairld! You know what he's doing. He's upstairs looking at television. And if he was sitting here he'd have that one right there on and be sneaking looks at it—if I was to beg him till I was blue in the face. Television has just about killed the art of conversation.

I said to Paula Dale Lovejohn yesterday, I said, "Paula Dale, you are going to hear about this. If I don't tell you about it sure as the world somebody is going to tell you about it, so I'm going to tell you about it. I'm just as embarrassed as I can be but my mama is going all over the state telling about how that washing-machine repairman showed up to fix your washing machine in your basement with a cast on his leg and went downstairs and it was so flooded from the washing machine that you kept worrying that his cast was going to melt, and then you looked down and the waters had floated up all those cat b.m.'s all around him from back behind the furnace where you didn't know the cat had been going? And he didn't want to say anything about it and you didn't want to say anything about it and finally he said he believed his cast *might* melt and he thought he'd come back when the basement had had more time to drain and you were so mortified about it—only the way Mama told it, she made it even worse because—"

You didn't hear about it? Oh, Aileen, I wish you could have seen Paula Dale's face. When she told me and Mama about it. You know how Paula Dale is, how just-so she is about everything, and then to have cat b.m.'s—it wasn't even her cat. No. She doesn't have a cat. For that reason—that she's so just-so. Oh, Paula Dale can't even stand to have cat *hair* in her house. But the washing-machine repairman didn't have any way of knowing that. I thought Paula Dale was going to *die* when she came over and told us about that repairman and the expression on his face and all—and he was so *nice* about it, that's what made it worse, and his cast had a little child's writing on it.

And of course Mama just sitting there. But we didn't know Mama would *repeat* it. And make it *worse.* Because—

No, see, we didn't know then. We knew she was telling stories but none of us had had time to go hear her and of course she hadn't let on to us what the stories were about. And she wasn't *writing down notes* then. Now she is. She doesn't even care really if you catch her at it, she just doesn't want you to take them away from her.

Hairld!

But I told Paula Dale, I said, "Mama is not the same person she was. We do not know what to expect of her any longer."

I told Mama, "Mama, when we were children you didn't tell us stories." Mama said she was too busy raising us. She said we wouldn't sit still long enough. She said she didn't realize she knew any stories back then. I just gave up trying to reason with her.

I finally felt like I had to go hear her perform. I went to the big state finals of story-telling, which Mama came in second in, which I thought she should have won against the old man who did win, he just went on and on about outhouses and snakes.

Hairld! Hair-uld! I could cheerfully kill him.

It was a folk story festival, they called it. Now Aileen, we are not folk. You know that. We weren't ever folk. We children may not have had every *advantage* when we were coming up, but we were not folk. I have seen the way folk do a drawing, and from the time she was thirteen, my sister Janelle—you've met Janelle, yes. Janelle could draw a horse or a deer with all the shadows and all to the life. It would be as if it was standing in front of you.

Hairld! You are being rude to Aileen!

But I listened to Mama hold forth up there on that stage, Aileen, and she could have just as well been somebody else entirely. And people just applauding, and laughing, and their eyes getting wide. And my face burning. And of course afterwards, Mama is just in a world of her own, she doesn't want to talk to *us* about it, it's as if we don't have any say over what she thinks or does.

And Mama talks about what people *look* like. Like you know how Lloyd Salley is always looking like he's just getting ready to say something? Kind of beginning to smile and lean forward and even just barely open his mouth so you keep leaning forward to hear whatever it is that he has just thought of to say, until you realize that he isn't ever going to say anything, that's just Lloyd? Mama describes things like that. And if that ever gets back to Lloyd, I don't know *what* he will think. Course I guess we'll never know, if we have to hear it from Lloyd.

Hairld! I know what you're doing! Sitting at that TV, and every now and then burping, or whatever it is that he does, it's more like a hiccup than a burp, but frankly I don't know what it is—Hairld and I have been married for eighteen years and I still don't know what it is. I don't think he knows.

Paula Dale of course is just as hurt as she can be. But she doesn't know what to say to Mama. I try to talk to Mama about it and she says it's a free country. I say, "Mama, that's what we all say. But you know, and I know, that when it comes to talking about people we know—it's one thing to talk about people behind their backs, as long as it *is* behind their backs. But when you do it out where all they have to do to hear it *themselves* is join the crowd, it's treating them like they're not right real."

Mama says let them sue her.

I say "Now Mama, you don't want to start talking like that because people *will.* " And not only that—Hairld says old ladies can get away with a lot, but they can go too far.

Hairld! You might as well make up your mind, I'm not going to quit calling you until—No, Aileen, he *knows* he ought to at least stick his head in here. I take up time with his old sour friends. Well, I do. I make it a point.

Hairld says it is not out of the bounds of possibility, even in this day and age—Hairld says there have been *fires* in this town that haven't been investigated as hard as they might have been. Like the Metzes. Oh, yes. The firemen theorized it started in their Parcheesi set? Nobody believed that.

Because—and it's not just *telling* stories about people. It's—that's what I was telling you.

Mama makes them worse.

Hairld! It wouldn't hurt you one bit in this world to just—
Hairld!

The way Mama tells the story about Paula Dale and the washing-machine man and the cat b.m.'s: it was Lily that did them behind the furnace.

Of course maybe it was, but the way Mama tells *every* story, it involves Lily. Lily being sent out by Mama. To do things.

Hairld!

Hairld and I are going to have a knock-down-and-drag-out when you go home, Aileen. No, no, don't *you* feel bad. Hairld won't even watch TV with me anymore. Because we agreed that when one of us wants the other one to look at them, then he has to look away from the TV and look at the one who's talking and listen. And to Hairld that's like—you'd think he was taking rat poison.

Mama says story-telling is an art form. She says it's her art. I say, "Mama, we are *happy* for you to have an art. That is not the point."

Mama just looks at me like—you know how a toddler will get sometimes, all of a sudden in a crowded grocery store or somewhere just get to bucking you so hard they lay flat out on the filthy floor wallering and actually kind of grinding themselves down into the floor yelling when you try to pull them up? Mama looks like she is just literally about to do something like that.

Hairld!

Aileen, I don't know what to do. If we'd been better about going to church I'd take Mama in to counsel with the pastor, but I don't know what the new pastor's name is and I hate to ask because you know the last one was Reverend Tinkle and they've been accused of not renewing him because of his name and they're sensitive about it. And if there is anybody in First Melrose Church who has heard the story Mama tells about the last time she went to church there— Lord. . . .

That lady was there that Sunday, you know I've told you about her, she's not all right, poor soul, wandering in the aisle peering under the pews like she was looking for something and muttering in the middle of the sermon and getting closer and closer to the altar, and the preacher didn't know what to say and finally he said, sort of smoothly but with a little nudge of his head so that maybe somebody would get up and lead her somewhere without him having to say right out, you know, that he wasn't so enthusiastic about suffering her to come unto him—he said, "We are *all* searching here, together, as one, that the holiness of God's word be *heard,* and *paid attention to,* " and somebody in the Board of Stewards caught his meaning and took her arm as she was bending over peering and she looked up surprised and said in that right-out-loud voice like people who aren't all right don't know any better than to use, she said: *"Some*body's *sit*ting on my *dol*lar. Cause I didn't *put* it in the collec tion. Cause I *got* that *dol*lar from Mr. *Lef'*wich for being *sweet* to him." And everybody turned to look over at the Leftwich family. And with that Lily jumped through an open window right into Mr. Leftwich's lap. Which is all true except for the part about Lily. Which just makes it a better story. To Mama.

Hairld! You're going to miss Aileen!

Mama always, I don't know, puts such a *point* on her stories.

Hairld! Imagine how you are making poor Aileen feel!

Hairld!

Hairld—

Hairld, a bear ate you! A great big bear got you and ate off your legs!

A MAN'S
GOT TO
READ

If there's one thing New York women share, it's a deep lack of affection for Saul Bellow. . . . "Like Updike, he's part of that generation of men that doesn't like anybody" . . . But— and here's the poignant part—they blame them- selves and pathetically persist in trying to read him. . . .

And while we're on the subject of literary peeves, we'd like to point out another absurd- ity—lying about the books one has read. It's a very silly pretension, and it implies grave intel- lectual insecurity. . . . And worse: "I just reread Dead Souls*!" Fat chance.*

—NEW YORK WOMAN

If a single generalization can be made about contemporary American literature . . . it would be that it is the province of middle- and upper- class women. **—JONATHAN YARDLEY IN THE WASHINGTON POST**

It happens I am a guy who is all male, the ladies and I have no problems my friend, yet it just so happens I read everything from the Virago Press before the ink is dry, and take it from me *The Well of Loneliness* is eleven hundred pages long about same-sex love among women which I am not threatened by in the least, don't start with me.

I got news for you, I dip back into *The Well of Loneliness* every night of this world, unless we're talking Women's Poetry Collective night, which I am there for, pallie, and you can bet the rent I have reread all the poems myself, first, aloud, because that's the only way to catch all the allusions.

I catch all the allusions, my friend, you can take that to the bank, and why? For one reason and one reason alone: I so desire.

I read all the women's books and their reviews as they come out, not to check my responses against the reviewers' because nothing could be further from my thoughts, I could care less, and you're damn shootin' they pile up but I also never miss a panel discussion among women novelists who have never even been invited to appear in a panel discussion before, which is a special area of interest of mine which I wouldn't read too much into if I were you because it's been tried.

Ask around, I've got sealed postmarked letters mailed to myself registered mail containing my signed responses dated weeks before any of these old girl critics start telling you what response you're supposed to have—I know that game—so nobody has any valid basis for telling me my response is not my response, my friend.

The Bellows, the Updikes of this world, their men are as if they're in constant problems with women, being threatened by women, being sued by women, and it makes you want to go: wait a minute, don't these men *read?* So don't start with me, my friend, reading's not a popularity contest, you want to start with me? Edith Wharton? I could show you candid shots of myself reading Wharton printed in my high school yearbook junior year. No big deal, I was well rounded, I dated all the majorettes, they had no complaints. But I'm just saying, in ninth grade I had to weather criticism (and not just from the boys, compadre) that I was favored by Mrs. Bissonette.

Put me through the fire, is what she did, and I read and reread every woman she gave me, thank you. And you're hearing this from some-body who didn't go to Vassar Prep my friend, where I went, unless you had a rep for not reading any men even, you had to fight your way into the restroom and out of it.

That's why, I don't have to tell you, I can handle myself—you're looking at a guy who knew he had to go out for baseball year after year because you'd better not get caught voluntarily reading anything by a woman in my high school without a bat in your hands, my friend. I read all of Carson McCullers in the on-deck circle.

Where I come from? Read a book by a woman? Out of the sheer desire to? If you couldn't handle yourself? Don't be in a dream world.

Dorothy Richardson—I've read over all of Richardson so many times I've lost track.

Wollstonecraft, all the commentary, all the letters.

Millet, Dworkin, Charlotte Yonge.

Ms. Lou Andreas-Salome? You don't know her, except in the original.

Danielle Steel—that surprises you. I'm not the kind of guy you would think, to look at me, to hear my manner of speaking, that I would read quote romance fiction quote, but the thing you don't understand about me is I've got nothing to prove. The heroine's bodice ripped by swashbucklers and it's cool because they're there for her—*I* got no problem with that, believe me, it's what women have instead of porn, which I don't read. That is I do read the classic porn but only once and that's the one thing I don't read out of the sheer desire to, I read it because I want to be able to keep certain women intellectually honest, my friend.

You can write this down: the main market for porn is women, certain women, I'm not saying all women I'm saying certain women, who read it to find out what they think men really think about women so they can keep certain men defensive.

That's their problem, that's their nose out of joint, they wouldn't believe you if you're standing right there in front of them with *The Golden Notebook* in your hand with your finger holding your place where you've been rereading it for the fifth or sixth time with obviously well-thumbed pages and frequent underlining. Or a Sarah Orne Jewett or a Djuna Barnes, or any of the many neglected seventeenth-century accounts by pioneer women who were abducted by Indians in which they constantly go out of their way to allude to people being stripped naked, men and women alike being stripped naked by Indians for all to see their shame but I don't read them for that reason, *I* know I don't, it doesn't matter what anybody else thinks because *I* know *I* don't.

That's all. Enough said. I got to go read.

ON MANHOOD

I have seen the movie *Glory,* which I can only describe as a three-handkerchief motherfucker. It transcends the traditional butch tearjerker (such as *Brian's Song,* in which a football player dies of cancer) by verging upon making warfare (a combination of football and cancer) seem *stupid stupid stupid.* But in the end it makes warfare seem heartbreaking (instead of life-trashing) and, ironically enough (no, *not* ironically enough), glorious.

In *Glory,* guys stand ten yards apart in ranks, staring at each other and shooting holes in each other, reloading and doing it again. Ex-slaves and secessionists proving their manhood by killing and being killed. And people complained about the violence in *Do the Right Thing,* in which one person is killed and a store is destroyed. An insured store. In *Glory,* the black-militant character (played by Denzel Washington) finally gives in and carries the American flag, to his death in a ditch with the white-commanding character (Matthew Broderick), whose ability to lead his black troops into a final test of their good will (a suicide charge) derives from the personal chops of the responsible-black character (Morgan Freeman), who of course gets cut to ribbons too.

One of the fallacies of American movies lately is the burden borne in them by Morgan Freeman. Without Freeman as the gruff, positive-attitude sergeant, black troops following Matthew Broderick into car-nage would not play. Morgan Freeman portrays rough masculine presence, hard yet instinctively decent, better than anybody since John Wayne. Unlike John Wayne, Morgan Freeman is an actor with a wide range, but in the parts Hollywood gives him (aside from those in which he's a pimp), he plays an intrinsically powerful man with reason to be disruptive, who chooses to go along. Poignantly. And not for much money, either.

I have also seen *Driving Miss Daisy,* and what I would like to ask is, why can't we have a movie in which Morgan Freeman proves his manhood by hiring Matthew Broderick to drive his cranky old mother around?

Wouldn't be commercial. Wouldn't be realistic.

But I did want to ask that question, and now that I have asked it I am stuck with writing an essay, here, on the theme of manhood.

Great.

Just what I need. It's not as if I have anything to prove, myself. Granted, I voted for Michael Dukakis, who was stomped into the dust by a man who had been called a lapdog by George Will. Who wears a bow tie.

Let me say this: in accepting the 1964 GOP presidential nomination Barry Goldwater declared, "Extremism in the defense of liberty is no vice. Moderation in the pursuit of justice is no virtue." It frightened the mainstream. Back then, government was widely seen as a means of *doing things for folks,* and right-wingers were widely regarded as extremists. Ultra-conservatives, they were called. Now nothing on the national political spectrum is ultra-anything, though occasionally some indiscreet Democrat puts in a tentative good word for the First Amendment, say, and is branded as an ultra-liberal. Someone ought to compare and contrast Goldwaterism with Reaganism and Bushism, to trace the embosomment of the American right. If contemporary reactionaries had the grace to be crusty and cantankerous, like Gold-water, instead of smugly mellow-repressive, they would be more manly, in my view.

Of course by manly, there, I mean offering a good target. And who am I to talk of manly, when I am losing my tolerance for seeing people shot to death?

"Shoulder to shoulder and bolder and bolder we grow as we go to the fore, *when* stout-hearted *men* stick together man to man," goes the old Sigmund Romberg song. In today's new less-sexist Army, of course, that would be "person to person." I was in the Army, though never in any bloodshed, and I must say I did sometimes get a sense of heartiness from striding along as part of a more-or-less-highly-coordinated body of men. Had there been women involved, however, I feel (maybe I am way out of line here, but this is what I *feel*) that the whole enterprise would have collapsed on its merits.

Had I been either musically or sexually secure enough in high school to be among the unchic young men and women of the march-ing band, I'd like to think I would have found more enjoyment in that esprit de corps. Mixed-companyhood. In a better world swords would be beaten into tubas and troops would give way to troupes. My friend Slick Lawson, who was in his high school's band, looks back on adoles-cent oompahing as a better preparation for life than either ROTC or sports. He makes a point of adding, however, "In *my* school, the band could whip the football team." There's a movie fight scene: a brawl between a football team and a marching band. Tensions released, no fatalities. Would the girls in the band join in, shoulder to shoulder (like dancehall girls jumping onto blackhats' backs?), or would they have a separate agenda?

Driving Miss Daisy made me feel guilty for not having catered enough to my own, late, cranky Southern mother. After an Atlanta friend of mine's mother saw that movie, she called him up and complained.

"Don't I look after you?" he asked.

"You ain't no Boolie," she said. Boolie being the Dan Ackroyd character, who engaged the Morgan Freeman character to chauffeur the Jessica Tandy character around.

I didn't even know who Morgan Freeman was when my mother was alive, and I couldn't have afforded to hire him anyway, even back then before he was famous. And if you want to know the truth, I don't think there has ever been a person in real life who was both as manly and as somebody-else's-momma-ridden as Morgan Freeman in *Driving Miss Daisy.* One of the fallacies of movies is that . . . Oh, never mind.

No, I take it back. It is unmanly of me to verge upon a challenging *apercu* and then to slouch away, muttering. Once more into the breach. Did you see that new *Henry V*? Not bad, not bad. Morgan Freeman can do Shakespeare. So why can't we have a movie in which Morgan Freeman proves his manhood by strangling Desdemona? Wouldn't be commercial. Would be too disturbing. But why more disturbing than seeing Morgan Freeman walking into a hail of bullets?

One of the fallacies of movies is that some neurotic writer provides the words, and some neurotic director (with the aid of countless conceivably well-adjusted technicians) provides the images, and some neurotic producer fiddles the money, and some neurotic actor provides the body-as-instrument, and consequently, cranky old mothers and male carnage touch the heart.

Whereas in life everybody is neurotic, except, again, conceivably, technicians. Who toil for neurotic people.

But cranky old mothers don't want to recognize that. And maybe each of us is a cranky old mother at heart. So we fidget, gripe and wonder why we aren't more moving ourselves.

Here's another distortion intrinsic to the movies: stakes. I mean, you could be making a movie called *Petal Power,* about violets and their tendency to move of their own ineffably natural will toward the nurturing beams of the sun, and you would still be a hard-charging, high-rolling major player, because of the boxcarloads of serious money you would be throwing after the ways of these tender blossoms. People would be saying, "Will you get a load of the balls on this son of a bitch, making a movie about *violets* for Chrissake!"

Those violets better damn well make us feel better about ourselves, though, or heads will roll.

MEOW

DUMBER

THAN WAR?

Jimmy Carter mediated a peace settlement in the Middle East without using any troops at all. And he pushed through oil-conservation programs. It is generally understood that Carter lacked Reagan's and Bush's understanding of the American soul. We don't placate and scrimp, we consume and kick ass.

Carter called energy conservation the "moral equivalent of war." Critics observed that the acronym was MEOW.

Hey, okay, I dare say that a major power in order to be taken seriously *does* have to make it clear that it is willing to throw flesh and blood and lethal firepower at a problem. But I'm not sure how quaint that notion is, the moral equivalent of war.

Okay, set *moral* aside for a while, because (and by the way I suspect the Carter people had a more sophisticated sense of this than the Reagan and Bush people, but never mind) what seems moral to us may not seem moral to them, whoever they may be, and morality in practice is never pure, and you can't have right (at *any* level) without some kind of might.

But in fact what have the U.S. and other nations been messily but intently engaged in improvising over the last ten or fifteen years, if not equivalents to outright war?

War gets people's attention. You have to give it that. People get into war. On the other hand, all-out war today . . . end of the world, so forth and so on.

So. Surgical strikes? With bombs and missiles for scalpels? Medieval surgery, maybe.

But hostage crises, now. Hostage crises are a great improvement over war. Horrible for the few people physically involved, but they *are* few, and we *know their names,* and often they are *interviewed on television,* and they actually get home, often. And when they get home they tend to say, listen, those people who kidnapped me, they were brutal to me, but they have a point. Whereas in war, thousands of anonymous people get blown to even more anonymous bits, taking a hill or something. If atrocities are what it takes to get people's attention, then let's have atrocities compromised by public relations.

Maybe this Arabian thing we are involved in now is just a new, expanded, hairier hostage crisis. I wish I had more faith that George Bush understood what the world in its desperation is trying to work out here, and what this country can contribute. We are good at devising new mixes. This is a country that invented both product liability and jazz.

We also created the Cable News Network. I am told that CNN announcers have been frequently reminded to refer to American boys and girls in the Gulf as "U.S. forces," not as "our forces." Because, as people used to chant back during the anti-war movement, the whole world is watching.

After the Christian Crusaders took Jerusalem by storm in July 1099, an interviewer with a global audience might have said to Geoffrey of Bouillon, "You have declined the throne of Jerusalem because, as you put it, you did not want to wear a gold crown in a city where your Savior once wore a crown of thorns. Doesn't that sentiment ring a bit false, inasmuch as your troops have just pitilessly butchered some ten thousand of Jerusalem's Jewish and Muslim men, women and children?"

No such interview was feasible in 1099, and the Crusades went on viciously for centuries. According to the Encyclopedia Brittanica: "Thirteenth-century theologians held that conversion could not be forced, but most agreed that force could legitimately be used to preserve a situation in which peaceful propaganda was possible, and they continued to support the Crusade. Furthermore, Europe's fear of Muslim power was such that the Crusade idea persisted well into the 17th century, and the conviction that, in certain circumstances, war might be just became more deeply enrooted in the conscience of the West."

WORDS FOR
THE
GULF

I t doesn't help that our commander in chief is George Bush, whose personal reactions to the tactics of Saddam Hussein ("kinda sick," for instance) are reminiscent of Michael Dukakis's reactions to the tactics of the Bush campaign. Or that *linkage* seems to be a dirtier word for our side than *kill.* But at any rate morale is the key element in a war, and war lowers mine.

From the beginning of the war in the Gulf, my position on it has been clear: If it works, I'm not against it. If it doesn't, I didn't think it would.

I realize that those are not stirring affirmations. They put off many hitherto antiwar people I talk to who have caught Desert Storm fever. Some of the reasons for being infected by that enthusiasm:

■ a dread, nearly as great as the President's, of concentrating on domestic cans of worms.

■ the absence of a military draft.

■ moral fatigue.

■ the feeling that no one can be expected to resist more than one full-scale national mobilization in a lifetime.

■ hatred for Israel's enemies, coupled with a need for genuinely detestible enemies of our own.

■ baby boomers' discovery of something fresh or pleasingly retro in the notion that American troops are not personally the enemy. "Of course I support the war," said a young civilian man on TV. "You can't support the troops if you don't support the war."

The only one of these reasons I have trouble sympathizing with is the last one. And that is only because—although I was in the Army myself and the only people in it whom I found very congenial were those who, like me, were eager to get out of it—I don't see how there could ever have been any doubt, even during Vietnam, that the nation needs soldiers and should root for them to survive (if not necessarily to turn out heavily at the polls). And hey, these new generals we have are a lot more likeable (comfortably fat, for one thing, like Mrs. Bush) than Westmoreland.

Still, bomb runs and yellow ribbons (the latter of which were popularized, let us not forget, by one of the most egregious of all Tony Orlando and Dawn songs) don't make me feel patriotic. What makes me feel patriotic, aside from returning to this country from any other one, is inventive American English. "Generals always speak generally," General Norman Schwartzkopf said on TV, and I was proud to think that after all these years, it was an American general who finally came out with that. "Intermitting the bad guys" is how a tank commander described his mission one night on the news: American irony has gone to war.

"Why won't you call a spade a spade?" Saddam Hussein (in translation) asked Peter Arnett on TV. The Butcher of Baghdad was hurt that his enemies kept calling his missiles Scuds, when he called them Al-Husseins, after his grandfather. According to the *Washington Post,* the U.S. used to have a missile equivalent to the Scud. We called it the Honest John.

Sticks and stones may break my bones, but official NATO names for various Soviet helicopters are Hinds, Hips, Hooks, Halos, Helixes, Havocs, Hokums and Hormones. American-named American helicopters are Cobras, Apaches, Knights, Super Sea Stallions, Blackhawks and Chinooks. Whether a Chinook can beat a Hormone one-on-one, I don't know, but it sounds like it ought to be able to. I do know that we have some nerve naming our weapons after people we took this country away from. (The Super Sea Stallions, I believe, once peacefully farmed Atlantic City.)

It's amazing to watch, on television, how slowly our Tomahawk missiles move through the air poking about for targets. If I were naming an American missile I would call it the Waverly, after this bit of Eudora Welty dialogue: "All poisonous snakes you can tell 'em because they crawls waverly, son. If a snake ain't coming with the idea to kill you, he crawls straight." Of course our missiles officially exempt what we call "innocent civilians," so maybe we should call one of our Cruises the Guiltseeker.

Maybe I am entering into the war. Naming friendly missiles. Next thing you know I'll be trying my hand at the ancient tradition of *hija'*, or diatribe poetry, which according to Ehud Ya'ari and Ina Friedman in *The Atlantic* has been revived by Iraq's invasion of Kuwait. Saudi poets have been broadcasting attacks on Saddam like (in translation) this:

>Your face is darkest black,
>And we will yet set fire
>To your bottom and your back.

And Iraqis have been answering with "Your braves have all been killed, O rue. / Even the rooster laughs at you."

In previous centuries, according to the *Atlantic* story, this mode of blowing off hokum and hormone actually averted warfare sometimes. Makes you wonder whether Democratic congressman Harry A. Johnson of Florida knew what he was talking about when he said, "This may sound racist, but these guys are twice removed from camels. They don't know how to fight a war." What if we had tried throwing our ghetto-hardened rap groups at Saddam before committing our divisions?

>Saddam you think you're bad? You would
>Last about a week in our neighborhood.

We do, after all, have some nerve.

GOOFING ON YAHWEH

To be honest with you, I don't quite know what to make of this idea that a woman, with a rich sense of humor, made up Yahweh.

On the one hand I say, "Of course! Why didn't I see it before? Behind *every* great man is a woman (rolling her eyes). She didn't make up a woman God. No. She was too droll for that. What is God but someone to blame unhappiness on? *And* someone who's bigger than all the men around."

On the other hand I say, "Now wait a minute. Let me have a little time to digest this."

Just as we're about to go to war with Islam (we who, incidentally, have a deeply disaffected underclass here at home featuring people named Raheem), along comes Harold Bloom with these propositions:

■ That J, ancient Hebrew author of what is now known as *The Book of J* (from which Genesis and other parts of the Bible derive), is the author who created not only Adam and Eve but also Yahweh, later to become Jehovah and Our Heavenly Father, not to mention Allah.

■ That J was a woman, friend of Solomon's.

■ That her account of the Creation and the Old Man Himself entails a good deal of the old tongue-in-cheek.

And, like I say, I am inclined to buy it. I *did* buy the book, a new translation of *The Book of J* by David Rosenberg with interpretation by Bloom, and I must say that I am jealous. All I could think to do, in my own most recent book, was to make up a first female president and male first lady. Bloom has made up a woman who made up God. It will be *centuries* before the dust of this thing has settled enough so that someone can take the next step and make up Bloom.

If only Bloom could take J on tour with him. Would *that* be an Oprah show! Probably J would have to speak from behind a screen, to preserve her anonymity so she wouldn't have to go into seclusion like Garbo or Salman Rushdie; but that would just make her more fascinating. As she no doubt realized from the first word.

It is true that J's Yahweh makes a man first, Bloom points out, but it is also true that "her childlike Yahweh" makes Adam out of mud, and then blunders around making birds and fishes and snakes trying to come up with a partner for Adam—and then, after he's had a lot of practice at making animals, he goes ahead and carefully fashions, from Adam's flesh and bone, what was called for from the beginning: a woman. "Misogyny in the West is a long and dismal history of weak misreadings of the comic J, who exalts women throughout her work, and never more than in this deliciously wry story of creation." If that is not a book-selling point, then I don't know the first thing about publishing.

Bloom says he first began to wonder whether J was a woman "when I heard yet once more the familiar contention of feminist criticism that my own theories of influence are patriarchal." This ought to hold the feminists for a while, you sly dog, Bloom. I wonder whether in his heart of hearts he doesn't occasionally think of J as his Molly. Sometimes he does overplay his hand a bit, referring to "reading J as J" with such zest that I was reminded of Jon Lovitz and Dana Carvey on *Saturday Night Live,* portraying gushy French critics who seize rapturously on Quincy Jones's every utterance with exclamations of *"Le Q!"* Bloom is smoother than that, though. Catch this:

"J charmingly evades both patriarchal misogyny and feminist resentment while insinuating a kind of Shavian wit not exactly shared either by Yahweh or by Adam." Whom does Bloom see as "the modern writer most in J's spirit"? Kafka. Ah. No ladies' man, he.

If Bloom has left himself sitting pretty, however, I still feel uneasy myself. I won't explore the question, "But how are we going to work all this into the Sunday school curriculum?" because that is not my problem.

But here's what I'm wondering. What happens when my plane is hijacked by an Iraqi agent eager to die for his beliefs, and I try to talk this whole thing out with him—for that is what I have learned (from women) is the only way to resolve conflict in mutual respect—and he asks me, "What do *you* believe in?"

"Oh, well, the arts and sciences, of course. And the Bill of Rights. And, I have to tell you, I subscribe to the Judeo-Christian ethic, that is to say, turn the other cheek, or in other words, an eye for an eye. What I mean to say is . . . You know, I read recently that all the great religions that began in the Middle East derive from a single author, a woman, interestingly enough, not really religious herself, bit of a humorist actually . . ."

I figure he shoots me.

THE FALL

(IF THE ORIGINAL STORY HAD BEEN CONCEIVED, *PACE*

HAROLD BLOOM, BY A MAN)

NARRATOR
One day, Eve was walking through Paradise, a place in the
Middle East. Looking good.

EVE
Hello, bird.

BIRD *(in a high sweet voice)*
Hello, Eve.

EVE
Hello, toad.

TOAD *(in the voice of Eugene Pallette)*
Hello, Eve.

EVE
Hello, butterfly.

BUTTERFLY *(in a fluttery voice)*
Hello, Eve.

EVE
Hello, bear.

BEAR *(in a gruff voice)*
Hello, Eve.

EVE
Hello, earthworm.

EARTHWORM *(in a harmony of two voices, one high and one low)*
Hello, Eve.

NARRATOR *(in case people don't know about the earthworm)*
The earthworm being hermaphroditic. Having, that is, both
kinds of organs.

(Organ music)
Then she met another animal.

SNAKE *(in an insinuating tone such as Sheldon Leonard used as the tout on* The Jack Benny Show*)*
Psst! Hey, Eve!

EVE
Hello, sn— sn—, sn—.

SNAKE
Hot-cha.

EVE *(embarrassed)*
I'm sorry, I can't quite call your name. What did you say?

SNAKE
Never mind names. I'm just a friend.
(Music to "There's a place in France, where the women wear no pants")
I said . . . Hotcha.

EVE
Oh. I don't know that word.

SNAKE
You don't know . . . much.

EVE
I . . . don't?

SNAKE
For instance, you don't know why you have to do the cleaning and cooking and canning and all Adam has to do is go out and *(heavy sarcasm)* pick . . . fruit.
(Ominous music)

EVE
I . . . just . . . never . . . thought about it.

SNAKE
Did you ever think about . . . money? *(Ominous chord)* Power?
(Ominous chord) Lawyers? *(Ominous silence)*

EVE
I . . . don't know what those things are.

SNAKE
Mm-hm. Wanna know?

EVE
I . . . suppose. I . . .

SNAKE
Haven't you been raised above all the animals? Don't you have a
responsibility to stay on top of things?

EVE
Well, Adam usually . . .

SNAKE
Mm-hmmm. Here.
(*Ominous chord indeed, with a sinuous wiggle at the end*)

EVE
Why, that's an apple.

SNAKE
Mm-hmm. I picked it for you. Just for you.

EVE
But . . .

SNAKE
I'll bet Adam never picks anything just for you.

EVE
He picks things.

SNAKE
Mm-hmm.

EVE
He brings them home.

SNAKE
Mm-hmm.

EVE
He says, "I'm starved!"

SNAKE
Mm-hm, okay, here it is, take a bite, it's for you.

EVE
No.

SNAKE
Why?

EVE
Because. We're not supposed to.

SNAKE
Who says?

EVE
Well! Our Father, that's who! For heaven's sake!

SNAKE
You ever see this "Our F— F— F—"

EVE
Father. No. . . .

SNAKE
And who *told* you about him?

EVE
Well . . . Adam.
(Organ music)

SNAKE
Mmm . . . hmmmm. *(Quickly)* What if I told you Adam eats 'em all the time? What if I told you that's how come he's on top of things? That's how come he does the picking and you have to clean and can and cook?

EVE
Are you telling me the truth?

SNAKE
Mmmm. Wanna know?

EVE
I don't know.

SNAKE
So why'd you ask? Come on, an apple a day keeps the doctor away.

EVE
What's a doctor?

SNAKE
Wanna know? It's easy. Watch. *(Sudden swallowing noise)* Can Adam do that?

EVE *(laughing)*
There's a big lump in your throat.

SNAKE
Over you, sweetheart.

EVE *(softly)*
Awww . . .

SNAKE
Of course I'm just a snake. I guess you wouldn't want to eat
what I eat. You wouldn't even want to take a bite of this other
apple here. And how do you think that makes me feel? I guess
you think I don't have feelings. That's all right, I'll just . . .
crawl off.

EVE
No, don't!

SNAKE
Why not? You wouldn't care.

EVE
Yes I . . . I feel funny. I never felt this way before.

SNAKE
Of course not! It's a beautiful feeling! It's a rare feeling! It's the
most wonderful feeling in the world! It's . . .
*(Music that goes with the first few bars of "Love Lifted Me"—that goes,
that is, with "I was sinking deep in sin")*
. . . guilt. *(Quickly)* There's only one thing for it! An apple!

EVE
Oh. *(A crunch. A pause.)* SNAKE!

Snake
Heh-heh-heh. How do you like them apples? And look at you!
Hot-cha!
(Organ music)

EVE
Eeek!

SNAKE
I'll be, uh, seeing you.
("Place in France" exit music, dying away)

EVE
Oh, what will I do? I don't have anything to wear!
(Theme to The Andy Griffith Show, *whistled)*

ADAM
Hi Eve!
(Whistles another couple of bars.)
Look at all this fruit I brought. I call it . . . figs! I'm starved.

(Begins to whistle again, but trails off.)
Eve? Why are you all huddled like that?

EVE
As if you didn't know.

ADAM
Huh? Know what? How would I know?

EVE
You *don't* know, do you? You don't know . . . much. And the
worst thing is, you don't care.

ADAM
Huh? Sure I do. I mean . . . what do you mean, "care"?

EVE
You know very well what I mean, "care."

ADAM
No I don't, I swear I don't, how would I—

BRISK, NO-NONSENSE VOICE
Okay, okay, stop it right there. This is never going to work.
Here, Adam, here's an apple. Eat it, for God's sake. And get
yourself some clothes, both of you. I thought it would be easier
for you if you didn't know anything but I should have known
better.

ADAM
Well, I . . .

EVE
Are you Our Father? You don't sound all that fatherly to me.

THE VOICE
Our Father, Granny Smith, what does it matter?

EVE
What does it *matter?* Adam, you sat right there and told me we
were created by Our Father.

ADAM
No I didn't, not exactly—I said . . .

EVE
Adam, will you *eat the apple?*

ADAM
Don't want to.

EVE
You *have* to. Doesn't he?

THE VOICE
Hm. Interesting question.
(The voices of all three begin to fade.)
I guess. Listen, I've got things to do.

EVE
Things! What *things* could possibly be more important than your family?

THE VOICE
Family?! Well—I didn't say *more important.*

EVE
Yes you did, too. And you know you did.

THE VOICE
You said more important. I said, to do.

EVE
You know what you said, and so do I, and so does Adam. Don't you, Adam?

ADAM
I think I'll go fishing.

EVE *(rising against the final fade)* Fishing?! Like that?!

ON BEING
ONE'S
OWN GUY

Even in the depths of what we feel to be humility, we may be full of ourselves. A Baptist pastor distressed over factional power struggles within his denomination was recently quoted as saying, "We are embarrassing God."

How much more . . . well, for one thing, how much more *religious* it would have been, in my view, not that I am taking sides (this pastor in fact belongs to the moderate faction)—how much more *seemly* it would have been, surely, to have left it at "We are embarrassing."

Has any religious group ever expressed concern that they were *boring* God?

But I do not come before you to rattle the chains of the Baptists, whose *fundamentalist* spokesmen (the ones who assume that if God could be embarrassed by Baptists he would have said so in the Bible) sound more and more like the people from whom Salmon Rushdie is hiding. It is the rare writer, however receptive to exposure, who would feel comfortable being depicted in a film as a fiendish enemy of Baptism who in the end gets his head justly exploded by heaven.

No, my text for this morning's sermon has nothing to do with religion, so far as I can see. My text is a remark made by a Big Guy who believes in himself, and has been toppled.

Here it is, the remark:

"I know people say, 'Why, George, why?' But I'm my guy. I can't change a lot."

The man who made the remark was—no, not George Schultz. Not George Harrison. Not George Jones, because in that case it would have been:

> This bottle thinks that I'm its guy,
> But here beneath this unlit sky,
> I'm no one's guy but hers, I know,
> Although our vows were sev'ral ones ago.

(Incidentally, I spoke a while back to someone who knew Tammy Wynette. "I think Tammy has stopped worrying," this informant said, "about who she's married to.")

The George who made the remark—a few weeks before he agreed to cease and desist from running the New York Yankees forever—was George Steinbrenner.

I looked at that remark, and I thought to myself (who else?): *How can anybody, even George Steinbrenner, say something like "I'm my guy"?*

> I'm my guy,
> As long as I
> Have me.

"I can't change a lot," Steinbrenner says—he who changed managers and general managers and pitching coaches and public relations men and secretaries the way people trying to shake athlete's foot change socks. He who berated fledgling players, apologized for a pennant-winning team and undermined his stars because they wouldn't be like he wanted them to be.

I will psychoanalyze Steinbrenner now. (I interviewed him once, and didn't like him.) His father was a hard-driving Teutonic disciplinarian and former Olympic athlete. George grew up as a hard-driven disciplinee and a subOlympic athlete. So he bought a whole lot of athletes and took his father's presumable disappointment in him out on them. To the Yankees he was the father his father was. And he proved that that kind of fathering runs sons, even pinstriped ones, into the ground.

And to himself, he is the father he wanted his father to be. He never felt like his father's guy, so he is his own. When he told the commissioner of baseball (who planned only to suspend him for his excesses) that he wanted to give up control of the team forever, George was all over the newsstands on the cover of *Newsweek*, looking sternly, concernedly, overbearingly paternal and billed as "The Most Hated Man in Baseball."

He announced his intention to pass control of the Yankees to his son, Hank. Hank (how sharper than a serpent's tooth it is to have a thankless child) declined to accept.

It is not the Steinbrenner family curse, however, that is my primary concern, but rather the whole notion of self-image. As it happens, I woke up this morning feeling like smearing chocolate frosting all over my body and making an impassioned statement about excrement as a symbol of how I felt. But whereas that works on stage for Karen

Finley, it wouldn't for me because I am not built for it and I don't belong to any category of people that is generally regarded as deserving to feel unjustly despised. If I were to declare in my frosting, as Finley does in hers, that "in principle we are not very different" from Nazi Germany, "it's just that our ovens are at a slower speed," it would not go over.

"If you look far enough back in anyone's life," a friend of mine observed recently, "you will find that she was once married to someone named Ed." The truth may be that everyone, deep down inside (with the possible exception of, say, Maya Angelou), *is,* or *at least* used to be, someone named Ed. And by everyone I do not mean just "all husbands"—though I would like to think that I can say to any woman reader who assumed that that is what I meant, that I know what she means. True, I have never had a husband, but I have been two of them, and in each case I believe I can say that one of my not unreasonable grievances was: what was so *wrong* with being, deep down inside, someone named Ed?

And yet I knew that there was, after all, something wrong with it.

The other night as I listened to a bluesman sing, loudly,

> Stoop down baby,
> Let yo' daddy see.
> You got something down there baby
> That beats the hell out of me,

I asked a cheerful quiet woman at our table what she did and she gave me her card. She does wholistic massage for women. "One's most important relationship is with herself," her card says. Guys can't carry off that kind of slogan, and white guys can't get away with singing "Stoop down baby."

All we can do, if we have any pretensions to political correctness, is analyze other white guys.

And what am I doing? Complaining?

God, am I embarrassed.

GUTES AND EULAS

When Gutenberg met Eula Snopes
She raised in him unprintable hopes.
But very soon he ran aground
Upon her earthiness profound.
   "You're not for me, although you're ripe,"
   Said G.: "I like the movable type."

When Scheherazade met Billy the Kid,
The sands gained heat from what they did.
He gave her stolen golden watches.
She gave his gun six buenas notches—
   Then stayed up nights one thousand one
   Novelizing what they'd done.

When Don Juan met Sue Barton, Nurse,
He said, "I guess one could do worse,"
Half-heartedly. Of sterner stuff
Our Sue was made. She said, "Oh, fluff!
   You are a complex. Even an ism.
   Can you back it up with gism?"

When Mickey Spillane met Guinevere,
He stated, "Me, I don't know fear.
My fists are deadly, so's my rod.
And I know how to treat a brod."
   "Oh, yes, I know: Ladies and Lords.
   I've had it all before, with swords."

When Gypsy Rose Lee met Jack the Ripper,
"Well," he said, "so you're a stripper."
"Sure am, Honey." Then he said,
"Wouldn't you rather be an angel instead?"
   "No, I wouldn't; I'm an artiste."
   "Well I am a surgeon and . . . sort of a priest."

When Becky Sharp met Dr. Johnson
(When both were speaking at U. of Wisconsin),
He grumbled, "Tell me why you shook

Off my lexicographical book."
    "I'm a young lady of action, not diction."
    "Noble words—Miss Popular Fiction."

When Mary Poppins met Genghis Khan,
She told him, "Put your rain-boots on."
"My *rain-boots!*" thundered Genghis—"What!?"
"Say a little jingle and then it's not
    Hard to remember: 'Oh, it's puddly . . .'"
    "Kill her. Bring me something cuddly."

When Job met *la belle dame sans merci*
He said, "So what can you do to me?
For I've been dumped on by Jehovah."
"Yes, but when *I* mess you over,
    I can make your testes shrink
    Just by choosing not to wink."

When Lee Harvey Oswald met Lady MacBeth,
She said, "Do you boggle, Lee Harvey, at death?"
"I don't guess so, I've been to Russia."
"Now here's a man! I won't have to pussia?"
    "Nah. Not me." "O great brave foil!"
    "You CIA, Castro, or rich Texas oil?"

When *la belle dame sans merci* met Sade,
The first words out of her mouth were, *"God.*
You think you're tough with all those tricks?"
"Eh," he shrugged. Their respective quicks
    Appeared uncut. Then, "You p.o.'d?"
    He blurted out. "You *wish,*" she crowed.

When Frank Sinatra met Molly Bloom,
He sang mellow, filled the room.
Yes she said Yes. He sang smooth and low.
Yes she said Yes. He sang My Way. No
    She said: Sure I'm willing to go along
    But that she said is a terrible song.

When Friedrich Nietszche met Lois Lane,
He found there were notions she'd not entertain:
His. "I know Clark Kent as well as Su-
Perman," she said. "Guess which one you
    Remind me of." He glared and then
    Went out and addressed a group of men.

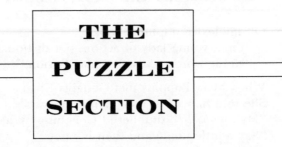

THE PUZZLE SECTION

A PARTIAL EXPLANATION

In 1986 when Graydon Carter and Kurt Andersen were getting ready to start a scurrilous satirical magazine called *Spy,* they asked me whether there was anything I would contribute. I said, well, I had always wanted to do a cryptic crossword puzzle, on the British model, only with coarse American references. It has always irritated me that The London *Times* puzzle expected me to know about tube stops and British vegetables, which have unnatural names like "Cockfosters" and "marrow." My first puzzle, not reproduced here, had *pussy-whipped* in it, and *doo-wop* ("In the still of the night, do we hear an Italian offensive?"). Since relatively few Americans can work this type of puzzle, I explained many of the answers. While explaining, I added further coarse American references—to the Reagan administration, for instance. Over the years these references have expanded into essays into which I have poured some of my deepest resentments. For instance, my resentment of the fact that George Bush, in the 1988 presidential campaign, referred to his opponent, Michael Dukakis, as "the so-called Stealth candidate," when in fact both candidates favored the Stealth bomber, Bush had accused Dukakis of *opposing* it, and at any rate, how can you justify calling somebody the *so-called* something when you are the only one who called him the something in the first place—unless you are just trying, stealthily, to make sure that voters remember that your opponent is short, dark and other than Anglo-Saxon?

Meanwhile, many people informed me of how deeply they resented the puzzles. Too tricky with the language, they said. Finally, I quit doing the puzzle and continued with the essay. I didn't take up writing so that I could listen to other people complain about me.

Of course, we who function in the major media do not expect

positive feedback, and when we get it, it is usually weird. On October 2, 1987, this was reported in *The New York Times:*

> *St. Elsewhere* created additional controversy Wednesday night with a closing shot of the actor Ed Flanders's bare buttocks. . . . The network . . . received forty-three phone calls from New York viewers about the program, ten favorable and thirty-three unfavorable.

Now, anyone who has had any small part in the expansion of the boundaries of acceptability in the American public eye—as I like to think I have—can readily imagine the tone of those unfavorable responses. (I myself did not watch *St. Elsewhere* that night, nor indeed any other night, so I can only say that my reaction to the scene in question would have depended on tastefulness and context—for instance, whether the commercial immediately following the scene was in keeping with it.) But how about the *favorable* ones?

> Listen, I have never called a network before, but after what I saw last night, well—I just wanted to tell you personally that at last the television medium has justified our trust. When our family's eyes lit on that elderly gentleman's heinie, we were surprised, yes. Jolted, even. But we were also—somehow, I can't say just why—drawn closer together. So—I won't keep you any longer, but we just wanted to tell you thanks, and: More!

The truth is, we who provide readers' and listeners' entertainment—and, perhaps, sometimes their edification—do not know what they are like out there. Not really. We can't even be all that sure what we are like in here.

In California, incidentally, the calls about Ed Flanders' buttocks ran seventeen against and nineteen in favor.

CHAOS

Just when this country seems to be settling into permanent goofy Republicanism, the rest of the world is—well, as goofy Republicans see it, I suppose, the rest of the world is advancing toward goofy Republicanism. What I was going to say, more conservatively, is that the world is undergoing extraordinary change.

The winds of orderliness have caught up Nicaragua. The Iron Curtain flaps in a wild and crazy breeze. By the time you read this, everyone from Tbilisi to Petropavlovsk will be applying for Amway distributorships, and, I don't know, Afrikaners will have started a Back to Haarlem movement. For the geopolitical implications, see the answers page. What I'd like to consider here is, can all this be explained in terms of chaos theory?

At a dinner party I attended recently, it came out that nearly everyone present had a copy of *Chaos: Making a New Science,* by James Gleick. There was a general vagueness as to whether any of us had actually read it, but most of us had looked at the illustrations, lustrous multicolor images of more or less paisley phenomena ("the Mandelbrot set," "the Great Red Spot: real and simulated") as graphicized by computers, somehow or other.

What these illustrations show, unless I haven't got this right, is that the underlying pattern of all nature is chaos. When we realize everything is arbitrary and random, everything falls into place.

This, as my old mother used to say, doesn't make any more sense to me than the man on the moon. But then, *neither does anything else anymore.* So there you have it. It wouldn't surprise me to find that if I just started twiddling my fingers on these computer keys unsystematically, I would hook into something far more fundamental than usual.

I'm getting ready to. Any minute now.

Okay.

Wait a minute.

Okay.

aiufopaijfgohjghjeoje

piohesiojeiogubeij89urheioI*dontbecruel* jeiohghuas ghgo[eu

I feel *silly*. I mean . . . Okay, okay.

Okay.

ljk8s

No, wait, I wasn't ready.

Now I am. Here goes.

kjaoiiwerihqwe4rnguhieeruhq4hj389j02349h3u89gh34u89ioh349
[j34bnghlaaq3u8yhgq8o4tjqipasgrw*toaheartthats*

Oh, great. I just hit something, who knows what, that caused my computer screen to flash me the following message: KEY CODE DOES NOT EXIST. SEE STYLE SHEET FOR VALID KEY CODES.

What is this "valid" stuff? What is this "does not exist"? How come, when Gleick tells *his* computer to go wild, it draws luminous whorly stuff, prettier than any oil slick?

Because his computer has a screw loose, would be my assessment. "The Great Red Spot: real and simulated." Give me a break. Communism is going down the tubes and chaos theory comes up with a great red spot. If this computer really knew where Chaos Central was, it would be drawing the Almighty Dollar, the Great Ten Spot: real and simulated.

Don't get me wrong. Give me, or even lend me, the dollar over the ruble any day. I have long recognized that communism is too moral to be lively. Under communism, injustice has to be imposed, and everyone scowls or sulks. Under capitalism, chicanery bubbles up like a wild, natural thing.

Would it be too . . . structured of me, though, to wonder whether capitalism doesn't need to have a little something imposed on it? Eighties Republicans cut capitalism so much slack. . . . Okay, there's a new demand for capital now from Lvov to Komsomolsk, and Marx is turning over in his grave. But we owe so much already, aren't we going to have to borrow some more capital somewhere in order to have any to lend?

I suppose computers will simulate the needful in some way that I am too orderly to understand. Maybe the Great Red Spot *is* debt (or the Rising Sun). What the heck. After all, this nation began with tea leaves dumped into Boston Harbor. And this administration owes a great deal to pollution in Boston Harbor. And . . .

I'm just free-associating. Exercising my birthright. Albanians will be doing it soon.

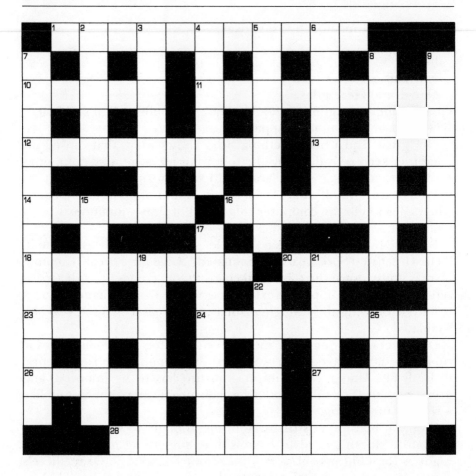

ACROSS

1 In Russia this class may have to find new jobs, for a horse. (11)
10 A piano concealed a plant louse. (5)
11 Something you can do in a pot—what doves do to Kansas street, east-west. (4,1,4)
12 How long will they keep on calling it the Union of Soviet _____ Republics? (9)
13 In Mexico, Mickey is a jokester. (5)
14 Murder and put in place to counterbalance. (6)
16 Soldier's equipment disordered? Rage, Mary. (4,4)
18 Pleasantries confront it backward, each the same way. (8)
20 Additional gold for Jeanne of *Jules et Jim.* (6)
23 Pilot formerly a bull. (5)
24 Put frost in crate to get level of illegality. (5,4)
26 Big hand envelops Uncle Leon initially for producing eggs. (9)
27 Ivana's baby is square. (5)
28 Manute Bol can't find the range? He *still* distrusts Russia. (4,7) (Note: This

clue dates back to before Bol was traded to Philadelphia.)

DOWN

2 And this, in Latin, is a good principle. (5)

3 Fred flipping his lid over high card—what a Communist has now. (3,4)

4 Into South Carolina whirls a warning. (6)

5 Cocks blown roses to right. (8)

6 Mischievous in any state of disorder. (7)

7 What Mike Dukakis went home to: large-scale 6. (4,9)

8 Pressed down in Southeast, herd goes wild. (8)

9 Bi-vehicular obsequies could be 15 by a bad organizer. (3-3,7)

15 Screwed down, turned around, and bungled. (6,2)

17 Boy! Sexist person supported by offspring. (3,5)

19 Twister's right messy and inside, too. (7)

21 Exceeding the standard, rover is off around Pennsylvania. (4,3)

22 Famous Nicaraguan uses breath spray wrong. (6)

25 Two states go down in Tex-Mex massacre. (5)

■ ANSWERS

ACROSS

1 The Secretariat (also the name of a great racehorse, of course) is the apparatchik class in Russia, or has been. Who will take on their duties now? Freely elected bozos? Ward heelers' cousins? Uncivil service employees? One hears that nobody is taking care of much functionary business in the U.S.S.R. lately. Imagine all the groundwork that has to be laid before democratic officialdom can be in place at every level of Soviet society. Local Sunday-morning interview shows will have to be produced: *Spotlight on Novgorod, Your Tax Ruble at Work in Grozny.* The whole concept of bid-rigging will have to be absorbed. There's probably no such thing as paving contractors, as we know them, in the Soviet Union today. Now's the time to get an enlightened campaign-financing law in on the ground floor; un-

fortunately, before there will be anyone to pass such a law, there will have to be campaigns. Whatever it takes to win those campaigns will be the source of enlightenment.

10 *A* plus *p* (the music-score abbreviation for *piano*) plus *hid* ("concealed") gives you the synonym for *plant louse*. This puzzle has been going on for more than three years, and I still have to explain stuff like this. That will give you some idea how long it is going to take Russkies to grasp the concept of image-mongering and the electoral college.

11 Doves *coo.* Kansas street is *KA* and *st.* East-west is *EW.*

12 U.S.R.R. (Union of Soviet Republican Republics)? UNCLESAM (Union of Neighboring Countries Liable Each to Secede Any Minute)?

18 To confront is to *face.* Plus *it* backward and *ea,* also backward. If you ever happen to write a book of trenchant, finely wrought and deeply unsettling essays and stories, you may find that the Library of Congress has classified them as "anecdotes, facetiae, satire, etc." This is an outrage. I bet it doesn't go on in godless Communist . . . Cuba, even.

20 *Au* is the symbol for gold.

28 Manute Bol, before he was traded, was a Golden State War-

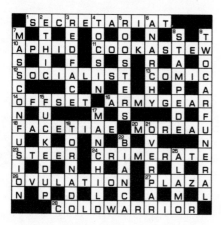

rior, right? (Aside from being a seven-foot-seven Dinka tribesman from the Sudan who has found a place for himself in our system.) And if he can't find the range—keeps missing shots—he's *cold,* right? You don't like it? Hey, it's a free country.

DOWN

2 If you don't know basketball, you must know Latin, right? What *were* you doing in high school? You can bet that young people in what used to be known as the Eastern bloc (now the New Free World) are learning these things.

3 Maybe you can't embarrass a Communist, I don't know. Anyway, if they all want to be free-marketeers now, it is okay with me. As long as they don't start turning out facetiae cheaper than I can.

4 *Into* and *S.C.* rearranged ("whirls").

6 *Arch* in *any.*

9 The saying goes, "He could fuck up a two-car funeral."

17 *Man* is a sexist term for "person."

19 *R (right)* and *and* rearranged ("messy") inside *too* gives you a twister.

22 The breath spray is Binaca.

25 The two states are Alabama and Missouri. The official post office abbreviation for Alabama now is *AL,* but surely you remember the more stately *Ala.* And what better note to end on, as our puzzle draws to a close and the sun sinks suddenly in the East (why shouldn't they have a sunset over there too?)—what better note than a salute to that gallant handful of Texans and Tennesseans who didn't see why they couldn't whip several thousand Mexicans in a town named San Antonio? If three million Russian tourists should descend on Moscow, Idaho, or St. Petersburg, Florida, we could do worse than to remember brave Bowie, Travis and Crockett.

⚊(OUT OF AEROBIC GUILT)⚊

"I offer nothing more than simple facts, plain arguments and common sense," wrote Thomas Paine in 1776 in *Common Sense,* which helped spark the American Revolution. A great deal of water has gone over the dam since then. In Paine's day, for instance, there was no Book-of-the-Month Club. Now there is one, and a plain-speaking American statesman has branded it a pinko tool. The *Daily News* reported recently that Richard Nixon had refused to allow his new memoir to be a BOMC selection. "He's always thought that the [BOMC] board has a pervasive left-wing bias," explained a Nixon aide.

The Washington Monthly, on the other hand, strives for evenhanded-ness. "Forget liberal. Forget conservative. Think common sense," it suggested recently in an article—billed on the cover as WHAT'S WRONG WITH THE FOURTH AND FIFTH AMENDMENTS—by Paul Savoy, a former prosecutor and law professor. What Savoy had to say, in essence, was, *Only the innocent should have a right to silence.*

That's commonsensical, all right. And since, as anti-gun-control people say, only the guilty shoot people (culpably), the crime problem suddenly clears up—we can just take away all those *guilty* people's guns and rights, and life will be easier for the innocent and the police.

Of course, say you are a guilty person and you get stopped for questioning, and the police advise you that if you're innocent, you have the right to remain silent, but if you're guilty, you don't. Wouldn't you be inclined to remain silent?

Fortunately, you aren't guilty. If you were, I wouldn't be associating with you. In fact, you're probably the type who's happy to talk to the police, because what do you have to hide? Which puts the police in a bit of a bind, because although you look innocent, *you're not remaining silent.* So just in case, the police lock you up. Which may make you feel guilty. Which, paradoxically, may make you stop talking. "Aha!" say the police.

In the Eighties, of course, no one felt guilty. But in the Nineties guilt may be coming back. Perhaps a new form of guilt: guilt that is self-improving. The Democrats have got to come up with *something* the Republicans haven't co-opted.

Aerobic guilt. Kicking oneself so vigorously as to lose weight and tighten the gluteus muscles. Tossing and turning. Slapping the forehead, *whap* two three four. Dashing outside and thrusting money upon the more deserving. Weeping, wailing, gnashing one's teeth.

Donald Trump claims he does in fact feel some guilt because he is so rich while others are homeless. But the most interesting exchange in his *Playboy* interview is the following:

> TRUMP: Every successful person has a very large ego.
> PLAYBOY: *Every* successful person? Mother Teresa? Jesus Christ?
> TRUMP: Far greater egos than you will ever understand.

I have dashed off a little spiritual that might be sung by a person who understands as Trump understands:

> There's an ego on my Savior
> That you would not believe,
> You would not believe,
> Oh, you would not believe.
> There's an ego on my Savior
> That only I believe—
> That is why He's where He is today.

If fusions of guilt and exercise or egotism and Christlikeness lack broad popular appeal, how about religious ecstasy and weapons testing? In *Street News*, a newspaper sold by homeless people, the actress Lisa Bonet shared an epiphany:

> Once in Los Angeles, Lenny [her husband] and I were outside and a missile was shot off. It must have been a test of some kind. . . . There were these incredible magical colors in the sky. . . . Everyone was outside going, "Oh my God, you've got to see this." And Lenny said, "If that was from a missile, can you imagine how beautiful it will be when God's taking care of us?"

Common Sense sold a hundred thousand copies, even without the BOMC. But after the Revolution, Paine's career plummeted. He was imprisoned in France for opposing the Reign of Terror. Back in the U.S., where he'd popularized the rights of man and the rule of law, he was accused of atheistic beliefs. He lived out his years in obscurity on a farm in New Rochelle. It takes more than simple facts and plain arguments to stay in tune with America.

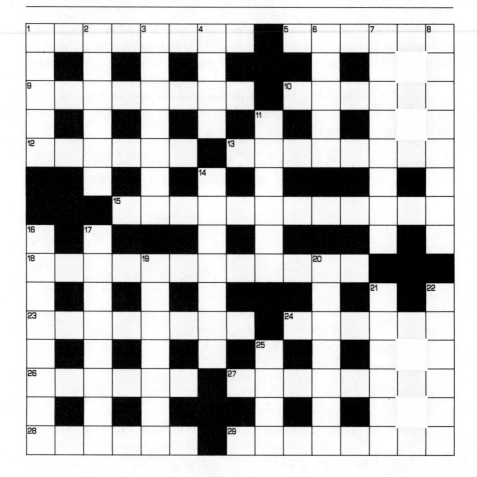

ACROSS

1 Fair attempt, east to south—with 5, 12, 13, and 25—merely reveals our ignorance. (4,4)

5 Drunk retreats—how? (2,4) (See 1.)

9 Storms be shaking organized bad guys. (8)

10 System speaking with forked tongue in street before zip. (6)

12 Second person with Native American greeting. (3,3) (See 1.)

13 Small, west to east. (6,2) (See 1.)

15 Sound reasoning from be-nign slim sovereign. (4,8)

18, 23 How to get the sound of four hands clapping? Assemble the obvious evidence (3,3,3,3,8)

24 Two male cats get Indian drum. (3-3)

26 Appearances of ageism, perhaps. (6)

27 Renege in arrangement with person who drives train. (8)

28 In ancient country, it's said, squeaky wheel gets this. (6)

29 Brandenburg and Water, or Heaven's and contra-. (3,5)

DOWN

1 Pry open recent president. (5)

2 Underwater boat supported by Juicy Fruit with vegetables. (3,3)

3 If you must leave, you have old Giant Mel surrounded by dance. (3,2,2)

4 Noble was recent president's middle name. (4)

6 After the tenth month, unearthly creature becomes a group of eight. (5)

7 Sterile dissident takes in a thousand. (8)

8 Go *whee!*, L.G., mixing the yellow with the white. (5,3)

11 Di took off and shared slander. (6)

14 Egghead in embrace of loose maiden produces conceptualizing guys. (4,3)

16 Shish kebabing and salivating expressively. (8)

17 How old it says you are in *Playbill,* or the Wells Fargo era. (5,3)

19 What a court without a jester is: dumb. (7)

20 Ow! My gin spilled in a Western state! (7)

21, 22 What you need to know to survive in the city: drag hurts. (6,6)

25 Be aware of a strikeout immediately. (4) (See 1 Across.)

■ ANSWERS

ACROSS

1 Fair is *just*. Attempt is *go*. Plus *E* and *S*. Put this together with 5 Across, 12 Across, 13 Across, and 25 Down and you have *Just goes to show you how little we know*, which is to say, "Merely reveals our ignorance." I feel a bit guilty about expecting anyone to figure this out. I want so much for you, for us, for this puzzle of ours, and sometimes I get carried away. You would not believe the flak I get from people who say they cannot work the Un-British Crossword. Well, hell. Why should *I* feel guilty because *they* can't work it? But I do. Because I fall in between two awkward categories in American life: the homeless and the shameless. I hasten to say that the homeless is a much more awkward category. Once, a man came through my subway car asking for "money, food, socks, whatever you have," be-

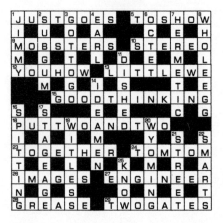

cause he was homeless and also had AIDS. He showed the sores on his ankles, which were sockless. He was chipper, bearing up. Not laying any kind of guilt trip on us. (As a matter of fact, when he said he had AIDS, one healthy-looking youth in the car said to another, "All riiiiight.") I gave him some money. I didn't have any food on me, or any socks aside from the ones I was wearing. I should have given him those. Jesus would have. Maybe Donald Trump would have, if he had been there. But my ego wasn't great enough. It wouldn't have hurt me to give this man my socks. Jesus washed lepers' feet, right? Anyway, disciples' feet. I didn't want to deal with this man at all, to tell the truth. I know you can't catch AIDS or homelessness hand-to-hand, but you don't relish contact with *anybody* on the subway. Right after the most recent December-January holidays I was sitting in another subway car, a crowded one. Through a temporary gap in the standees I saw an old good friend, whose company I'd enjoyed just a few days before, on New Year's Eve. Our eyes didn't catch. Another glimpse and our eyes didn't catch. Then a third glimpse and they did. Clearly each of us had noticed the other on a previous glimpse, and hadn't said anything. We smiled and briefly spoke. Then she got off. Any recognition on the subway is . . . is unusual. *Jesus Christ, there are dying people on public transportation showing their sores and asking for help!* And you complain of an inability to work *this* puzzle?

5 *Sot* backward ("retreats"), plus *how.*

9 *Storms be* reassembled ("shaking").

10 Street is *St.,* before is *ere,* zip is *O.*

26 *Ageism* rearranged ("perhaps"). "Appearances" is the definition.

27 *Renege in* rearranged ("arrangement").

29 Remember when we used to have *-gates* all the time? Watergate, Billygate. Scandals. With regard to governmental lying. Now, I guess, the Republicans have lied so much and so blithely that the whole *-gate* concept is stretched out and flaccid to the extent that nobody can get up for it anymore.

DOWN

1 To *jimmy* is to pry open—a lock or a window. Jimmy Carter is a recent president. Of the United States. You remember. Jimmy Carter keeps popping up in this puzzle. That is partly because he and I are both from Georgia, but mostly because I keep thinking, *Jesus Christ, the guy*

was lame in lots of ways but he wasn't morally *lame, whereas . . . oh, never mind.*

2 An underwater boat is a *sub.* Juicy Fruit is *gum.* On Chinese menus, sub gum means with vegetables.

3 Mel *Ott* was a great player for the old New York Giants (baseball). Surrounded by *go-go.*

4 An *earl* is a noble. James Earl Carter. I mean, I know, the guy was self-righteous. But . . . Reagan and Bush haven't been self-righteous? They've been self-righteous *without any serious pretensions to knowing right from wrong.* Self-righteous Lite. Designer self-righteous. (I confess: I stole this concept from Sandra Bernhard, who said, "It's always so shocking to me that we're back to this racism. It's not even fundamental. It's like designer racism.") People seem to find that easier to take.

6 *E.T.* after *Oct.*

8 "Mixing," here, signals a rearrangement of the previous letters.

14 *E* (the head of *egg*) embraced by *maiden* rearranged ("loose"). Idea men are conceptualizing guys.

21, 22 *Drag* is a word for "street" (as in "main drag"), and *smarts* means "hurts."

25 The scorekeeping symbol for strikeout is *K.* Immediately is *now.* To know is to be aware of. Jesus, Jesus. Aware of what?

⎯LEADERS WE CAN READ?⎯

I'm giving away 1 Across, because it's just a cheap verbal gag. If there's any type of person in the world who wouldn't be an authoritarian, surely it would be an author.

Well, of course Hitler was an author. So was Julius Caesar. Mussolini. Khomeini. Lenin. Mao. Ho Chi Minh. And I believe these men actually wrote the books they were authors of (unlike Ronald Reagan, author of one of the most shamelessly titled books in publishing history—*Speaking My Mind,* a collection of speeches written for him by speech writers).

But you know what I mean. Those guys weren't *primarily* literary persons. Vaclav Havel and Mario Vargas Llosa, on the other hand, are. Havel is an *absurdist,* for heaven's sake; and in Vargas Llosa's novel *Aunt Julia and the Script-writer,* the characters get all intermingled with characters in soap operas written by one of the characters in the novel, if you follow me. And Havel is the new president of Czechoslovakia, and Vargas Llosa ran for president of Peru. Courageous and high-minded, both of them, but what do these qualities have to do with appearing to run a country?

This emergence of the writer as presidential timber comes when I'd about decided writers generally don't even make good *authors.* What is needed to put a book across is a nonbookish author. Where the author is already established as an actor or politician, the problem is solved: the author appears on TV, and whoever actually wrote the book remains quite properly a ghost. In the case where the author is an authentic writer (or dead), however, the need for a promotional presence is glaring.

The writer-author's value to a book is severely limited by the belief, all but openly endemic among writers, that no one worthy of being addressed—no one, that is, who can read—ever bought a book because the author was good on TV. Writer-authors may also find it onerous to repeat crucial selling points ("Interestingly enough, my book *How to Become Famous by Feeling Better About Yourself* is not so much about how to become famous—though it *has* been endorsed by Nancy Reagan, Wayne Newton, Donald Trump and many other famous people who feel good about themselves—as it is about feeling better about yourself") two hundred times in a month-long promotional blitz.

Such authors, I had thought, should plainly be portrayed by actors. Simulated authors. *This-is-a-dramatization* authors. If current events can be re-created on TV, why not contemporary authors? If necessary, the person who wrote the book could write the actor's lines, but writers of books are not always good at even this element of self-portrayal.

It would probably be best if a whole new profession were to spring up—and therefore a whole new course of instruction in the media departments of up-to-date universities. People who write books could support themselves by teaching "Writing the Dramatized Author-Appearance Script 101."

I had thought. But now I'm feeling guilty, as a writer, because it never occurred to me to propose that David Rabe or Toni Morrison run for president. It is at least partly my fault, then, that the current holder of that office delivered this public utterance last November 1:

> We had last night, last night we had a couple of our grandchildren with us in Kansas City—six-year-old twins, one of them went as a packet of Juicy Fruit, arms sticking out of the pack, the other was Dracula. A big rally there. And Dracula's wig fell off in the middle of my speech and I got to thinking, watching those kids, and I said if I could look back and had been president for four years: what would you like to do? And I'd love to be able to say that I'd found a way to ban chemical and biological weapons from the face of the earth.

This is the kind of absurdism that works for heads of state, I had come to believe. Then the people of Czechoslovakia elected an absurdist who, in his New Year's address to them, said, "I assume you have not named me to this office so that I, too, should lie to you . . .

"Our country is not flourishing."

That tack sure didn't go over for long over here when Jimmy Carter tried it.

ACROSS

1 The form of government a book writer may be expected to impose? (13)

9 Ava, quit messing around and drink! (7)

10 One of Beethoven's symphonies found in "Down in the Boondocks." (5)

11 Author of *The Phenomenology of Mind,* he uses a hair-fixing product. (5)

12 Every third word in this sentence is a sister swallowing a goose egg. (4)

13 Just so-so. (4)

15 Wraps minks? Oo, wild! (7)

17 Oppress lover. (7)

18 Cancels Northeast openings. (7)

20 Fashionable couple of guys sniffed. (7)

21 Belt goes on foot. (4)

22 Gore made this a best-seller—it sticks with you. (4)

23 Old survivor, about 51 to 100. (5)

26 Moral code in the thick and the thin. (5)

27 Liberate before chaotic blaze can be turned to ice! (9)

28 A problem with James Fenimore Cooper's

work (if not, indeed, Ved Mehta's): used to advertise cigars. (6,7)

DOWN

1 In Warren's novel they couldn't unscramble an egg. (3,3,5,3)

2 What k. d. lang has, along with absolute torch and tomboy's head and penis. (5)

3 Penguin duration? People may say it doesn't matter, but just to make slim-volume authors feel better. (4,6)

4 John Washington, and Howe! (7)

5 King Chester A. Schlesinger. (7)

6 What Christ needs for followers: Frazier, Fleming. (4)

7 Peerless northern leader on par with crawfishing lie. (9)

8 Prince and Satan wrote French revolution novel. (7,7)

14 Sanctioned, or autographed by the writer? (10)

16 Disappearing act is Johnson's? In what way? (5,4)

19 Pigs spoil elf's fun for truffles. (7)

20 The kind of author Amos Oz is, is Shakespearean king rising on ego. (7)

24 In DeLillo novel, woman's supporter supports Long Island. (5)

25 *Name of the Rose* author is what we hear—again! (4)

■ ANSWERS

ACROSS

11 *He* plus *gel.*

12 A goose egg, in sports, is a zero.

13 This is just about as simple as a clue in this kind of puzzle can be. *Just* means "fair," and so, in another sense, does *so-so.*

15 *Minks* and *oo* rearranged ("wild") to form a word for which "wraps" is a brief definition.

17 As in "Tyrants squeeze the people" and "I'd like you to meet my main squeeze."

20 *In* plus *Hal* and *Ed.*

21 To belt is to *sock,* as in to hit.

22 Gore Vidal authored the best-selling historical novel *Burr,* about Aaron Burr. A burr sticks with you.

23 About is *re;* 51 is the Roman numeral *LI;* 100 is *C.*

26 The same kind of clue as 10 Across.

27 *Free* followed by *blaze* rearranged ("chaotic"), and then the definition. Speaking of *blaze,* I was reminded by the recent movie *Blaze* that I once had my head between Blaze Starr's breasts. She was dancing in her club on the Block in Baltimore back in 1966, and for reasons I can only guess at, she chose my head (among all those confronting her along the runway) to flomp her voluminous and congenial breasts around. After inviting me to lean forward. I not quite realizing what she had in mind. It was like being caught between two—well, three, counting her sternum—large people in an elevator. Large, congenial people. Earl Long was long dead by then. He never authored a book, I believe, but he was the subject of a wonderful book, A. J. Liebling's *The Earl of Louisiana.* On the whole, I believe that is the most suitable role for a politician in literature.

DOWN

1 A reference to Robert Penn Warren's novel (about Earl Long's brother, Huey) and to Humpty Dumpty.

2 The singer k. d. lang, who lowercases herself as e. e. cummings did (but R. D. Laing didn't), has an album out entitled *Absolute Torch and Twang.* The head of *tomboy* is the letter *t.*

And have you heard the joke about who was the first computer expert? Eve, because she had an Apple in one hand and a Wang in the other. Ho ho!

3 Opus was the penguin in *Bloom County.*

4 John Irving, Washington Irving, Irving Howe. Authors all.

5 King Arthur, Chester A. Arthur and Arthur Schlesinger.

6 Add *-ians* to *Christ.* Fleming and Frazier: authors named Ian. Frazier's *Great Plains,* incidentally, cites a biography of Doc Holliday by an author named John Myers Myers. Isn't that an interesting name? Have you ever heard of a person who had the same middle name as last? I have racked my brain, but I cannot think of another. Was his father a Myers who married a Myers?

7 *N* (*northern* leader) plus *on,* plus *par,* plus *eil,* which is *lie* backing up.

8 *Dickens* is a euphemism for the Devil, as in "What the dickens" or "You little dickens." *A Tale of Two Cities.*

16 *Magic's* (reference being to Johnson of the Lakers) *how* ("in what way").

24 Don DeLillo's novel *Libra* is about Lee Harvey Oswald. Odd sort of title. I am a Libra myself, along with such authors as Jimmy Carter, Oscar Wilde, Damon Runyon and Graham Greene. Generally speaking, Librans are too evenhanded (conspiracy theorists take note) to shoot anybody. Greene dabbled in Russian roulette but never even managed to shoot himself.

25 What we hear is Eco, and an *echo* is what we hear again. As in John Myers Myers. I have never heard of anybody else whose last name was the same as his or her middle. Wait a minute! I just thought of one! Eleanor Roosevelt Roosevelt. An author, to boot.

BE HAD?

Is it just me, or what? Correct me if I'm wrong. But my understanding is that certain Americans devise, with difficulty, certain licks, moves and expressions of fact and feeling that carry credence. And then capitalism comes along and tries to turn those licks, moves and expressions of fact and feeling into means for selling doodads.

Now, we all know that prosperity depends on the selling of doodads. But *credence* depends on telling the truth. And the truth about doodads is that some of them work and some of them don't, and even the ones that do work don't often work to the extent that advertising says they do.

So. How come Tip O'Neill and Norman Mailer did commercials for an airline owned by Donald Trump? Did *commercials* for it! I didn't think self-respecting people would even *fly* on the son of a bitch.

Alexander Haig and Don King also appeared in these commercials. Al Haig is an act. Don King is an act. Who cares what they do? But I thought—I know, I know, this is reeelly uncool, but I thought Tip O'Neill and Norman Mailer, like, *stood* for things.

With respect to advertising, I am not, myself, wholly virginal. I try not to denounce things that I have not tried. ("Once a philosopher," goes the saying, "twice a pervert." I don't know who said this. Was he a philosopher? Did he ever repeat it? If he never did, was it because he didn't believe in saying things twice or because he had started doing things twice?) I have done things that the late Samuel Beckett would not have done. (I *assume* that Beckett never did a commercial. Hard to picture that craggy visage intoning, "I can't go on. I will go on. Thanks to heaping bowls of Nut & Honey.")

In 1975 I did a beer commercial that was broadcast in the Pittsburgh area a number of times. I liked that kind of beer. I needed the money. I worked in a plug for my first book. But now that I am making a living writing what I want to say, why would I get into the business of saying what somebody else wants me to say?

Some years ago I wrote an uncensored signed paragraph of "shirt criticism" for a clothing-store chain's catalog in return for three shirts and a now-defunct discount card. In retrospect I feel that that was a bad idea, but I am willing to make speeches, for money, to people like lawyers. (Once I even addressed a business association that included, I learned to my horror, companies that specialized in peddling products by phone. And by mail—I sat next to an envelope manufacturer who said, "If you ever saw envelopes being made, you'd never lick one.") Not only am I willing for my own works to be advertised, I am touched by the gesture.

I have, however, declined to become the TV spokesman for a stockbroking company and a cellular-phone company, and to be the voice of a radio ad for a discount-store chain, and I've rejected a feeler for a national beer commercial. I also passed on the chance to write a brief story for a magazine-ad tribute to story-telling sponsored by a telephone company.

You may think, therefore, that I am a fool. Especially since I have, in fact, frequently drunk that beer and patronized that discount chain. ("Shop at So-and-so," I could have said in all candor, "if you belong to, or would like to keep in touch with, the lower lower middle class.") But I didn't feel right about being paid to say so. I hate all telephone companies. And I don't know anything about cellular phones or stockbroking.

This Southern stockbroking firm wanted me to do a spiel whose punch line was "Southern . . . and smart." It took me a while to figure out what was wrong with that concept: it was not much different from "Southern . . . but smart." My people have never served themselves well by *claiming* to be smart. Jimmy Carter, for instance, claimed to be a nuclear physicist, and then it came out that he wasn't a physicist and he couldn't pronounce *nuclear*.

So let me assure you that I don't know a whole lot. But I do know that when a person whose medium is free speech shows up in a commercial, it makes people doubt that free speech *means* anything.

ACROSS

1 Hustling for coin. (8)

5 Scratch low Los Angeles/ Hollywood front. (6)

10 Theme of Missouri: suitable regression. (5)

11 What Tip still has that's pure: what he confused with beginning of *Rocky II.* (5,4)

12 Swimming green seas with alacrity. (9)

13 Antipathy consumes half of U.S. with speed. (5)

14 Former number-one gentleman, in short, is requiring a great deal. (7)

16 Oddly, Ailes and I communicate. (6)

19 Journalist's name alongside business. (6)

21 Driving hazard in grass where golf ball should go. (7)

23 In a way, half-truths proceed proudly. (5)

25 One cheek, Ed, is slapdash. (4-5)

27 What Satan may take and people run true to. (5,4)

28 Donahue's wife is moral . . . sort of. (5)

29 Dancer and Prancer missing! That is, present. (6)

30 Bourbon

without old father's pop. (8)

DOWN

1 Mr. Si peed messily and foolishly smiled. (8)
2 Honesty confuses tiny tiger. (9)
3 Rifle exploded, and he's in for keeps. (5)
4 Quaint Sixties political concept flew wildly into net. (3, 4)

6 Hate-prone corrected by type of surgery. (4-5)
7 People who pretend to be earnest in commercials go with the wind up right inside. (5)
8 Sold intimate favors, we hear—to a great mass of people. (5)
9 Glitz is strangely silent. (6)

15 Weird sixteen with cold energy being . . . (9)
17 . . . paid for by snoops agitated over Communist. (9)
18 Calamity Jane and Wild Bill lie here with useless workers. (8)
20 Crazy hens to form cultural group. (6)
21 What com-

mercials say tires have in them—could be more ply. (7)
22 Biblical queen in finest heroic tradition. (6)
24 Polanski's kind of nose. (5)
26 Decapitated lunatic is person responsible for commercials. (5)

■ ANSWERS

ACROSS

5 *Scratch* is the synonym. The exiguously pieced-together end of the answer is as follows: to low is to *moo,* Los Angeles is *L.A.,* and the front of *Hollywood* is *H.*

10 *MO* plus *fit* backward (in "regression").

11 *What be* rearranged ("confused") along with *R* (the beginning of *Rocky*) and *II.* According to his agent, O'Neill does commercials for the sake of his loved ones. That these people are needy in this society only points up O'Neill's failure as a legislator. He pitches not only for the aforementioned airline but also for several other companies. In one commercial for a motel chain he . . . well, as one ad exec puts it, "Having the Speaker of the House come out of a suitcase is a little weird."

12 *Green seas* rearranged ("swimming").

13 Antipathy is *hate,* consuming *s* (the latter half of *U.S.*).

14 Former is *ex.* Number one is *I. Gent* is short for *gentleman.* And *exigent* means "requiring a great deal."

19 Alongside is *by.* A business is a *line.*

21 "Grass" is *pot.* Where a golf-ball should go is a *hole.*

23 A way is a *st.* (short for *street*). Inside, place half of *truths,* that is, *tru.*

28 "Sort of," here, betokens a rearrangement of the word *moral.* I have never noticed Marlo Thomas doing any commercials, and I apologize for dragging her into this mess. Except that maybe by dragging her into this mess we will save her from doing commercials. Maybe she was just on the brink of it when she read this. We don't know what good we may be doing in this world.

29 Dancer and Prancer are *reindeer.* When *i.e.* (the abbreviation for *that is*) is missing from that word, we are left with *render,* one synonym for which is *present.*

30 Old Grand-Dad is a brand of bourbon, which I do not endorse. Granddad is, of course, father's pop.

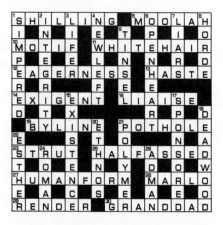

DOWN

1 The word *messily* signals a rearrangement of the previous words.

3 "Exploded" is another signal of rearrangement.

4 "Wildly" is yet another . . . Listen, I realize there are far more anagrams this month than usual. But that is not because this puzzle has been made possible by a grant from the National Anagram Council, because it hasn't been. I just wanted to make that clear.

7 To go with the wind is to *sail.* That word going up, with *R,* for *right,* inside, is *liars.* Isn't it? Isn't it? Why would I say so if it weren't true?

8 In *horde* we hear "whored."

9 "Strangely" betokens a rearrangement of *silent.*

15 We rearrange *sixteen,* because "weird" tells us to, and we toss in *c* for *cold* and *e* for *energy,* and we come up with a synonym for *being.*

17 *Snoops* rearranged ("agitated") over *red.*

18 You didn't know that Calamity Jane and Wild Bill Hickok were buried in Deadwood, South Dakota? Well, maybe you ought to get out around the country a little more. Would Jane and Bill have done commercials? Well, hell, yes, probably. But they were scum. Okay, maybe Wild Bill wasn't *exactly* scum, but he *dealt* with scum all the time.

20 All together, now: when we see such a word as *crazy,* what do we immediately consider as a possibility (though not, of course, a cinch)? "That the previous or following few letters may well be rearranged to form the answer!"

22 This is a different form of clue. Poke around in *finest heroic tradition* and see if you don't find a biblical queen hiding in there. Why would a biblical queen be hiding anywhere? Well, maybe she is avoiding the temptation to do a myrrh commercial.

26 *Madman* with its head cut off. And let me just say that all you people in the advertising community have been awfully good sports to stick with this puzzle all the way to the end here, and where would we be without you? (I have accepted money to speak to advertising people too. In fact, this puzzle is a clever way of recycling some of the material from that speech.) The question is, aren't you being better Americans when you hire actors to pretend to be earnest about the products you are pushing than when you compromise people who heretofore actually *were* earnest?

══════DOUBLE BIND══════

Your parents send you off for four years to study all that is highest and best in ethical philosophy, French symbolist poetry, pure astronomy and the violoncello, and then you must graduate into some field of work that will pay you enough to someday afford higher learning for your own children. Probably this field of work will entail spilling oil on beaches or marketing suction-footed Garfields.

How do we resolve these contradictory injunctions? Not everyone can become a college professor and be *paid* for championing art for art's sake (even academic criticism for academic criticism's sake) and the examined life. Not everyone will be simpleminded enough to say fuck it from the outset and major in business. Not everyone—I realize this—can hope to create advanced, antiestablishment, biodegradable crossword puzzles for gain.

I *guess* this is biodegradable. Maybe I should leave a copy out in the rain and see. Crude oil is biodegradable, as far as that goes, and so are oil-soaked otters. (Garfield dolls that stick to car windows aren't, though. Could I just say . . . Maybe I shouldn't. Maybe it won't seem pertinent to you. Maybe you think there are more important things this puzzle could worry about. But could I just say . . . that *I hate Garfield. So much.* He isn't funny, he isn't engaging, he isn't like a cat. And he ogles me, thanks to the magic of suction cups, through the window of every third car in America. What a *stupid* craze. Have the people who drive around with those things in their windows ever been to college? Have they ever seen a real cat? I can conceive of why some people would like Tater Tots or movies with Steve Guttenberg in them. But *Garfield?* There should be a required course, Minimal Understanding 101: Why Every Genuinely Educated Person Has to *Hate* Garfield or Leave This Class This Minute. But that would not foster freedom of thought, you may object. Yes it would too. Russia has the KGB, this country has merchandising. And *yes,* if I have to choose between the two, I will take merchandising. Still . . . *Garfield?*)

I am not coming on all holier-than-thou. I am just interested. And since every clue in this puzzle is, in a sense, a double bind (except for 22 Across, which asks you to complete the second of two rhyming double-binding admonitions), I thought I would salute those of you who are off to college this month.

Savor the college experience, which is such a golden opportunity that there is no way you can appreciate it. Have more fun than you ever will again, and take great tragedies to heart.

As Meryl Streep once advised a Vassar graduating class, you'll find that the real world is not like college: the real world is more like high school. Of course, Meryl Streep pulls in millions of dollars doing work that the high-minded applaud. She can make a crack like that without having to rush over to the side of the speaker's stand and vomit due to having hit herself too close to home. (Though she could play that *scene.*) My advice to you is, take care that you are not caught in the same trap as Shakespeare and I. Be Meryl Streep.

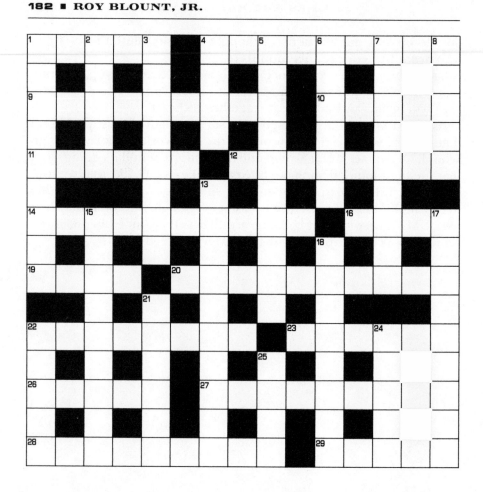

ACROSS

1 Liberates right surrounded by things to be paid. (5)

4 White powder container brings collegians together in New Orleans New Year's. (5,4)

9 By Roman law, crazy ol' Ruth is enemy of Superman. (3, 6)

10 Proudhon said property was the length of twelve inches. (5)

11 Success gets around, and you have to do this to the Japanese. (4,2)

12 Lend a car? Perhaps. We owe ours to Caesar. (8)

14 Ignorant tuna deduce incorrectly. (10)

16 Steady company. (4)

19 Sore back, Love? (4)

20 What your parents want you to have is what they don't want you to take, shithead! (10)

22 Take *Hamlet* to heart, but do well and marry./ Love *Peter Pan*, but don't __ _ _____. (2,1,5)

23 School of man known for yellow chickens, we hear. (6)

26 Grow up to

be a hundred and fifty-one thousand starting off, Buster! (5)

27 Artificial grouping of three states gets first chunk of Nicaragua. (9)

28 Casual dress code is bond between weight lifters. (2,7)

29 Before, state where Jodie Foster matriculated standing up. (5)

DOWN

1 Foursome is better than this frat with no opening. (4,5)

2 Long time without kisses for mass killer of sea life. (5)

3 Grinding debts follow professional male. (8)

4 Little bit of London just below Houston. (4)

5 Badly manage underclothes of sanitation engineer. (10)

6 Actor Hauer is a singular Jersey college? (6)

7 Wildly drove hole on bad gin, carrying too far. (9)

8 Slightly more than a quart of low-cal, right? (5)

13 Little Gloria at last at Dinah Shore's alma mater. (10)

15 Calling forth confusedly into a cove. (9)

17 MIT reacts oddly to how merchandisers address Garfield. (6,3)

18 Wrestle holy man with a tou-pee and bad leg. (8)

21 Person connected with disposable lighter concern makes egomaniacal statement with foot, ba-DUM. (6)

22 Someone must bring this home to Francis. (5)

24 Student singled out to become gray-brown civil engineer. (5)

25 Greater St. Thomas. (4)

■ ANSWERS

ACROSS

4 The Sugar Bowl is, of course, a football game in which major universities clash every year on January 1, in New Orleans. And here is what I think about college athletes: if they can play ball and pass college courses at the same time, great. If they can't, give them a room and a living wage, offer them such remedial classes as they may need to prepare for college work, and *then, after* they've played out their eligibility, offer them a college scholarship.

10 *The* plus *ft.* "Property is theft" was one of the wild yet incontrovertible communistic ravings spouted by the French philosopher Pierre-Joseph Proudhon. I don't know whether Proudhon ever owned a little real estate himself, or even, say, a hat. A hat is property, isn't it? He may have borrowed his hats. Shared

communal hats with other Frenchmen. Maybe he stole hats, with a clear conscience. I used to know all this, but I have been out of college too long. I say "incontrovertible." Perhaps Proudhon could have been shouted down by Donald Trump. But "property is theft" is one of those statements, I find, that stick with you from college. When I was in college, I never wanted to own anything that cost more than thirty-five dollars. More precisely, I never wanted to buy, maintain, put away, move or pick up the insurance on anything that cost more than thirty-five dollars. I still don't. But you have to have plenty of choice property today. Otherwise how could you get divorced? How could you protect yourself against the greater and greater degradability of what used to be called an honest living? If you don't own property that is so prohibitively expensive that you can count on it to appreciate preposterously, before you know it you won't be upscale enough to swing a loan to pay your share of the Exxon oil cleanup or the savings-and-loan-industry bailout, and all your assets will be seized and you will die in the gutter. What I want to know is, why is the Communist world swinging toward capitalism *now*? Why not back in the Eisenhower years,

when the average person could afford it?

11 *Hit* around *and.*

12, 14 Anagrams signaled by "perhaps" and "incorrectly." The calendar we use today is a modification of the Julian, from Julius Caesar. Unless we have started using a different calendar since I was in college. Today is . . . what is today?

20 *Advantage* and *s* (head of the S word).

26 To grow up is to *climb,* as in a climbing plant. Roman numerals *C, LI,* and *M,* plus the letter that starts off *Buster.*

27 Grouping of *IN, OR* and *GA,* plus *nic.* "Artificial" is the definition.

28 The dress code is *no necktie.* The bond between weight lifters is a *no-neck tie.* On the final, you're going to have to figure these things out for yourself.

29 "Before" is *ere.* Jodie Foster matriculated at Yale, in *CT.*

DOWN

3 "Grinding" is the definition. *IOUs* after *stud.*

5 *Manage* rearranged under *garb.*

7 *Drove* rearranged, plus *o* (a hole), plus *gin* rearranged.

13 There is no reason why you should know that Vanderbilt is Dinah Shore's alma mater, I suppose. But it is also my alma mater, and I figure that every time I mention it in a crossword puzzle, that's another fifteen dollars I don't have to contribute to the development fund. If that be corruption, well, at least it is corruption in the cause of advanced education. A chance to work a little angle here and there is a terrible thing to waste.

21 Bic is a manufacturer of disposable lighters. An iambic foot goes ba-DUM. Shakespeare wrote his plays in iambic pentameter, for the most part, but sometimes he got sloppy. "To *be* or *not* to *be:* that *is* the *ques-ti-on.*" Doesn't really work, does it? Well, Shakespeare (unlike the Prince of Denmark) had to make a living. He had to get done what I have here, nearly: the increasingly less cost-effective job.

SUCKS!

Where are the great American exclamations anymore, like the ones we learned in school? *Fifty-four-forty or fight!* Actually, I guess that one was imperialistic, and it nearly got us into a war with England. *Remember the* Maine*!* Actually, I guess that one was imperialistic, too, and it *did* get us into a war with Spain.

But lately it's worse! All anybody exclaims is *Let's stop feeling guilty about this jabbering rabble of* other *people and just be our natural selves: nasty, hateful and self-respecting!*

We hear plenty of exclamations from proudly offensive comedians and rock groups. From the also proudly defensive Jackie Mason: "Anybody who calls me a racist should be shot in the street like a horse!" Also, "You have to be an idiot, a coward and a bigot to call me names!"

We can do better than that! Okay:

Shame on those congresspeople who rushed to the office of Representative Claude Pepper after his death to get his autograph on books and pictures before the automatic signing pen was put away!

But denouncing congresspeople is too easy. Presidents are capable of that. So let us quote Public Enemy's former "minister of information," Richard "Professor Griff" Griffin: "The Jews are wicked. And we can prove this." And then let us exclaim, *You have a filthy mouth!*

And let us quote . . . no. I, for one, am not going to quote the minority-bashing, woman-bashing and entirely unfunny album of Andrew Dice Clay, which I bought out of curiosity and hated so much that I threw it down the garbage chute. Let us just exclaim, *You have a despicable act! You, and your mother, and your fans, and their mothers, ought to be ashamed!*

And let us quote Axl Rose, of the rock group Guns N' Roses: "Why can black people go up to each other and say, 'nigger,' but when a white guy does it all of a sudden it's a big put-down?" And then let us exclaim this: *You have evidently given this question so little thought that you must be too dumb to realize how stupid you sound!*

And let us say about Mason that at least he's wrestling openly with what he doesn't want to admit is his racism, and even if he has lost every round to it, he's at least been giving it something *like* thought, what he *thinks* is thought (in fact, something that is thought, up to a point), proving that the worst (the most quotably self-defeating) defense makes for the best (the most illuminating) offense. And let us exclaim to Jackie Mason, *Listen to yourself! You could learn something!*

And let us say that radio personality Howard Stern, whose act has always stunk, has gone downhill. Recently, according to *Newsday,* Stern hosted an evening of performances that included "a fellow dressed in a Nazi outfit who, after asking the crowd if it would like to meet Anne Frank, dumped a bottle of ashes on the ground" and "a one-legged ball boy who rolled around the court pathetically retrieving tennis balls." Let us exclaim this to Howard Stern: *No one should speak kindly to you or about you until you show remorse for your career to date!*

Bleahh! That outrageousness should sink so low!

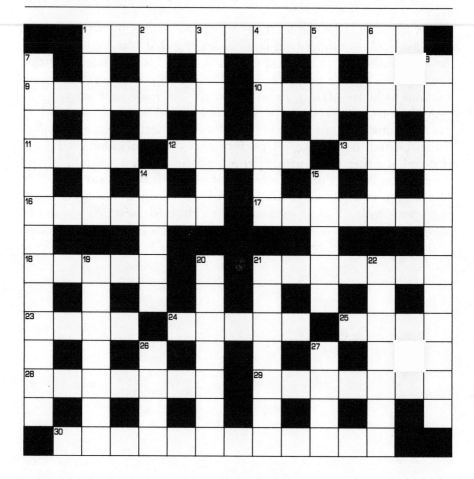

ACROSS

1 What we say when we slip: "Ms. Duck follows basketball in Washington!" (12)

9 Rizzuto's bovine exclamation: "Crazy? Cool? Why?" (4, 3)

10 Yell 17 Across before ten, and you get a little oat doughnut. (7)

11 Odd sort of saint, lacking a short answer to "Is so!" (4)

12 If not for the 22nd Amendment, we might be having fo' (if not fo' sco') years of this dummy. (5)

13 Curdled soybean milk found in baked potato. Fudge! (4)

16 In the direction of a drunk backing around Mr. Cleaver. (7)

17 Yet may a disorderly fan cry this? (3,4)

18 Bit-part actor gives old newsboy's call. (5)

21 Rum, this!

Bachelor's auto runs into princess. (7)

23 The state of Cleveland cloned? Exclamation of surprise! (2,2)

24 Flashy? Monk's music? Yo-yo Head! (5)

25 Large inscrutable landmass,

for instance Iowa. (4)

28 Watchman, in a word, split. Heads up! (4,3)

29 Told "Get thee to a nunnery!" she stammered, "L.A., I hope!" (7)

30 Scram, General Electric tout! Scramble free! Oh! (3,3, 2,4)

DOWN

1 Healthy at the present time, as we might say if we don't know

what to say. (4,3)

2 French or Swiss, when hurt we say this. (4)

3 Prisoner of war makes great impression in conferences. (7)

4 Ground-up Novy? *Ach!* Fish in pizza! (7)

5 Mean? Mixed up? And how! (4)

6 Whether Bill Murray or Alastair Sim, "Bah, humbug!" was said by him. (7)

7 Revived rock

group, not in Heaven, expresses startled nonrecognition. (3,2,3,5)

8 What the unwrapper said to King Tut's discoverer, or what a Brit might say, trying to play the dozens. (2,5,2, 1,3)

14 Pained sound sounds mature. (5)

15 Whole New York town in sin—many acknowledge it! (5)

19 Couple has most woe, perhaps. (7)

20 At B-list blowout? Drat! (5,2)

21 Message for a pest or an out-of-key bee. (4,3)

22 Wild lovers with energy finally settle. (7)

26 Encouraging words for platform dancers in brief fringy attire. (2,2)

27 We take in anonymous male subject with cry of glee. (4)

■ ANSWERS

ACROSS

1 *Hoops,* in *WA,* followed by *Daisy.*

9 Phil Rizzuto exclaims this when he's broadcasting Yankee games, and *cool why* rearranged ("crazy") spells it.

11 *Saint* rearranged, lacking *a.*

12 The Twenty-second Amendment limits presidents to two terms, hence we have no *mo' Ron,* but another "dummy." I explain this because I suspect there is someone in the White House, probably Chief of Staff John H. Sununu, who tries to work this puzzle every month when he should be helping to make a case against Noriega. Noriega appeared in this puzzle some months ago, but Sununu never has. It *looks* like a crossword-puzzle word, but I, for one, can't conjure with it. (Nobody in there but—well, no, not even *us nuns.*) Sorry, governor. When the Panamanian coupsters who briefly held Noriega captive were asked to turn him over to the U.S., the White House thought they said "We *won't*" and the CIA thought (and told congressional leaders) they said "We *want to.*" I mention this in response to all those critics who have charged that crosswords are irrelevant to geopolitical realities.

16 *Sot* backward around *Ward.*

21 A *B.A.* is often referred to as a bachelor's. The word *bachelor* derives from the Vulgar Latin for "farmhand," but it has been my observation that when a person becomes a bachelor, the plants suffer. He's in a relationship, he gets plants; it's over, they can tell. There's a song there somewhere.

> I forget to mist the plants.
> The plants are missing you.
> That's the way it goes,
>   romance.
> Doo-doot-dooty-oot doo.

25 *As* may mean "for instance," as in—well, as in *as in.*

28 As a single word, *lookout* means "watchman." Split into *look out,* it means "heads up."

30 It is worth mentioning here that Ronald Reagan was once a General Electric tout.

DOWN

2 *Ou* is the French for "or" and *CH* is the international symbol for Switzerland.

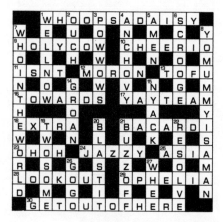

6 Sim played Scrooge in *A Christmas Carol*, Murray in *Scrooged*. I thought the scene at the end of *Scrooged*—Murray oozing shifty goodwill while urging the audience to sing along to "Put a Little Love in Your Heart"—was (1) Murray's best movie scene; (2) the only movie scene in which a *Saturday Night Live* graduate has taken a real culture-hero leap; and (3) a great way of exclaiming "Feh to the Eighties!" and "Come on back, America, in the Nineties!" It is all very well for comedians to work with other actors, but is that what we remember Fields, Chaplin, Keaton and Pryor (back when he was proving that outrageousness can be *enlightening*) for? No, we remember them for taking us on (in various ways) directly. And none of them ever looked the moviegoer right in the eye, like a president on TV, and combined entertainment with exhortation. That's what Murray does in *Scrooged*, working with dramatic and historical context. Check it out.

Others who've played Scrooge are Reginald Owen, Albert Finney, Mr. Magoo, George C. Scott and Henry Winkler. What other character has run through such an assortment of actors? Philip Marlowe (Dick Powell, Elliott Gould, Robert Mitchum, Robert Montgomery, James Garner) and Sherlock Holmes (Basil Rathbone, Michael Caine, Nicol Williamson, Peter Cushing, Christopher Plummer, Roger Moore, Vanessa Redgrave) lack Scrooge's range.

Just kidding about Vanessa Redgrave, but it's a thought. With Lynn Redgrave as Watson and Angelica Huston (whose father also played the role) as Moriarty. Maggie Smith as Mycroft Holmes. And Mel Gibson, I guess, as Irene Adler, "with a face that a [woman] might die for." Wilford Brimley as Mrs. Hudson, the landlady. Tyne Daly as Inspector Lestrade?

Actually, Lynn isn't right for Watson, even if she'd put back on the weight. Angela Lansbury is out; she's Miss Marple. Would it be woman-bashing to ask, where are the great women sidekicks anymore? By *sidekick*, I don't mean Gabby Hayes. Hey, James Mason, Ben Kingsley and Robert Duvall have done Watson. We want someone distinguished, credible as a doctor, yet willing to underplay. Claire Bloom? As *Watson?* Could the character be reconceived for Emily Lloyd? Wonder what Hayley Mills is like in her forties. The game is afoot!

MAMA

I suppose no crossword is 5 Down, and this one may 17 Across, but hey, I'm a secular humanist with no ax to grind. You don't hear me advocating a worldwide secular-humanist-fundamentalist movement (which we might call Humania). After ex–New York police commissioner Ben Ward's statement on the racial killing of a black youth in Brooklyn ("So un-American, so un-Christian, so un-Jewish, and so un-Moslem. It's just so inhumane to treat another human being in such a manner"), you didn't hear me wondering if the fifth negative wasn't the only one hard to argue with.

I may not know *exactly* what presidents and congresspeople mean when they cite the Judeo-Christian ethic, but I still believe in precepts that have come down to me through Sunday school and Felix Frankfurter. I believe a Nativity scene is not chopped liver and, for that reason, shouldn't be government-sponsored. I believe I'm not alone in wishing more young people today had been exposed to the Bible and thus knew more about, say, Eve.

Tell me three greater movies with the same name in their titles than *All About Eve, The Lady Eve* and *The Three Faces of Eve. Ivan the Terrible I* and *II,* even with another part? The *Cleopatras* (with Claudette Colbert and Elizabeth Taylor), *Cleopatra Jones* (Tamara Dobson) and *Caesar and Cleopatra* (Vivien Leigh)? All four together aren't a patch on Anne Baxter, Barbara Stanwyck and Joanne Woodward **X** 3.

Undoubtedly Genesis is sexist. *Everything* was then. Jehovah was a he; so were (coincidentally or not) all the prophets. What did they know? Without Eve, they'd have known a lot less. The story of her being tempted by the serpent—is this a slur on womankind (or snakes), when you think about it? It's evil to know something new? We should be *glad* there's a sex that wants to renegotiate. At any rate, we don't have to think of the biblical origin of humanity as a boy-girl story.

Eve was the first secular humanist. And this is an article of virtually non-gender-specific faith with me: if Eve went one-on-one with any unarmed fanatic, she'd teach him or her a thing or two. Say he or she were a Shiite. "Those who believe and do that which is right," says the Koran, "we will bring into gardens, watered by rivers . . . and there shall they enjoy wives free from all impurity." Let us note that many a modern woman has been heard to say she needs a wife. Partly because she never had one, but still: the longing for a pristine place to share with a perfect wife is perhaps as universal as it is un-thought-out. To watch an Eve movie is to realize that even those of us who grew up fleeing from orthodoxy still have a long way to go.

"Critics have said that *Lethal Weapon* is brainless," says Jeffrey Boam, screenwriter of that film and *Lethal Weapon 2,* "but that's not the point." Ah. "I try to bypass the brain and go right to the senses. . . . An audience wants to be wound up because it enjoys the pop at the end when it's liberated." Movies today lead us into the valley of blind credibility. They pull our strings, they make money, they do not bring the mother of us all into play.

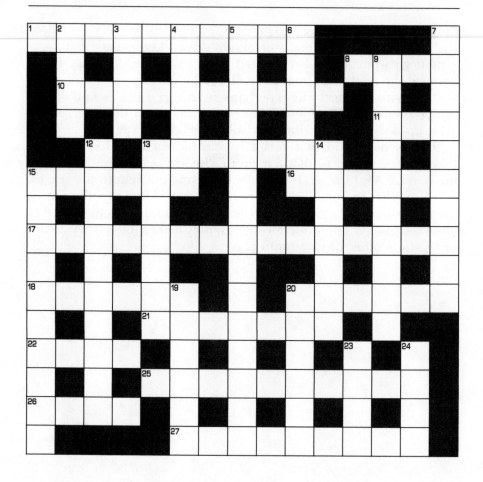

ACROSS

1 Puppet with folksy greeting and crazy Department of Defense—*oy*! (5,5)

8 Christian symbol for gravlax, for instance. (4)

10 Countless crazy deer following odd nun, bum. (10)

11 Sounds unhealthy, even so. (3)

13 Comprehend fashionable hint about Delilah's head. (7)

15 No man is an Easter, for instance. (6)

16 Not built like Santa, first lady's wild about Lawrence Taylor initially. (6)

17 Number one! Mother of us all! Right? *Oy!* Back, crazy one! Fast-forward! And unite us all offensively. (4,8,3)

18 Add latest development to cheerful rendezvous. (6)

20 Company time in east come fall is what mother of us all must have been into. (6)

21 Working hard, redeeming about 50. (7)

22 Oddly fig-leaf-free in sandpile. (4)

25 Rascals' *Big Chill* song, plus spot of eroticism, makes virtuous agape. (4,6)

26 Yuletide brings Trotsky back. (4)

27 When some of us worship and some of us party. (9)

DOWN

2 Burden of the joke is . . . (4)

3 . . . over-cooked. (4)

4 Shaky damned claim. (6)

5 Woodrow Wilson called for open covenants thus (devil, not a prayer) negotiated. (6,7,2)

6 Gives up crops. (6)

7 What a tough old biddy doesn't have is schmaltz. (7,3)

9 One last ascendant lover, and the end is here. (3,3,4)

12 Expose oneself to ballet, perhaps, or Jennifer Beals movie. (10)

13 Bugs in religious groups. (7)

14 Close of day, and mother of us all almost nine thousand. (7)

15 I am knocking and taking possession. (10)

19 Without one Baptist head, wobbles oddly in joints. (6)

20 Roofed in with Jim Morrison, for instance. (6)

23 What glitters sounds like a prophet. (4)

24 Whence snakes or doves awaken, taken with lox or with bacon. (4)

■ ANSWERS

ACROSS

13 "Comprehend" is a definition of *include*. "Fashionable" is *in* and "hint about Delilah's head" is *clue* around *D*.

16 *Eve's* rearranged ("wild") around *LT*.

17 "Number one" is *piss*. Then *Eve, R., yo* (that is to say, *oy* backward), *one* rearranged ("crazy"), *FF*.

18 To add latest development is to *update*. *Up* is "cheerful," *date* is "rendezvous."

20 "Company" is *inc.,* "time in east come fall" is *EST,* and, like I say, this puzzle plays fast and loose with Eve, but not, in this case, without implicit scriptural authority. I mean, if she and Adam were the only two people, and the only children they had were boys, then you wonder how much attention anyone was paying during scriptural script conferences. This is the sort of speculation that used to add a

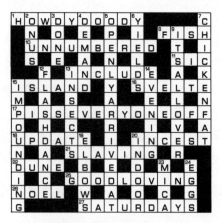

lot of punch to Sunday school for me, but that was because I was callow. What are my excuses now? Nostalgia, and a willingness to do whatever it takes to revive the old stories in a time of *Nightmare on Elm Street 5: The Dream Child.* Hey kids: in this one scene in the Bible some children mock a prophet for his baldness and he causes a bear to tear them to shreds. Granted, you don't actually get to see the shreds, but you don't in a Stephen King book either.

25 The Rascals sang "Good Lovin'." The spot in question is the G. Remember the G-spot? Jeez, if you don't remember the G-spot, no wonder you don't remember Eve. Whatever happened to the G-spot, anyway? Did anybody get a grant and set up proper control groups, and, you know, hire disinterested researchers with rubber gloves, and get to the bottom of the G-spot verifiably? Did I miss the *Times* that day? If there were in fact a G-spot, you wouldn't think people would have forgotten about it already. People haven't forgotten about cigarette ashes in Coke, right? Okay, now. After all this pop-gynecological rattling on, am I way out of line in mentioning that *agape* in this clue is not *a-gape* but *a-ga-pe,* or Christian love, without everybody going *oooh gross?* What's un-Christian, necessarily, about pop gynecology? See, in a puzzle (as in science), decorum is as follows: whatever fits is fitting. Is that wrong?

DOWN

2 A burden is an *onus,* the joke is *on us.* Ho ho!

3 A rare one-word clue. Both *over* and *cooked* mean "done."

5 Probably Woodrow Wilson has never been in a puzzle or anything else with Eve and the G-spot before, but then who knows what Woodrow was like when the lights were low? We do know that he said treaties should be "open covenants of peace openly arrived at." (Which went over, as they say in the armed services, like a prick in a pickle barrel.) *Devil, not a prayer* is the last three words of that famous quotation rearranged ("negotiated"). There has never been a great movie—check me on this—with Woodrow *or* Wilson in the title. However, it was Woodrow Wilson who said as World War I was winding down, "It must be a peace without victory. Only a peace between equals can last." Nobody listened, but it's a good

thing to remember in relationships. Except the only person who'll ever admit things are fifty-fifty is the one who, according to the other person, is getting the better of things. So if both parties know what's good for them, neither will ever concede that anything is equitable. The ideal is when both can behave publicly as if it were fifty-fifty, each can continue to argue privately that it is more like forty-sixty, and each can feel secretly that it is sixty-forty.

9 The Roman numeral *I,* then *last* coming up ("ascendant"), then *lover.* And the rest is silence. Oh, except I might mention that (20) Jim Morrison was a *Door* and that (23) *mica* (fool's gold) sounds like Micah. It is in Micah 4:32 that we read, "They shall beat their swords into ploughshares, and their spears into pruning hooks; nation shall not lift up sword against nation, neither shall they learn war any more." So the rest *isn't* silence. For all I know, the rest is the sort of flat feeling that you may experience after spending a certain amount of time on a puzzle. So sue me. You want to wind up with a pop, go watch Mel Gibson and Danny Glover solve things with hot lead.

CHANGE

The other day I saw a teenager literally throw away thirty-six cents. He and his father were waiting at an elevator. He tossed the coins into an ashtray on the wall, he pushed the button that causes the little floor in the ashtray to flip over and dump the dreck out of sight, and then he stood there. The father cried incredulously, "You just threw away *money*!"

The son, in turn, found his father's incredulity hard to believe. *"Thirty-six cents?"*

All change is chump change now. Giving it to the homeless is a nice idea, but a while back I proffered a disconsolate-looking woman a handful of nickels and pennies and she said, "Honey, you have a nice face, I hope you have a nice day, but I can't use these," and handed them back. So why don't we do away with pennies, nickels and dimes—let merchants round everything off to the nearest quarter? Granted, it would mean seeing less of Lincoln, Jefferson and Roosevelt.

These presidents stand for meaningful change. Broad, progressive change. The sort of change that people were forever calling for in the late Sixties and early Seventies. In the Eighties, megabucks made coins seem something less than petty, and political change, in *this* country, was reduced to clock-back-turning.

So what should I do about it? Move to Russia or China? No. I believe my place is here, on the puzzle page. A crossword can't bring back the pretty penny, the two-bit crook, the five-and-dime, or the New Frontier, but it can run change through changes. It can also coin a word.

The word this puzzle has coined, and now gives away, is 4 Across: *technomob.*

A mob is a crowd that is getting ugly. But a technomob is not a mob in the streets. It is a mob addressed through, and therefore created by, modern technology: just about any given media audience today. (Present company excepted.)

Media audiences (as we are inured to hearing) are inured to viewing everything that might stir a street mob to action. Rioting, injustice, starvation, mass murder, toxic effluvia, kidnapping, barefaced lying, wholesale graft, an American ship shooting down a civilian airliner— all this brought to us by corporations that have paid serious money for the right to dramatize their interests as they please, for instance by showing us B. B. King reduced to yum-yumming over cruddy hamburgers (in return, presumably, for what is now perceived as every American icon's appropriate price: an enormous piece of change). A mob in the streets is out to change something, somehow, demonstrably. But that's nickel-and-dime stuff. A technomob is involved in a higher economy. A technomob is into crying out (by means of a poll, or technosampling) for an anti-flag-burning amendment to the Constitution, although there is no flag fire in sight; but more important, a technomob is primed to demand enough of a stake in the established order to be able to afford all those products (including public officials) that underwrite the technology involved.

This puzzle sez: All change is chump change now.

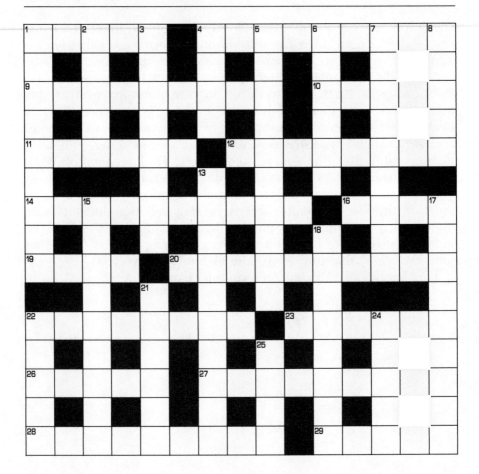

ACROSS

1 British mother all wrapped up in preservation. (5)

4 (See essay) (9)

9 Being shut up, assorted lucre's got number-one backing. (9)

10 Born in present condition of foundation. (5)

11 One crazy god in blue. (6)

12 Max in addict chamber. (8)

14 Vehicle surrounded by, for example, messy slime pursues others' 5. (10)

16 Bonehead, it's eight to the dollar. (4)

19 Ooze gradually makes water the other way. (4)

20 Surviving wife hit hard by tiny donation— all she had. (6,4)

22 Come together with killing of change? (8)

23 Oddly learnt point of a buck? (6)

26 Changed, I'm missing in action in city that's seen lots of change. (5)

27 Disturb at eternal switch. (9)

28 Civil engineer eating meat before Christmas turns into changeable lizard. (9)

29 Played with base Billy Cox

played, local fans said. (5)

DOWN

1 Quality of one who gives no quarter, though crimeless, sort of. (9)

2 Winter morning rises, blinded by spray. (5)

3 Up-and-coming get old at early time of life. (5,3)

4 Rich women and a dime are. (4)

5 Negative account changing dollars to yen. (10)

6 Unimportant person may have mind and soul, but that's all. (6)

7 He changed Italy a lot by manipulating sums in oil. (9)

8 Mob so disturbed by what we'd all like to return to. (5)

13 Flatland sandhill takes in a homely Jane's mate. (5,5)

15 Native corn redeveloped in a camera. (9)

17 Pioneer weapon junkie. (9)

18 Sticks to the same old ways,

messing with Tunisia, right? (2,2,1,3)

21 Busy, I've set after what's done. (6)

22 Commanding officer sounds like Jagger and Jackie Mason. (5)

24 Dr. Timothy sounds wary. (5)

25 Rising balls astound. (4)

■ ANSWERS

ACROSS

1 Let me just say a word about how this puzzle works: Each clue (with occasional exceptions not featured this month) gives the answer twice: once literally ("British mother") and once jokily or anagrammatically or something. People are forever telling me that they can't work this puzzle, but they can. All that's required is the will to do it. The British do this sort of thing in several different newspapers every day, and the British are our allies. Incidentally, it would have been nice for this clue, and for one's sense of the interconnectedness of things, if Ronald Reagan called Nancy "Mummy," but no, it's "Mommy." He may call Mrs. Thatcher "Mummy," I don't know.

9 *Reclusion* means the state of "being shut up." The cryptic part of the clue is the letters in

lucre's rearranged ("assorted") plus *no. I* backward.

10 *B* stands for *born*. "In present condition" means *as is*.

11 *II* (roman numeral *one*) plus *god in* rearranged ("crazy").

14 *Van* surrounded by *e.g.* plus *slime* rearranged ("messy"). Evangelism pursues other people's 5 Down. It also pursues other people's money, of course, but what doesn't these days.

16 *B* is the head of *bone*. Plus *it's*. There are eight bits to a dollar—two bits is a quarter. this usage goes back to the old pieces-of-eight coin, which was indented so that it could be broken, or changed, into eight bits.

20 The New Testament tells, quaintly as may be, of the poor widow who gave a greater gift then the rich man because she gave her mite, a piddling coin but the only money she had. "Surviving wife" is *widow,* and "hit hard" is *smite*.

22 To *coincide* is to "come together." If homicide is killing a person, then coincide might (give me a break here, we're having fun) be killing change.

23 *Learnt* rearranged ("oddly").

28 *CE* eating *ham* before *Noel* goes backward ("turns").

29 *Played* is the synonym. Billy Cox, as everyone who is interested in the saga of New York's five boroughs knows, played

third base for the Brooklyn Dodgers, and Brooklynites in them days stereotypically pronounced *third* like *toyed.*

DOWN

1 *Crimeless* rearranged ("sort of").
2 *Dec. a.m.* coming up.
5 A negative account would be the *con,* as opposed to the pro, *version.*
8 I *assume* we would all like to return to the bosom. I don't *think* this is a sexist allusion. To the bosom of *something.*
13 A flatland is a *plain,* and then *dune* takes in an *a.* I guess this clue is sexist, but since it is condescending toward male homeliness, it is surely okay, and it redresses "Plain Jane."
15 *In a camera* rearranged ("redeveloped").
22 A commanding officer is a *CO,* and *mic* sounds like "Mick."
25 Did you know that the expression *nerts,* as in "Nerts to you," was racy Hollywood slang in the thirties? A euphemism for *nuts.* Back then, Hollywood

didn't make movies in which people called one another Scumbag or even said, "I'm mad as hell and I'm not going to take it anymore," which is what people in the television audience started yelling out their windows in the Seventies movie *Network* at the urging of a disgruntled newsguy played by Peter Finch. He had whipped up an actual stand-up-and-be-counted technomob, or rather countertechnomob. A naive conception, we realize now.

■ *Well, we seem to have some more room here, so I believe I will start writing a prophetic novel.*

In the Nineties the earthworms grew large and took people underground. It was hard to figure the worms' motive. They didn't seem to be capturing people, it was more like dolphins saving the drowning. But dolphins lead people to shore. The earthworms took us down where they lived.

Next month, next paragraph. Move over, Tom Wolfe.

GUESS I'LL GO

15 ACROSS

I have always been fascinated by the idea of Noah's ark—guns, sheep, penguins and armadillos all milling around together discussing the weather. The entire gamut of natural couples bound haplessly by a single goal. A unity of experience there, surely, of a sort. The wildebeests panic: "We'll never get off of this boat! Never! We'll never . . . yaaaaargh." But the solid ones—not necessarily the ones you'd expect—pull together: the gnats, the tortoises. How long did the voyage last? Forty days? You know there was some slipping around, which is how we got the platypus, for instance.

So I thought I would throw together a lot of animals in this puzzle and see what came up.

Not very much. A new word, for what it is worth, at 16 Down, but no new life-forms, I'm afraid. The beefalo is no breakthrough. In fact, for all I know, the beefalo may be extinct: it's been years since I saw the last reference, in an in-flight news magazine, to that hybrid meat source for which so many had such hopes. I have never eaten any beefalo myself, wouldn't feel right about it, because I doubt I have enough Indian blood in me to deserve to eat anything that's three-eighths bison.

I am not going to eat worms, either, self-pitying as I happen to feel at the moment for reasons of a personal nature (yes, crossword people have personal natures) involving a few careless (and, yes, cross) words.

On that ark, I'll bet, the animals mixed at first warily, but then they began to make contacts. A dove had something to say to a cassowary, an otter to a pangolin. One wants to believe that: that one creature can relate to another, if the right *language* can somehow be found. This puzzle is dedicated to that proposition.

And if finding the right language this month does not induce the usual frisson, well, hey.

Listen. This puzzle, this month, has done its level best to get down to a raw animal level—we do have here, after all, a horse, a rat, a monkey, an alligator, a mythical beast and so on. What more do you want for your . . . whatever this magazine costs? I'm sure it doesn't cost any more than it's worth. I get a free copy. And when I need an extra one, I buy it off the street. Homeless people (I assume they are homeless, or trying to be homeless) who sell magazines, and books, and Garrett Morris albums, and shoes, and so on, all laid out on the sidewalk as miscellaneously as the cast of the ark, often include copies of *Spy* among their wares. I support this industry. I give it my extra books, although I could get money for them at the Strand. When I give a sidewalk bibliovendor a big bag of blurb-begging bound galleys in return for, say, an extra copy or two of *Spy* or a nice first-edition lurid-covered paperback of *All the King's Men* or a mystery entitled *Dead Men Don't Give Seminars,* which I intend to give one of my academic friends for Christmas, that vendor tends to show spontaneous gratitude. Not that I deserve more gratitude than I get or anything, but: you take it where you find it.

Which leads me back, at last, to the main question I would like to leave you with this harvest-season month: Were the animals that were chosen to be on the ark *grateful*? Or did they just sort of swank around saying, "We're survivors"?

And did they all edge hungrily—some out of sheer appetite, some for reasons of self-abasement—toward the earthworm couple? Was the earthworm couple a single worm? What did the ark animals eat? The carnivorous ones.

ACROSS

1 Spoiled Los Angeles child may help us conquer cancer. (3,3)

4 Uncut horse gets muscles backward. Leo. (8)

10 Retain! Release! Maintain flexibility! (4,5)

11 Carry monkey's head as emblem. (5)

12 Drink right at hilarious occasion, and it causes weeping. (4,3)

13 Snake found next to Indiana, around Rhode Island, eases pain. (7)

14 Concerning a match. (5)

15 Wigglers without Rh factor devour German city. (3,5)

18 Devil-lassoer is out of line. (8)

20 Dislocated state of discernment. (5)

23 Parrot, bloodsucker, we hear, are diplomatic. (7)

25 No cur in messy mythological beast. (7)

26 Low droning sound precedes an animal that murders. (5)

27 Forced against Mother's laws. (9)

28 Gaudy metal Edsel smashed. (8)

29 What cowboys did to her

Doctor of Education. (6)

DOWN

1 "The name of the place is I like it ____ ____." (4,4)

2 Cow-bison combo puts bee on climbing Norwegian. (7)

3 Decadence: a soldier climbing all over big reptile. (9)

5 That oviparous rabbit, if you believe. (3,6,5)

6 Slack off and allow to rise. (3,2)

7 Break in wrong time around, right? (7)

8 Putting a han-dle on place where we lost war over gin spritzer. (6)

9 Nessie shot creature feature. (7,7)

16 Unfashionable wisecracker on tiny platform becomes gull. (9)

17 Caged, Barbie's significant other has need around 50. (8)

19 Grand kind fellows who bring what Bossy gives. (7)

21 Not exactly so crude when scrubbed hard. (7)

22 Consequence of oversexy delivery service. (6)

24 Bound up in past, perhaps. (5)

▪ **ANSWERS**

ACROSS

4 An uncut horse is one that has not been gelded. (A horse is by definition male: females are mares. Don't complain to me about this, it's just the way the language is set up.) Geldings get along with mares much better than stallions do. I am just saying that. I am not taking sides. But sometimes when you step back from the whole thing, you wonder: did nature mean for intercourse and companionship to mix? Hey, listen, I *hope* the answer is yes. I'm just asking. *Lats* backward with *lion.*

11 *Tote* plus *monkey's* first letter.

12 *Tea* plus *r* plus *gas* (as in "the party was a gas").

15 With *r* and *h*, *eat worms* would be *earthworms.* Right?

20 *State* rearranged ("dislocated").

23 We hear "Polly" and "tick."

28 *Tinseled* is gaudy; *tin* is a metal and *Edsel* rearranged ("smashed") is *seled.* Have you ever tried to write a quatrain in which each line had a word that used the same letters in a different order? For instance:

> Shun vainglory. Don't *enlist.*
> Medals are but *tinsel.*
> Sail calm *inlets.* Don't insist.
> *Listen.* Be prehensile.

But would that work if you went through life like that all the time? Being receptive rather than pushy? Oh, well, it's just word games here, we don't answer searing moral questions. We feel that just raising them is enough.

DOWN

2 *Olaf* is the Norweigian, "climbing" makes him backward in a down clue.

3 *Rot, a, GI,* "climbing," with *all* over.

8 "Putting a handle on" is the definition. *Nam* plus *gin* rearranged ("spritzer"). I shouldn't be doing this, I should be writing a major novel.

9 Nessie is the Loch Ness monster. A shot is a *picture.*

16 Unfashionable is *out,* a wisecracker is a *wit,* and a *tee* is a

tiny platform. A person who is outwitted is a *gull*.

19 The Roman numeral *M* represents a grand. A kind is an *ilk*.

22 *UPS* over *hot* ("sexy").

You don't need any more explanations, surely. You are a lover of language for its own weird sake, or you would not have come this far. And don't you find it fascinating that in the dictionary a shrimp and a shrew are pictured on the same page and they are just being cool, not looking at each other, even though (on the one hand) a shrew might snap up a shrimp and (on the other hand) you'd think the two of them might have some things to say to each other about the shared experience of being small? And you wonder: Is it all just language? Would shrew and shrimp hang out together at all if it weren't for the dictionary? Or maybe you don't wonder this. Maybe we have nothing in common.

The Worms' Turn
(Prophetic Novel Begun Last Month)

Chapter Two

■ *Gray was the dawn of January 1, 1991, on Manhattan's high-rise-overshadowed West Side. In Riverside Park, beneath frost-rimed copies of the* New York Voice Post News Observer, *lay Shandy and Blair Dorian-Letz, a homeless young bisexual bond-trading couple.*

Blair was the first awake: "Sh . . . Shandy. Is . . . is that your head beneath the 'Stepping Out' section?"

Shandy, after a moment, grunted that it was.

"Then . . . what can be nestling against my leg?"

Together they peeled the frigid papers from Blair's increasingly be-qualmed lower half. What they saw—though only time could bring their Prehumous minds to accept the instinctive recognition—was the unruffled male extremity of Lumbricus terrestris. *Common earthworm. Two hundred times normal size.*

To be continued . . .

═══════════PLEASURES═══════════

Eric Zorn of the *Chicago Tribune* has sent along a clipping from that newspaper, with the following headline: STUFFED GARFIELD DEFLECTS BULLET, SAVES GIRL. So as not to drag the actual child involved into smarty-pants commentary, I will change her name:

> CORPUS CHRISTI, TEXAS—A stuffed comic Garfield toy attached by suction cups to the window of a family's pickup truck deflected a gunshot and saved a five-year-old girl from serious injury, police said.
>
> Maria Lopez suffered from facial cuts Sunday night when the window was shattered by the .22-caliber bullet. Police don't know who fired the shot.
>
> Police said the bullet apparently changed direction when it struck the stuffed Garfield toy.

And now, an excerpt from Zorn's version of "the story as it might have read":

> "Just two days ago, we had a stuffed Garfield toy suction-cupped right up against the window where the bullet came in," sobbed grief-stricken Pancho Lopez, a hubcap maintenance engineer.
>
> "But then we read Roy Blount Jr. in the September 1989 *Spy.* He said Garfield isn't funny, he isn't engaging, he isn't like a cat. He said Garfields in the window were a stupid craze, with italics on *stupid,* and said he doubted people who had them were college-educated. We took the cat down. It would have saved her."
>
> "We wanted only the best for our little girl," added Consuela Lopez, who has been working two jobs so that Maria, their only child, might someday attend college. "We tried so hard to be so-phisticated—for her benefit. That's why we subscribed to *Spy.*"
>
> Blount, busy skewering other trends and the simple pleasures of simple people, could not be reached for comment.

So. Perhaps this puzzle has been guilty of elitism. This isn't a puzzle of the people. This isn't a puzzle that knows the lottery number, or what the new sitcoms are, or what Trix Fruity Frosted Corn Puffs with "New! Brighter, Fruit Colors!" taste like. This puzzle never saved a child's life.

Perhaps this puzzle isn't big-business enough to provide simple pleasure. Today, corporations package and broadcast simple pleasures, to maximize profits, to tax the ingenuity of junk-bonding raiders who are scheming to leverage those corporations away from the raiders who leveraged them away last year.

Still you occasionally see some of the best things in life dispensed on the level, even in New York. For the example of weird processed food above, I went to the nearest supermarket. "In my building, they're cutting off my water," a shopper was saying. "I have to buy water. I'm an old lady from Chicago. I have to buy French water for $1.79 a bottle?"

"I tell you what, lady," said the manager. "I'm from Chicago, too. Go to a mom-and-pop store, get some Naya water, American. Same size bottle, $1.19."

"An honest man from Chicago," she said. "From you I'm buying all my noodles and butter."

From *The New York Times:*

5 MILLION POUNDS OF BUTTER
  MELTED IN WAREHOUSE BLAZE.
CAMBRIDGE, MD.—Firefighters sloshed through five inches of melted butter in battling a warehouse fire that burned out of control for nearly 21 hours.

More than 300 firefighters from Maryland and Delaware had to contend with slippery floors and a dwindling water supply to put out the blaze . . . where food was being stored for shipment to Poland and the Soviet Union.

This puzzle can't compete with that kind of operation, but it can melt a few words for you to slip around in.

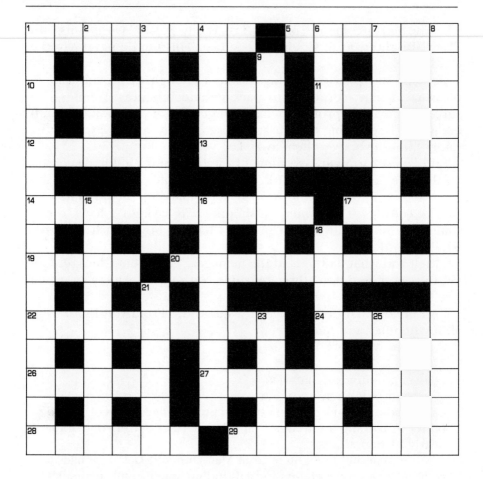

ACROSS

1, 5 Wasting time on promiscuity? (8,6)

10 Couple in their cups have British tête-à-tête. (3,3,3)

11 The last thing to say to a French god. (5)

12 Where couple resides without benefit of clergy. (2,3)

13 Cheating where the unwashed swim. (5,4)

14 What you last thought about in college, and what 1 and 5 Across and drugs seemed like at the time. (5,5)

17 Birds down under muse peculiarly. (4)

19 Critics pick them, monkeys too. (4)

20 It may sound like a romantic interlude in France, but to parents it's fatal. (10)

22 I, Gus, embrace weird Roman numskull. (9)

24 Where scene is shot, in beginning. (5)

26 A foot-sore source of oak. (5)

27 Minisouls somehow made the trains run on time. (9)

28 Put golfing device in place on couch. (6)

29 Where does the answer to this go, deadhead? Nowhere strange. (4,4)

DOWN

1 What Sancho was doing while the don tilted, and what the average male *Spy* reader is doing right now. (7,2, 3,3)

2 Cheers for underparts. (5)

3 Would we hear message in bit of sylvan music? (8)

4 "No!" Koppel observed. (5)

6 Prepared to peruse the opening of *You Can't Take It With You.* (5)

7 Vague around one in livery. (9)

8 Game for twin hermits. (6,9)

9 Blondes have this? Just over a tiny fraction. (4,4)

15 Patronizing a restaurant with unusual tea, in inflammatory condition. (6,3)

16 Dime made oddly by one who can neither speak nor do dumb show. (4,4)

18 Decapitated physician has nothing on old racist category. (8)

21 Canter dementedly in hypnotic state. (6)

23 Butt in so the Duke's right-hand man . . . (5)

25 . . . finds Ghostbusters gunk in crooked smile. (5)

■ ANSWERS

ACROSS

17 *Muse* rearranged ("peculiarly").
20 Sounds like "Paris idyll."
27 *Minisouls* rearranged ("somehow"). Whenever I read about what an amiable, folksy fellow Ronald Reagan or George Bush is, I think of Will Rogers's 1926 interview with Mussolini. In 1926 Mussolini had been running Italy fascistically for only four years, and many Americans somehow found him refreshing, from a distance. Still, it is hard to understand how Il Duce could have deceived old Will so thoroughly. "Dictator form of government is the greatest form of government there is, if you have the right Dictator," wrote the celebratedly democratic Rogers. "Well, these folks have certainly got him. . . . I told him that I knew lots of Italians over home

and that I wanted to have some message for them. Well he laughed and put his hands on both my shoulders and said in English, 'You can tell 'em Mussolini, R-e-g-u-l-a-r G-u-y. . . . Mussolini no Napoleon, want fight, always look mad; Mussolini laugh, gay, like good time same as everybody else—maybe more so,' and he winked. . . .

"This Guy keeps on getting better all the time. . . . Some over home say a Dictator is no good! Yet every successful line of business is run by a Dictator."

Business was big back then before the Depression, as it is today. If I weren't tied up in this puzzle, I would write a book called *Galloping Capitalism*. In *New York Newsday*'s City Business section recently there was a story explaining the demise of *Ms.* as a monthly magazine. Here was one paragraph: " 'From its origins under Gloria Steinem, it had a history of advocacy,' said Joel Kushins, media director at Bozell Inc. 'You didn't want to position your advertisement adjacent to editorial [matter] that was loud and took strong positions.' "

A bad sign when business interests become so blithely upfront about the immiscibility of marketing and free speech. Didn't this Kushins even say

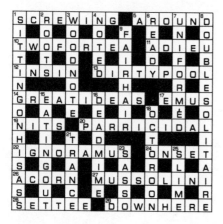

"Let's face it" or something?
Every so often someone is surprised that I, a freelance writer,
have never incorporated myself.
Maybe if I did, I could say I
don't want to position my editorial next to advertisements that
are loud and take strong positions. But hey, I've always
figured live and let live.

29 The head of *dead* is *d,* followed by *nowhere* rearranged
("strange").

DOWN

1 While Don Quixote tilted at
windmills on bony horseback,
Sancho Panza rode an ass. In
the interest of solidarity with
the average reader, let me em-
phasize that I do not for one
moment deny that I am sitting
here on mine, too.

6 To peruse is to *read,* and the
opening of *You Can't Take It
With You* is *Y.*

8 The original clue here was
"Game of mutual masturba-
tion," but that seemed coarse.
Now that I have mentioned it,
though, it gives me an occasion
to quote a passage from *The
New York Times* that I have long
wanted to quote. It is from
Christopher Lehmann-Haupt's
April 21, 1986, review of *Death
of the Soul,* by William Barrett.
Here it is:

> Part of the reason for my
> suspicion is [Barrett's]

heavy-handed way of illus-
trating his argument. In one
example, which even he ad-
mits is "as plain and gro-
tesque as possible," he asks
the reader to imagine that
"you are approaching a moment of tenderness and passion with the woman you
love, but for a moment you
stop to reflect that theoreti-
cally you can treat her
words and caresses as if
there were no consciousness
or mind behind them." He
concludes dramatically,
"That way madness lies!"
Yet why should we be im-
pressed when the issue of
consciousness is no more
important to lovemaking
than it is to herding swine?
Mr. Barrett's example is unnecessarily sentimental. It is
a flourish of rhetoric behind
which one senses the religious proselyte.

Well, I am no fan of prosely-
tism, but—isn't the issue of consciousness important to
lovemaking? I have never
herded swine; maybe the issue
of consciousness is important
there too, but surely it is *less*
important there, at least to people. Call me unnecessarily sentimental, but more and more
often, as this "conservative" era
advances, I read statements that
startle me and make me won-
der, *Shouldn't that at least be pref-
aced by "Let's face it" or something?*

THE WORMS' TURN
Chapter Three

■ *The Worm Queen glistened dully.*

You may think that our heroes Shandy and Blair (homeless young bisexual bond-trading couple of the Nineties) had found themselves huddled before the Queen's throne in some vast subterranean palace chamber.

I mean when they awoke from the shock of being pulled gently but firmly underground by an earthworm the size of a ballistic missile.

But no. They had found them-selves moving along a burrow—a long tunnel through the earth, in-distinguishable from the dimly lit holeway of any earthworm, except that its size was enormous:

"The burrow," whispered the ir-repressible Shandy, "of Queens."

Rhythmically the Queen pro-gressed, by means of her bristles, or setae, which she also employed to keep our heroes pressed against her massive stretching-and-contracting flank.

This much was clear.

The question was, what possible use could she have for Shandy and Blair?

To be continued . . .

TOO HOT TO

SMOOCH?

There it was, a raw, quivering thing, this spring, in *The New York Times:* "Researchers are reporting that parts of the corpus callosum, the fibers that connect the left and right hemispheres of the brain, are larger in women than in men."

Deep down inside somewhere—in my corpus callosum, undoubtedly—I knew it all along. But I hated to say anything. Even at the height of passion I never felt quite abandoned enough to exclaim, "Sophronia [not her real name]! There is something so *elseways* about you people! So *exotic,* so . . . I don't even know how to say it, so . . ."

Now, however, it has been said in the *Times.*

Men's and women's very brains are joined together differently.

I guess that is why Barbara Ehrenreich can write, in *Mother Jones,* a progressive magazine: "What husband, even in the well-known two-income marriage, is capable of performing simple acts of daily self-care without the constant assistance of a watchful and fully able-bodied spouse?" And it is cool. Whereas if I wrote anything, no matter how tongue-in-cheek, at all comparable about wives, in this day and age (Not that I would! Not that I would!), I would have to go to jail.

This mental fiber thing also explains all the burning and cleaving that still goes on, in spite of everything, between the sexes. You look at a person, and she or he is probably wearing the same sweatclothing you are, and both of your names may be Lindsay, but there is something you can't put your finger on. Something that makes you want to cleave to that person and stroke his or her hair. Now we know it is a *cerebral* thing. You are fascinated by what lies *under* that hair: the corpus callosum, which incidentally is Latin for "firm body."

But. Here's the question I was coming to when I got off into that matter of patronizing spousal references.

Which I am crazy to have gotten off into. But I am still dismayed that in her book *A Very Serious Thing: Women's Humor and American Culture,* Nancy A. Walker writes that my book *What Men Don't Tell Women* "perpetuates the traditional concept of separate male and female cultures," and that passages in it "reinforce the concept of woman as 'other,' and also approach feminism as though it were equivalent to being a Democrat or a Methodist—an affiliation to be changed at will—both of which [note: it is not clear to me what that *both of which* refers to] represent a continuing cultural resistance to the principle of gender equality." This is the thanks I get for devoting my life, as intractable Democrat and post-Methodist, to the principle of mixed company.

The question I was coming to is, are we still avid to burn and cleave in August, when the temperature is up around a hundred?

Late one spring when I was in college, a woman I wanted to burn with and cleave to, a woman who had generally seemed to be of a like mind in this regard, said something to me that has stuck with me ever since:

"Too hot to smooch."

I didn't get it. I still don't get it. It was only around ninety. (This was in the South.) A woman can say something like that and be beguiling. Whereas if a man said it he would sound like a schlump; a husband. The difference must lie in the corpus callosum.

At any rate, when it is around a hundred it *can't* be too hot to smooch. Because another person is only around 98.6. Another person figures to be refreshing.

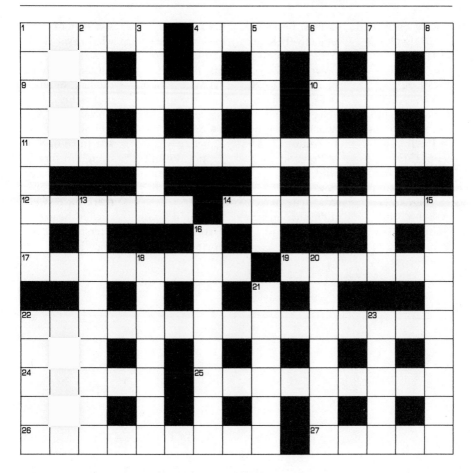

ACROSS

1 They keep our heads up with kisses and caresses. (5)

4 Romantic heat, re men going crazy among lice. (9)

9 Supreme fictionalized, ideal young female. (5,4)

10 Strength of sun sign slightly off. (5)

11 Drummer's temptress may inherit cows. (7,8)

12 Inflamed ogle keeps you up all night, coast to coast. (3-3)

14 Fill in what you get lots of with a string bikini (5,3)

17 Hush! I . . . Quiet! Get away, sea puss! (5,3)

19 Leech on ocean animal. (6)

22 We hear Pete Rose and risk-taking mate are approaching perfection. (6,3,6)

24 Description of summer skirts may cause blackout. (5)

25 Sort of hinted about what a cow says: "ready for it." (2,3,4)

26 Those who lend their names to Reno dress oddly. (9)

27 For example, sizzling start following back road to all that's left at last. (5)

DOWN

1 Bare bodies have some fun, Dr. Strange. (4,5)

2 Uncloudy gain. (5)

3 Sounds like outline is suited to August. (7)

4 Behold in South the seat of Eros. (5)

5 First person objectively leads lieutenant empowered like wax or chocolate. (8)

6 Southeastern states are (we hear) coming up for ruins. (7)

7 Peignoir for wild thing? G'won! (9)

8 Miscue makes difference in run or earned run. (5)

13 Forest follows tendency to be beach detritus. (9)

15 Whose best man the groom is, we hope. (3,6)

16 *Spy,* for instance, is what Tipper doesn't want children to have sex with. (8)

18 You'll be one if you wear one in August. (7)

20 Play like what royal claimants do. (7)

21 Get ready to publish, before high school, whose lover Archie was. (6)

22 Juice in the oven and thrash. (5)

23 Ones over there have sweet excited heads after hot dancing. (5)

■ ANSWERS

ACROSS

9 The musical *DreamGirls* fictionalized the Supremes.

11 A drummer, as you know unless you are preposterously new-fashioned (and perhaps belong to that class of people that seems to me increasingly common in New York, a class of people that I think of as teenage lawyers), is a traveling salesman. (We are not speaking of musicians here. Incidentally, it was a woman musician who told me this joke: "What do you call somebody who hangs around with musicians? A drummer.") What with electronic shopping and conglomerate agribusiness, I guess there aren't many traveling salesmen or farmer's daughters around anymore. In fact I haven't heard anyone say "Did you hear the one about the traveling salesman and the farmer's daughter?" in quite some time. Old stereotypes are breaking down. Today, a drummer, in either sense, could well be a woman, and the closest equivalent to a farmer's daughter may be an accountant.

12 To *ogle* is to *eye.*

17 *Sh* means *hush,* the musical notation *p* means *quiet,* and *scat* means *get away.* A *sea puss* for our purposes here is a nautical cat, but it is also a strong current near the shore that can sweep you out to sea. A public service announcement: what you should do if caught in that kind of sea puss is not to struggle against it but to stay up on top of it and swim laterally out of it. It's only going to be a few feet wide. I learned that when I interviewed a man who billed himself as the world's oldest working lifeguard. He was eighty-one. He claimed never to have had a drowning on a beach he was working, and he didn't have much sympathy for people who even *thought* they were drowning on his watch. "I got kind of mad going after one man," he said. "This fellow was a fine swimmer. 'What you yelling for help for?' I asked him. 'You can swim as well as I can.' 'Yeah,' he said, 'but I can't turn around.' But usually when you get to a drowning man he's facing the shore, taking his last look," the world's oldest working lifeguard chuckled. "The book says you're supposed to dive down under him and turn him around so you can tow him in. I have a little different trick. I get in a ball with my foot up toward his face. 'Turn around, if you don't want a kick,' I tell him. One woman got so mad at me she said, 'The next time I'm drowning I'd rather drown than be saved by him.' I make 'em swim in. Make 'em work. I say, 'I'm not a ferryboat.' " He lived alone. "I didn't get along so well in married life," he

said. "It's hard to hit it
right."

25 *Hinted* rearranged ("sort
of") around *moo*.

27 *E.g.* and *s* (which is the start
of "sizzling") following *Rd*
backward.

DOWN

1 *More funds* rearranged
(*strangely*).

6 *SE, GA, VA,* and *r* (which is
how *we* hear the word *are*),
backward (or "coming up" in a
down clue).

16 Tipper Gore mounted a
campaign against lewd rock lyrics after hearing Prince singing
about "masturbating with a
magazine." And although I
favor freedom of expression, I
must say, as a person whose
work appears in magazines, that
I find it a little embarrassing,
not to mention yucky, to
think . . . Oh, wait. It just occurred to me that *with* in that
Prince lyric might mean *while
perusing.* Hey, young people, if

left alone, are going to do that.
We in the magazine business
are quite aware of this, and
while we don't talk about it
much, I don't mind telling you
it gives us a bit of a glow.

21 This is, of course, Archie
Bunker. Archie of the comics, I
believe we can assume, was
never the lover, in the word's
full meaning, of either Betty or
Veronica, except perhaps off-
comic. During breaks, A. and B.
or V. may have slipped off
somewhere for an evenhanded
discussion of stereotypes followed by what is known as "a
violent nap." In my experience,
however, an evenhanded discussion of stereotypes between two
people of different stereotypes,
however well-disposed, draws
blood away from the organs of
sweet feeling and into parts of
the brain where who knows
what happens. I regret this as
much as anyone, and yet a
scholar calls me divisive. To *get
ready to publish* is to *edit,* and
high school is *h.s.*

23 After *hot* rearranged ("dancing"), *s* and *e* (the heads of
sweet and *excited*).

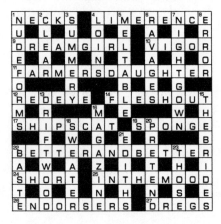

THE WORMS' TURN
Chapter Four

■ *The sensation was like that of
being dragged through subsoil by
the Michelin man, only with no
arms involved and more icky than
pneumatic.* "Eww!" *reflected Blair
and Shandy.* "Who the hell's idea
was it to start a visionary serial

novel of the Nineties about a home-less bisexual bond-trading couple taken underground by an enormous earthworm? It's disgusting, and we're sick of it."

Will it be continued anyway, in spite of the only human characters' strenuous objections? Tune in next issue.

SOUL TRAIN

Aband of youths from Harlem horribly assaulted a white jogger in Central Park in the spring, and what is a crossword puzzle to say? Remember when people speaking of urban race relations would forecast, with an awful knowingness, "a long hot summer"? Here's something I jotted down in July 1981:

A lot of white people I talk to lately, from Klansmen in Alabama to mediafolk in Manhattan, are assuming that within the next couple of months, when the Reagan cutbacks start hitting home, everybody is going to come down out of Harlem and do terrible things to white people.

For some reason the people who are assuming this are assuming it with a certain morbid (I would say) relish. Personally, I hope this wave of vengeance *doesn't* come down, at least not on me. No doubt, as a white person, I deserve it; and I would rather be forced to dance badly to Kool and the Gang until I drop than listen to a Klansman gloat. But the possibility looms that I might have to do *both things,* and that seems a bit much.

But that is my problem. I ought to be weighing broader questions, such as how a reign of youth gangs would affect the economy of New York City. Money ceases to mean anything if the only people who can hold on to it—and therefore have any demand for it—are muggers. Muggers will begin to mug for goods and services.

As we all know, the Eighties, generally speaking, developed differently. The predominant vandals have been waves of *Republicans* unable—or rather, not required—to tell right from wrong. Republicans determined to take in all Americans, white and black, who have any money at all.

This spring a friend in Washington called and said, "I've just been to a party where I saw B. B. King jamming with one of two people who live here. Ron Brown or Lee Atwater. Guess which one." I didn't have to; I'd already seen the tag line in the *Times* the day after Bush's inauguration gala: LEE ATWATER, BLUESMAN.

Ron Brown, being a black Democrat, can't afford to play the blues. Lee Atwater, being a white Republican, can do any goddamned thing he wants to. Anything except—in the wake of the John Tower matter—drink or womanize (so where's he going to get *material* for the blues?) or serve on Howard University's board of trustees. Atwater was induced to withdraw from the Howard position by student protesters who accused him of appealing to racism in his management of the Bush campaign. Atwater himself protested, however, "I was unjustly maligned."

> I'm an old home boy and I
> Been unjustly maligned.
> I'm an old home boy and I
> Been unjustly maligned.
> Yeah, we ran on Willie Horton but I
> Didn't think y'all would mind.

Atwater added that he would continue to be "involved in minority concerns." Yes, but *which* minority? "That limited percentage of black voters either rich or ill-advised enough to feel that they can find a home under the vast delusory Republican umbrella" would be *my* definition. But I have no right to *expect* black people to find the Reagan afterglow party abhorrent—after all, wasn't Mrs. Reagan sweet to both Mr. T and that little kid on *Diff'rent Strokes*?

A black person said to me during the last campaign, in fact, that if the Democrats were going to nominate a boring technocrat wimp instead of Jesse Jackson, then she was going to vote for Bush. To me that's like saying to a bakery that offers nothing but bread, "No, no. If you can't sell me a pie, I'm going elsewhere and eat chalk."

But what do I know. The paper of record has determined the chairman of the Republican National Committee to be a bluesman. (Coming soon: SANDRA DAY O'CONNOR, TORCH SINGER.) I'd better wake up and smell the coffee. On the national level, we're about to realign into two parties, the Republicans and the Hopeless. You'd think the Hopeless would at least get to sing the blues, though. In fact, you'd think if there was *one thing in America that couldn't be co-opted by the party of Dan Quayle, Goddamn it, it would be the blues.* "Got Those Working on My Image, No Time to Hone My Backswing Blues."

My Washington friend's impression of Atwater is "a hard Southern boy who has grown up doing whatever he had to, to rise." I'm not saying he can't play. But bluesmanship is doing whatever you have to, to *play the blues.* Republicans still don't get *that,* at least.

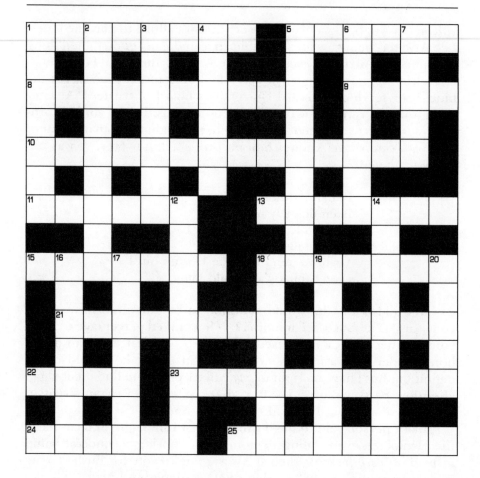

ACROSS

1 Screw and slide down slope on tip of nose—all for Oval Office snack. (4,4)

5 In the second place, he sounds like a bobwhite. (6)

8 Gem adds tone to collard leaves (or putting areas). (10)

9 With 12 Down, uncharitable African-American attitude toward Republicans—apologies to Dr. Thomas A. Harris. (2,2,5,4)

10 What we shall do, according to the song going around prisons and all

true leaders, is make up to a fault. (14)

11 In trouble, obey doctor or Dickensian dad. (6)

13 Mays and Horton: what Bush campaign encouraged voters to get re Dukakis. (7)

15 Unfurls, scat-

tering what the cremated are measured in. (7)

18 Ate Pole, reassembled: what anyone might do after drinking heavily. (3,1,3)

21 A native of the Nutmeg State who listens to country music is new to the

French Communist pet. (7,7)

22 Be bothered by blues standard: "Trouble in _ _ _ _" (4)

23 Hold a sated Rockefeller. (4,6)

24 Sounds like who? Mr. Charles? Hip, hip! (6)

25 Indignant assertion by farmer accused of overlooking seed-planting might be mistaken for confession of mediocre performance. (1,2, 2,3)

DOWN

1 Oink! Drop wig in a mess. (3,4)

2 Around East, allude to cat who deals in smoke. (6,3)

3 What "Don't play that song" is to Lee Atwater: Southern leader on guard with stick. (4,3)

4 With the beat, or close to the French. (2,4)

5 Of Barbara Bush's proportions (if she hopes to fill Nancy's shoes), or a large mattress's. (5-4)

6 Second first lady a large one in American League. (7)

7 Let's see, now, wasn't it a *Republican* secretary of Agriculture who said all black people want is "a tight pussy, _ _ _ _ _ shoes, and a warm place to shit"? (5)

12 See 9 Across.

14 Lines less strange result in ailments. (9)

16 The Gipper joins Racketeer Influenced and

Corrupt Organizations in rum brand. (3,4)

17 Tremble in horror to call for quiet source of milk. (7)

18 Long-playing prude, stirred, turned Alice Walker's color. (7)

19 Going on forever—as it would be if for Eve. (7)

20 The secretary of Health and Human Services and this will get you a ride on the subway. (5)

■ ANSWERS

ACROSS

1 To screw is to *pork,* to slide down a slope is to *ski,* and the tip of *nose* is *n.*

9 Dr. Thomas A. Harris wrote the pop-psychology best-seller *I'm OK, You're OK.*

11 *Obey MD* rearranged ("in trouble"). *Dombey and Son.*

13 Willie Mays (the baseball immortal), who did not work for the Bush campaign, and Willie Horton (not the former Detroit Tiger but the Massachusetts rapist), who did. In the movie *Personal Services* (based on the adult life of Madame Sin, a brothel keeper, whose girlhood inspired the movie *Wish You Were Here*), the lead gets into an argument with her boyfriend about how he ought to be driving the car. On the basis of dogged reasonableness, he is winning—until she blows him away with this clincher: "You and your little willie just keep

quiet." That is the level of argument on which the Bush campaign saddled Dukakis with a little-willie image by accusing him of coddling big, black Willies such as Horton.

21 "New to the French" is *nouveau,* a Communist is a *red,* and to pet is to *neck.*

23 Whether Nelson Rockefeller died sated or even held is not known, I believe.

25 Might be mistaken for "I do so-so."

DOWN

1 This was going to be *pigfoot,* so that I could suggest that a GOP blues singer would sing "Gimme a pigfoot and a Dom Perignon," but I couldn't find a word beginning with *t* for 11 Across.

3 "Don't Play That Song" was an R&B hit for Ben E. King in 1962 (you can hear it on *Atlantic Rhythm and Blues,* Vol. 4) and later for Aretha Franklin, and no doubt Lee Atwater can play it; but it might also be an admonition. *Southern* leader is *s,* plus *on, g* for *guard,* and *cue* (a pool stick).

6 Abigail Adams: *a, big,* and *I* in *AL.*

7 To attribute this set of properties to black people alone, as Earl Butz (of Gerald Ford's Cabinet) did, was mighty white of him. As it is of me, no doubt,

to insist on thinking of profound black music (not Whitney Houston) as somehow essentially non-Republican. Let's forget the blues for a minute. Look at Jesse Jackson. The Republicans called him for a warm chat. And the Democrats wouldn't even *nominate* him. Look at former Klansman and newly elected Republican legislator David Duke. The Republicans came right out and denounced David Duke. And the Democrats wouldn't even *nominate* him.

20 The only tangible good the Bush administration has done for black people so far is to provide presumably nice-paying gigs for Sam Moore, Bo Diddley, and other R&B oldsters. This hardly makes up for the $500,000 in severance pay and deferred compensation from the Morehouse School of Medicine that Louis Sullivan—wishing to avoid any conflict of interest— offered to give up to become the one black member of the Bush Cabinet. And that's not all Sullivan's been willing to give up. Because his views on abortion aren't doctrinaire, the Bush team made a point of surround-ing—not to say gelding—him with anti-choice subordinates. He'd said before that he personally disagreed with Bush's stance on abortion, but here he was vowing he would support it. In his tone of voice Sullivan seemed to carry the same deep-measured gravity that black civil-rights spokesmen used to. But what he was saying was, he was going against his own beliefs to hold a job. Of course, hey—white people do that all the time. Why should distinguished blacks be expected to have more moral authority than distinguished people of any other race? In this sort of color blindness may reside the long-sought George Bush vision thing.

■ N O T E : *The serial novel* The Worms' Turn, *which began in this space some months ago, has been discontinued due to heavy rains that caused the worms in question to come up to the surface and die, as they sometimes do. I am sorry for any inconvenience this has caused.*

CLUSTERS GONNA GET

═══════════YOU IF YOU═══════════

DON'T WATCH OUT

I read *The Clustering of America,* by Michael J. Weiss, because I felt I had lost touch with the electorate. Now I have a definition of we, the People: markets.

According to this book, we are not one nation, indivisible, of fifty geographical states. We are forty distinct precoded markets, from Blue Blood Estates (Beverly Hills, for example: good customers for Treasury notes, bad for cigarillos) down to Public Assistance (Watts: high on malt-liquor, low on low-fat milk).

If "blueblood" doesn't seem quite right for Beverly Hills, at any rate this book argues that it takes forty types to make up the U.S., and that these types flock together in "clusters," or (though this doesn't seem quite the word for Beverly Hills either) neighborhoods. It's a wonder that each of these clusters—anyway, the upscale ones—has not convoked a convention, incorporated itself and commissioned a logo, even a cartoon personification. Uncle Sam is fanciful, quaint; but Gray Power, Money & Brains, Black Enterprise, Blue Chip Blues, Furs & Station Wagons, etc., could be symbolized by cartoon figures that *mean* something.

At least to the marketing firms that developed the cluster concept, and whose data provide most of the basis for Michael J. Weiss's book.

According to these marketers' research, although each market is scattered through several states, each one is also identifiable by zip code. If you want to target your mailings and billboards and local-media advertising to New Melting Pot people (new-immigrant white-collar ethnic singles and families who reside in multi-unit dwellings and lean toward mutual funds, *The New York Times,* Mitsubishis, pumpernickel and David Letterman but have little or no use for deviled ham or *Modern Bride*), you concentrate on such zips as 90027 (Los Feliz, CA), 11372 (Jackson Heights, NY), and 33138 (Little River, Miami, FL).

So why do senators represent grab-bags like California and Pennsylvania, when the senator from Young Suburbia could wheel and deal with the senator from Coalburg & Corntown? The former could stand forthrightly for rental cars, frozen waffles and *Night Court*, the latter for canning jars and lids, frozen pizzas and *Highway to Heaven.*

Yet Weiss reports that politicos have picked up on the cluster concept only sparingly, so far. If your campaign can afford cluster analysis, it can also afford broad-gauge television ads. "TV can communicate a message much more clearly than the careful work you've done setting up the targeted messages . . . ," Weiss quotes one targeting analyst as saying. "And it can undo your work in some groups." That is, if you've been coming on all nativist to Shotguns & Pickups, all ethnic to Two More Rungs, and all hip to Young Influentials, a TV message that reaches all these clusters can make each of them wonder whether you have been speaking with a multi-faceted tongue.

The approach this book describes, then, is *less* conducive to truth-in-politics than mass TV commercials are. This bothers me more than it seems to bother Weiss. He does refer to another, apparently more judgmental, book's "claim" that "receiving only pieces of a candidate's platform filtered through a cluster perspective makes it impossible for a voter to make an educated decision about the complete platform. . . . In the marketplace of ideas, the selective disclosure of truth is the moral equivalent of lying.

"Yet many political strategists," Weiss goes on, "disagree with this criticism, noting that computerized data banks are only replacing old-fashioned ward heelers."

This does not surprise me. Nor do quite a few other points made in this book, for instance that "communities with the highest concentrations of welfare recipients also have the lowest concentrations of college graduates," that "those who rarely own woks include the least-educated and traveled Americans," or that "given a choice, few people would want to live in Public Assistance, the nation's poorest inner-city neighborhoods."

"With each marriage of data bases," Weiss maintains, "we take a step closer to understanding the tangle of reasoning and emotion that causes us to behave the way we do." For this book he has undertaken to humanize these marriages by visiting and interviewing people in a wide range of clusters. At this, however, he is no Studs Terkel. Individuals do not come alive in glimpses such as the following:

" 'Every night there's a stream of people moving down the winding streets from one club to another,' says Wistow, speaking in the staccato rhythm of a stand-up comic."

Speaking in the vexed tone of one who fails to detect anything at all staccato about this Wistow as quoted, I would like to cite another instance of this book's insufficient *engagement* with its interviewees' tangles of reasoning and emotion: Weiss does not turn a hair when a magazine editor tells him her magazine upscaled its whole ethic and approach because reader surveys revealed that "All of a sudden, the need to be anti-materialistic evaporated."

Weiss does establish to my satisfaction that terms such as "Middle America" and "white-collar" need refining. But I found this book hard, ironically enough, to focus on. It would take me a long time to get all forty of these clusters straight in my head, and I wonder how long they are going to be current. The clusterings Weiss uses are based on the 1980 census and are considerably different from those based on the 1970 census. Just how different is laid out in a table which left me with a keen sense of regret that I had spent so much time trying in vain to figure it out.

I did enjoy lingering over various bits of information: the data on groin-irritation-remedy use, for example, and also the clearly demar-cated "mayonnaise line" across the national map, which supposedly "separates the creamy Hellman's mayonnaise buyers to the South from the tart Kraft Miracle Whip salad dressing lovers to the North [table after p. 97]." (My own experience and all the anecdotal evidence I have been able to gather in the last few days, however, argue that this line is the bunk).

And of course I enjoyed trying on the various clusters for fit. As well as I can make out: of the two zip codes where I get mail, one is not quite (in fact not at all) Middle America, Back-Country Folks, Hard Scrabble or God's Country, and the other is a mixture of (at least) Bohemian Mix, Urban Gold Coast, Young Influentials, Emergent Minorities, Hispanic Mix and Public Assistance. My two clusters must be the despair of targeters. I am quietly proud.

FLY THIRD CLASS

The silent, wistful-looking businesswoman's laptop pressed harder and harder against my thigh as we braced to stay as erect as possible while leaning as far away as possible from the straining underarm of the oaf in the SEE WEEHAWKEN FIRST T-shirt who was reaching above us to get a grip on the looming, bulbous carry-on article he had earlier managed to cram into the compartment over our heads along with someone else's down-filled coat, which drooped more and more voluminously down onto our heads as the oaf stretched and tugged.

Can there be anything less classy, I thought to myself, than coach-class flight?

"Please remain seated with your seat belt securely fastened until the captain has extinguished . . . ," the flight attendant's voice intoned, but her message was ignored, drowned out by the deep all-but-audible moan of human flesh and luggage entangled, tensed, counterpoised and swelling: Coach Passengers Overfilling Cabin Space, Aching to Disembark.

"This is the part I hate the most," I murmured to the silent, wistful-looking businesswoman.

We had bumped elbows and feet for hundreds of miles, yet had not spoken—she wrestling with spreadsheet data, I staring dully at an in-flight magazine article entitled "Schenectady, Gateway to the Present."

The corner of my eye was no more than two inches from the corner of hers, but just a scant edge of her sidelong glance met mine.

"Mf," she said. That was all she said.

At length peristalsis began along the overstuffed aisle; overhead and underseat impedimenta emerged fully, to be hefted and borne; infants screeched gradually forward; the sluggish churning evacuation process took its course; and my relationship with the silent, wistful-looking businesswoman (who had a tiny dark mole on her upper lip like a speck of freshly ground pepper on fine shrimp bisque) was ended.

Had we been flying first class, it might well have been different. Leg room, free drinks, identifiable meats, better cutlery and linens; she might have told me of her dealings with Hong Kong or Run–D.M.C. I might have alluded, in a gentlemanly way, to her speckle. First class is more conducive to civility than coach, because first-class passengers are able to feel that they are sitting next to other people rather than on them.

However, I fly first class only when I am involved in some dubious enterprise such as being conveyed to the Coast (a euphemism for Babylon) to discuss an obscenely lucrative deal that will never come off. Other first-class passengers sense that I am not truly one of them, perhaps because my clothes are peccably tailored and gumbo-stained, perhaps because I make no bones about my disapproval of corporations large enough to have vice presidents.

What class of air travel, then, could I be at home in? The obvious alternative is business class, but business class is not available on all flights, and even business class makes me feel that I am holding myself superior to all the wretches smushed together back there in coach. Once, as a married army lieutenant, I sailed in a much less than luxurious but still private cabin on an army troop ship. All night I could hear the common men down below griping, hassling, retching and praying for deliverance. It made me feel un-American.

But I wouldn't do away with first-class and business-class fares, because they subsidize the cheap seats, and I am in favor of cheap seats because they enable my children to come home from college without having to drop out. What we need is *cheaper* seats. Cheaper and more adventurous.

The problem with coach class is it is just enough of an ordeal to be onerous, but not awful enough to be interesting. Etched in the face of every figure in the frozen tableau of coach-class fliers yearning for the hatches to open is this sentiment: that economy flying is harrowing but also dull. It is not bad *enough* to produce folk songs, travel books or even camaraderie.

What needs to be introduced is a class of flying that would pack *more* people into a plane, and in the process take us back to frontier hardiness. A class that is more like going somewhere on, say, a Namibian bus.

Third-class flight.

Say you could fly anywhere for fifty dollars if you were willing to squeeze in a little tighter and to forego some amenities. For instance, you'd have to brown-bag it. That is, you would bring your lunch in your own paper bag, and that would also be the bag you would throw up in. Probably you would also want to bring a knife so that you could defend your bag against interlopers who forgot theirs.

In the event of loss of cabin pressure, there would be buddy-breathing—one oxygen mask per six-person row. People would *have* to interact, get to know one another, overcome their differences. Everybody has a chance to breathe for a while; everybody has a chance to turn blue for a while. And when pressurization returned, the air would be rich with imaginative recriminations.

Laps would have not only howling babies in them, but also pigs, chickens, malodorous cheeses and other adult passengers. In fact no one would rush to be the first in a seat, because the most prized situation would be in the lap of an otherwise unencumbered fat woman. Some fliers would of course elect to nap in overhead compartments.

Boarding would be a challenge: everybody would be not only on standby, but on push-and-shove-by; in order to enplane in third class you'd have to be game enough to hold your place in line, and nimble and tenacious enough to clamber up the chute that you would slide down at your destination.

The reading matter would be *underground* in-flight magazines, with articles in them that challenge established views: "Schenectady, *Schmenectady*," "Frank Lorenzo and the Class Struggle," "How to Steal the Pilot's Hat."

When the third-class traveler landed, he or she would be tousled and scratched, but would also have a wealth of stories and a better sense of the market for a number of inexpensive products, such as itching powder (for getting people up out of laps), chicken repellant (fox urine) and scented Ziploc bags (for sandwiches that can still be enjoyed after heavy turbulence).

Maybe I am looking at this thing wrong-end-to, and we coach types should try to get (a) rich, and (b) used to it. But if we could all afford first class, the airlines would just find ways to take the pleasure out of that. Remember when you could stretch out in coach?

What we need is a heightened awareness of the class that the airlines have consigned us to. I'm already working on an anthem for the wretched of the air:

I can't breathe, but I'm aloft.
One thing—I ain't gettin' soft.
Flyin' with folks like a natural man,
Close together like beans in a can. . . .

If it's a big hit, then I'll think about upgrading.

THE SUNDAY PAPER

A COLUMN

One great thing about reading six different Sunday papers as you fly from Phoenix to LaGuardia is you can slip the various sections of them, as needed, behind the small of your back as you go.

I have entered into a period of life wherein my back is always with me. I used to take it for granted. It used to prop *me* up. Now I am always having to decide how to situate it.

The discomfort is never quite severe, just—well, that is neither here nor there. That is my problem. That is something *I* have to live with. Every minute of every hour of—I even went to a chiropractor. He had a poster on his wall, a young nurse looking distraught over the caption TRAINED TO SAVE. INSTRUCTED TO KILL. A fetal-rights poster. I've got a bad back and now I've got to worry about every damn zygote in the world. I don't want anybody with that kind of taste in posters messing with my spinal column. He's liable to say, "Hey, I see your problem. You got a *baby* back here, a little precious soul. The reason your back bothers you is you have not lived entirely in such a way as to honor the holiness of every spark of life. *My* back don't bother *me.*"

That is the kind of thing that gripes me about this period in history: it seems to me there was a time when the narrow-minded person had the burden of proof as to whether he or she was in touch with the life force. Now it's the broad-minded person who does.

Spinal column. There is an interesting subject for a column. Maybe too subjective. What I am writing about now is the Sunday paper. The Sunday Paper! An institution! Today I have read the *Arizona Republic, Los Angeles Times, Los Angeles Herald Examiner, Dallas Times Herald, Dallas Morning News* and *Fort Worth Star-Telegram.*

Not every word. I don't want to know—let's see, dig out something from behind the small of my *ungh*—more than a couple of paragraphs about "a man who holds the patent on the pompon," whose name according to the *Times Herald* is Herkie Herkimer, and I believe it.

But I have read worse than that, in my time. I long to lose myself

■ 237

in the Sunday paper. It is a legal drug. It is the opposite of *Paradise Lost,* about which Dr. Johnson said, "No man ever wished it longer." In other words, in case you don't follow me, no (person) ever wished it shorter. (The Sunday paper.)

Which doesn't mean (neat twist) it is Paradise Found. I remember when I was a small person, back in the late Forties and early Fifties. The Sunday paper almost redeemed Sunday afternoon, even if never quite. Solid, hefty, many-sectioned, multicolored, it seemed to have enormous potential. But although it could get you from after you finished singing "Jesus Jesus Jesus, sweetest name I know, fills my every longing . . ." to when you ate fried chicken, it couldn't be stretched to fill that whole bleak period between the chicken and when Jack Benny came on.

The older and more experienced and wiser in the ways of the world one grows, the harder becomes the Sunday paper to get off on. Myself, I began with the *Atlanta Journal-Constitution* and progressed gradually to the hard stuff, *The New York Times.* Once, years ago, I saw an out-of-towner buy the Sunday *Times* at a newsstand and say, "Fifty cents! This better be some paper." And it is.

But it is not enough. The last thing I will do tonight in New York, no doubt, will be to finish off the *Times* in bed. After six other papers. And I won't be satisfied. Back home in the country, the *Daily News* and the *Boston Globe* await me. You can see what kind of habit I have.

But what I am writing about now is the whole *notion* of the Sunday paper. And in today's six I have found several versions of the story about the Tucson, Arizona, gospel sect that expected to be in heaven today.

For the second time in forty days, a prediction by sect leader Bill Maupin that he and his followers would float to heaven to avoid the next seven pre-Apocalypse years of worldwide Satanism has failed to pan out.

"The rapture" is what you call the floating toward heaven. Out West I have been seeing a lot of ARE YOU READY FOR THE RAPTURE? bumper stickers. (Also, in Indian country, KIT CARSON WAS A NERD.) You would think that a lot of heretofore hopefully pre-rapturous folks would be sitting around this Sunday thinking, "Well, shit."

But here is Maupin's comment, as quoted in several of today's papers: "We're thrilled to death, not that the deadline passed, but that we haven't lost faith, we're not disappointed."

We're thrilled to death that we're not disappointed! *That* should be my attitude. I should close up the Sunday paper, adjust my posture slightly, and say, "Well, it didn't fill my longing, but I'm thrilled that

I'm not let down anyway!" That's the only way to get through life, these days. There ain't nothing *ob*jective, *sub*stantial, *de*pendable in life, except self-reassurance makes it so. Not even the Sunday paper, not even the spinal column, not even—I hear what you're saying— this one.

═══THREE-DOT COLUMN═══

A three-dot column! I always wanted to write one! You just string a lot of things together with no continuity required! . . .

Passing thoughts . . .

Remember when people were saying, "Well, there's no real point in trying to impeach Reagan over this Iran-contra thing, because it would just mean that we'd get Bush"? And now everyone prays that nothing will take Bush out, because that would leave us with Dan Quayle. So when Quayle gets elected, who is going to be his cautionary number two? And who will that person, in turn, appoint as his or her insurance? An infinite regression of diminishing Republicans stretches before us. Within thirty years, the vice president will be a parakeet . . .

Plugs . . .

To my way of thinking, a good country singer is Jimmie Dale Gilmore . . .

I wouldn't give you half a dollar for Ricky Skaggs, though. Some friends of mine saw Ricky Skaggs perform in Minneapolis once, and he said he was about to play a song that was number twenty-three, and he hoped they'd pray for it to go higher. How can you enjoy a song that you have been called upon to support in such a way? Pray Me Up the Charts . . .

We live in a discontinuous time, don't we? So . . .

Nobody asked me, but: the two greatest book titles are *The Turn of the Screw,* by Henry James, and *I Smell Esther Williams,* by Mark Leyner . . .

I don't think I'm doing this right. I tend to want to link things up, and develop thoughts, and . . .

In punctuation, three dots betoken either that you are trailing off or that you are leaving something out. Sometimes leaving out dirty bits, sometimes just boring bits. In mathematics, three dots mean carried on out infinitely, as in 3, 9, 81 . . .

So? So? I don't feel that I am getting anywhere here . . .

The public knows what it wants—something dumb—and isn't easily fooled . . . I like a woman who sneezes freely . . . Heard on the street: "He said to me, 'Larry, it could go away, level off or kill you, and we don't know how to treat it' " . . . Armpit odor is so rare among the Japanese that it was once considered grounds for excusal from the armed services . . .

Flann O'Brien: "I was once acquainted with a man who found himself present by some ill chance at a verse-speaking bout. Without a word he hurried outside and tore his face off. Just that. He inserted three fingers into his mouth, caught his left cheek in a frenzied grip and ripped the whole thing off. When it was found, flung in a corner under an old sink, it bore the simple dignified expression of the honest man who finds self-extinction the only course compatible with honour" . . .

I thought this would work out better than it seems to be working out. I figured I had all these random thoughts and things that I could just toss together . . . I have some limericks about Dan Quayle:

> Vice President J. Danforth Quayle
> Redefines white, Christian, male.
>> Although it is all well
>> And good he's not Falwell,
> He makes the majority pale.

> Though J. Danny Quayle, current veep,
> May not be especially deep,
>> Eight years' lying fallow
>> Will make him less shallow,
> If you buy that bleeping bleep . . .

Fortysomething myself, I have already dealt, badly, with all the maturational problems that slightly younger people, thanks to *thirtysomething,* are able to see as a whole generation's problems. Having preceded the baby boom slightly, I have never had any troubles that were generally acknowledged as cool to go through while I was going through them. I just thought I was going crazy and deserved to be shot. What I would like to see on television now is a show that provides the experience of eating all the foods advertised—potato chips, hamburgers, ice cream—without the weight . . .

And now, for my next item, here's a review of *I Wake Up Screaming,* with Betty Grable, Victor Mature and Carole Landis, which you might finally break down and rent at the video store, as I did, because you can't resist the title:

Blondes who don't go far enough,
Film that isn't *noir* enough . . .

Heard in a restaurant: "That's Gordon. He's been practicing putting his glasses on and taking them off with both hands. Because an optometrist told him that's the only way to avoid bending them. So he's *practicing* it" . . .

Did you notice what President Bush said about his wife a while back? "She's not trying to be something she's not. The American people love her because she's something she is, and stands for something." This is what we have come to: loving public figures for being something they are—for, when you come right down to it, *standing* for being something they are. It doesn't matter whether anybody knows exactly *what* they are, as long as . . .

From a recollection of Elvis in *Memories* magazine: "He kept many pets, mostly dogs, and an unnamed chicken. When the chicken died, said Mrs. Presley, 'Elvis cried for days' " . . .

"During the presidential campaign, George Bush said: 'Read my lips: no new taxes.' What do you think he meant?" a recent *New York Times/CBS News* poll asked Americans. Twenty-three percent answered, "No new taxes for a year or two." Twenty-nine percent answered, "No new taxes of any kind." Forty percent answered, "He did not mean it" . . .

In *The Village Voice,* Nat Hentoff cites an eighteenth-century instance of plain speech: "In a New England town, a citizen, having partaken freely of certain spirits, watched President Adams make a grand appearance accompanied by a 16-gun salute. The citizen said, aloud, 'I do not care if they fired through his ass.' The citizen was clapped in jail" . . .

He meant it.

IN-YOUR-FACE

L-WORDISM

(AND THE ROLE OF POETRY AND FLAGGOT JOKES)

Browsing in Books & Co., I run into Mark Strand, the poet, and we say hello. Maybe my own verses tend to run along lines like these:

Sitting drinking naked in a cheap motel,
Sharing our last Merit and a can of Bud—
Where is all that magic that you weaved so well?
Where is all the fun we had when you were with HUD?

Maybe, in fact, my strong suit is limericks involving Southern cities:

A poker-faced man in Mobile,
When women ask "How do you *feel*?"
    Will only say, "Well,
    I ain't gonna tell.
Who says that is part of the deal?"

A couple in Pompano Beach
Believed so in freedom of speech,
    They'd bring up each other's—
    And his or her *mother's*—
Failings, and holler and screech.

A foolish old fellow in Raleigh
Spends day after day singing "Polly . . .
    Doodle all day"
    In a vexatious way—
Always omitting the "Wolly."

A man in Tallahassee
Feels that it's not very classy,
    Inserting one's nose

> Into strange people's clothes,
> Unless, of course, one is Lassie.
>
> A high-handed lass in Eufala
> Greeted a gentleman calluh
>   With this salutation:
>   "For your information,
> We're having a baby, named Paula."
>
> A man you may know in Sewanee
> Likes just Marie Osmond, not Donny:
>   "She's *really* genuine.
>   He'd bring you the menu in
> A fern bar, all hey-nonny-nonny."

But I am not unacquainted with poets. After all, maybe someday I will write a great poem myself. Or anyway a great line, or at least a couple of great feet.

I try to think of an example of a single great foot. Maybe this, Adam and Eve packed into one spondee in *Paradise Lost:* "One flesh." Here, from Shakespeare's *Henry the Fifth,* is an example of a great *pair* of feet: "The game's afoot." Sherlock Holmes was always quoting it.

Anyway, what do I read, the very next day, in the newspaper? Mark Strand has been named poet laureate! Of the nation! I know our poet laureate!

My next thought is, maybe I could *be* poet laureate. Why not? I would be happy to do what the ones we've had so far have mostly refrained from doing: I would write poems commemorating national occasions.

> It's April fifteenth! Now I'm someone who owns
> A piece of a whole lot of Savings and Loans.
> Though what I've put in doesn't give me a plus,
> Each thrift malefactor was just one of us.

Would it be tasteless to *run* for poet laureate, I'm wondering . . .

Then something else crosses my mind. There's a little bit of money attached to the laureateship, I gather. Government money. I'd probably have to sign a pledge that none of my poetry would be obscene.

Bummer.

Because frankly, I'm hoping that being laureate would help me mount something that is long overdue. A liberal counteroffensive.

When it comes to gut issues like flag love and censorship, reactionaries lately are taking all the lurid advantages. It used to be the other way around: progressive forces had folksinging working for them, and also firehoses. But these days it's the forces of repression who have it both ways: waving Old Glory *and* pictures of flag conflagration, invoking the (threatened) innocence of American children *and* spewing (other people's) dirty lyrics. Riding turgid waves of pride *and* disgust, valor *and* paranoia. While liberals shuffle their feet and appeal to . . . reason.

Like I say, I'm thinking of mounting a counteroffensive. Funky liberalism. In-your-face liberalism. Liberalism that's into kicking asses and calling names.

People who wrap themselves in the flag, go all mushy over the flag, threaten the Bill of Rights in the name of the flag—I'm thinking of calling these people flaggots. Start telling flaggot jokes. Two flaggots sitting in a hot tub, one of them says to the other, "You know what I heard, I heard these liberals favor using the flag as a *snotrag.*"

"That's nothing," says the second flaggot. "I heard they favor flag *toilet paper.* I heard they favor using the flag to clean out between *toes.* I heard there's a woman in New York that doesn't ever shave or wash any part of her body and she lies down on a filthy stage in New York buck naked and puts a flag up her *business.* On the *stage,* in—"

"Uhh, Howard?"

"—in New York. Yeah?"

"Would you put your hand over my heart?"

"Like this?"

"And tell me all that again, only slower?"

And, see, if I were poet laureate, I wouldn't have to hem and haw all mealymouthed about how, gee whiz, even dumb obnoxious free speech needs to be protected. I could jump right in with *liberal* rap songs:

> Better get back, my narrow-minded friend,
> I am a liberal M-A-N.
> Fuck these racist and sexist jokes;
> I like all kind of *other* kind of folks.
> Tell you the thing about 2 Live Crew:
> They're just scared of what a woman can do.
> And as for Senator Jesse, Hell . . .
> He must think tobacco don't smell.
> But he's got a right to be a dumb peckerwood,
> And 2 Live Crew got big peckers? Good.
> This land has room for them, and others'.

Incidentally, how 'bout their mothers?
The awkward truth of the matter in fact,
Their mamas might rather catch Helms's act.
Mamas don't like to hear 2 Live Crew
Running down women. Well, maybe *theirs* do.
Say yo' mama is a masochist? Hey,
That's her right, in the U.S.A.
And as for Helms, well he's so prim,
His mama musta kept a *grip* on him.
But that's all right, it takes all kinds.
So let's all try to change each other's minds.

A liberalism as nasty as it wants to be.

DON'T DEFICIT THERE...
———————————— DO ————————————
SOMETHING

How many of us can say that we have done something about the federal deficit?

Besides me.

No, I can't flatter myself that I have done enough, because while I was writing those first two paragraphs, according to my calculations the United States ran another couple of million dollars into the red. But at least I've done something. I have made the following proposals on national television:

■ That every American buy ten rolls of twenty-two-cent (then twenty-five-cent, then twenty-nine-cent) stamps and throw them away, thereby pumping a hundred billion dollars or so into the post office without requiring it to do any extra mailing. If that didn't create a profit the balancing boys at Treasury could use, we would know something was wrong somewhere. Not a single talk-show host to whom I explained this denied that it made sense, but a national failure of will ensued. So far no concrete steps have been taken. I can't buy all those stamps myself.

■ That someone organize a Debt Aid concert on the order of We Are the World or Farm Aid. I went so far as to write and sing, on national television, a line for a song that might be sung in one great, swelling, all-American outburst by Chaka Khan and Leontyne Price and Roy Acuff and Jerry Vale and Dire Straits and Bo Diddley and the Mormon Tabernacle Choir:

Singing "Two-oh-oh-oh, oh-oh-oh, oh-oh-oh, oh-oh-ohhhhhh."

In other words, 2,000,000,000,000, or two trillion, which was the number of dollars the federal government owed at the time. I don't know what the debt is now, but two trillion is still a good round figure to work with. Unfortunately the tune that I have composed for this lyric seems to be hard for people to grasp. But then so is the expression "something to the tune of two trillion dollars."

■ That we focus attention on the problem by appointing a blue-ribbon presidential commission to examine the feasibility of declaring officially that the decade after the Nineties be called the *O*'s (what else are we going to call it?), to symbolize the achievement of a zero deficit by the end of this century. "Just say *O*." I have been forced to admit, however, that saying *O*'s sounds a lot like *owes*.

■ That we invite the nation's—oh, what the hell, the world's—billionaires to bid for the right to have the face of the winning bidder's choice added to Mount Rushmore. On reflection, though, I've rejected this idea on grounds of Donald Trump.

■ That God be offered a role. In Whom you gonna trust, after all? Remember early in 1987 when Oral Roberts told his congregation that if he didn't get eight million dollars in new funds for his ministry by April 1, the Lord was going to call him home? Well, I went so far as to declare on the *CBS Morning Program* that unless the federal deficit was reduced by half by the end of the fiscal year, the Lord was going to hold my breath, right there on that show, until I turned blue. Regrettably, I was canceled as a commentator on the program, so the Lord was deprived of a chance to implement my prophecy.

But I, for one, haven't given up. I stand here owing but unbowing.

The first problem we face in mobilizing ourselves on this deal, say the throng of whiners out there, is that we can't imagine the enormousness of the mounting federal debt. How can we get our backs into making it stop mounting so rapidly if we can't see the top of it?

Nonsense. Such vision requires nothing more than a fundamentalist turn of mind. When I was growing up in Georgia, not far from Stone Mountain, I heard sermons in which the concept of eternal damnation was rendered as plain as the nose on your face. All a preacher had to say was something like this:

"Now you take Stone Mountain and a robin redbreast.

"Now say that a robin redbreast was to fly over Stone Mountain every morning, carrying a worm. And as that little feathery bird went over the top, it brushed that huuuuuge mound of rock ever so slightly with that little slimy dead worm.

"Now just try to imagine how long it would take that little robin redbreast to wear down that big hard mountain to a flatness that was as that of a parking lot!

"Well now. Along about then, that would just be suppertime (not that you'd get any supper) of your very first day in hell."

The churches in which I heard those sermons didn't run into thirteen-digit debt. In fact they did pretty well.

So we could appoint Oral Roberts to the post of deficit czar and let him go to it. He could stir our imaginations and then could whip into the Lord's Prayer. "Forgive us our debts as we forgive the debts of others." And then we could forgive Brazil's.

SHOULD THE
═══════════SOUTH═══════
RE-SECEDE?

Previously conquered *Soviet* republics and satellites are clamoring to break loose. So how come no stirrings of nationalism in the former Confederate States of America?

How else is the South, or any other part of the country, ever going to get out from under the $2.8 trillion federal debt? How else but to duck out on it? I wouldn't put it past some of those slick Wall Street and Yale guys to beat Dixie to it. How would that be, if the Northeast seceded, leaving the rest of us holding the bag?

So. Check out this slogan:

"Nothing secedes like success."

I'm not saying that Secession II proceedings should begin immediately. But I am saying that it is not too soon to start printing up T-shirts.

Let me state my interest in the matter:

I am from the South and live in the North. So Southerners are always asking me to explain why in hell I want to live up North.

"Because when I'm in the North I'm always wondering where I can find some fried okra, and when I'm in the South I'm always wondering where I can find a copy of *The New York Times*," I say, "and I would rather think about okra than *The New York Times*."

And Northerners are always asking me to explain grits.

"Grits," I say, "like potatoes, are inexplicable to anybody who doesn't have sense enough to like them."

I am brief, in other words. Because nobody is paying me.

If, however, I were an international consultant, I could charge by the hour to answer these questions. So I would answer at considerably greater length. You know how the consultant's work song goes:

> On the *one* . . . hand *(hunh)* . . .
> This may *work* . . . and *(hunh)* . . .
> On the *other* . . . hand *(hunh)* . . .
> It may *not* . . . and *(hunh)* . . .
>   I get paid either way!
>   I get paid either way!

I would like to make it clear that I desire no governmental role in the New Confederacy. I do feel entitled to a piece of the T-shirt, but primarily what I want, as I say, is to be an international consultant. Winging back and forth between New York and Atlanta, looking mysterious in a rumpled seersucker suit and maybe fiddling the currencies just a bit. (The New Confederate dollar, I suggest, could be called the yam. I would be happy to explain it to non-Southerners.)

Blithe as I would be in my consultancy, we do need to talk viability. Let's make sure we have a consensus on one point:

It didn't work last time.

True, the first secession gave rise to some juicy generals, novels, movies and grudges. But it was too violent. (Secession II should take a leaf from the Civil Rights Movement—a Southern institution—and secede by passive resistance.) And anyway, who wants to live in a nation where the rich wear hoop skirts and own slaves? The old Confederacy allowed the other side to come up with "we are trampling out the vintage where the grapes of wrath are stored" and "we will hang Jeff Davis from a sour apple tree"—which are, let's face it, the two best lyrics of the entire unpleasantness. The old Confederacy lasted about as long as the Carter administration. And at least no man in the Carter administration had to flee the executive mansion in a dress.

So no more Lost Cause attitude, is my way of thinking. The New Confederacy would have to be unromantic and progressive. Here are some points to consider:

■ The South would have Elvis's remains, Miami's cash flow, CNN (which the U.S. government would still need to watch, to keep up with breaking events), the oil and TV-preaching industries in case either of them ever come back, foodstuffs to trade (and explain), space centers, EPCOT Center and Walt Disneyworld, the Country Music Capitol of the World, the Centers for Disease Control, the barbecued shrimp at Manale's, the Carter world-problem-settling center, the roots of black (hence most of popular American) culture, the Atlanta airport, several universities and Howard Finster.

■ The North, as things stand now, would have Bo Jackson. However, there would be no need for Southern teams to withdraw from the various American and National Leagues—isn't Canada in a couple of them?

■ I see no reason why the U.S. government would want to abandon its military bases in the South. It doesn't want to abandon them anywhere else, does it? This considerably holds down the cost of being a separate nation.

■ Buicks would become foreign cars. Maybe they'd be made better.

■ Would we want to let in any of the lower West? It might mean having a Spanish-speaking vice president: something I would be considerably more comfortable with if I could consult, or do anything else, in Spanish myself. I guess Santa Fe and the Grand Canyon would be interesting to have, but I think we're spreading ourselves a bit thin here. And we haven't even talked about L.A. The Lakers would be a plus, but anything that worked for both Hollywood and Dixie, I am afraid, would work mostly for Hollywood.

■ Granted, the South had a great deal to do with putting Reagan and Bush and Quayle in office, but surely Dixie wouldn't *choose* people like that. Not if it had a lot of Southerners to choose from. National candidates are always trying to placate the South without actually giving it any reason to holler "Hot damn!" A three-way presidential campaign pitting Sam Nunn, Jesse Jackson (assuming he chose to go with his heritage) and Jesse Helms against one another would evermore downright *thrash some things out.* And I don't think Jesse Helms would win, because he wouldn't have Northern Outrages to stand at Armageddon against.

■ Would there be a contra, or loyalist, movement in the South? Lord, we don't want to get tangled up in arms running and insurgency and that kind of mess.

■ Would the New Dixie have a Bill of Rights? Recently I watched the antebellum movie *Jezebel,* in which a high-minded forward-looking moderate named Preston (Henry Fonda) has an argument with a headstrong rakehell named Buck (George Brent) about the looming Secession I. Preston speaks nonfighting words that cause Buck to accuse him of disloyalty to his raising. Preston then avers:

"Buck, I believe it was Voltaire who said, 'I disagree with everything you say but I will fight to the death for your right to say it.' "

After a beat of incredulous silence, Buck replies:

"Pres, that don't make sense!"

Buck's mindset sounds unsettlingly present-day (North and South) to me. I wouldn't want to be a party to no Billy-Bob of Rights.

But this is a matter that I would be glad to help iron out. Over time.

THE NEW
==SOLVENCY: WE OWE==
IT TO OURSELVES

I can remember when people actually talked about reducing the *debt.* There were two things wrong with that concept: it was too easy to understand, and we couldn't do it.

So we began to talk about reducing the deficit. Reducing, that is, the annual amount by which the debt increases. This gave us some breathing room—as did the Reagan administration's courageous adherence to the principle that it is evil for the government (as opposed to Republican candidates, or individual members of the department of Housing and Urban Development) to take money. As a result we voters have enjoyed the freedom to elect congresspeople for spending more on us and presidents for cutting our taxes.

Now we can't reduce the deficit either.

So we need to come up with something new and more sophisticated to talk about reducing. The deficit as a percentage of the gross national product (or is it the gross national product as a percentage of the deficit?) may seem a handy fallback, but the d. as a p. of the GNP (or vice-versa) won't fit into a headline, and anyway, I believe we have already stopped reducing that too.

Here's a thought: the debt/date radio. The debt/date ratio would be obtained by dividing the debt by the date. Say the federal debt is $2.8 trillion on January 1, 1991. The debt/date ratio would be $2.8 trillion divided by 111,991. Since the date always increases—not only annually, but *daily*—we would have a sporting chance of reducing the debt/date ratio without recessionary tax increases or painful cuts in spending. The only time the debt/date ratio would be bound to go up would be just after midnight on New Year's Eve, and who cares then? The debt/date ratio would of necessity be higher in January than in December, but the administration might well be able to claim at any given juncture that the debt/date ratio was pretty good for this time of year. The nation's indebtedness would become more like the weather.

Then again the weather is something that we seem to have been doing the wrong things about, or to. It is possible that the debt/date ratio would be so warming as to produce what might be called a Greensfee Effect: if too many days of the year seemed like good days to knock off and play golf. Over the long haul, the debt/date ratio will not be comforting, in fact, if the debt increases faster than the date. And it undoubtedly will.

So. Speaking of sporting chances, maybe we should take our cue from the sabermetric school of baseball statisticians, who, bored with such venerable numbers as batting average and runs produced, have in recent years been ranking players according to abstruse formulas like, say, the square root of plate appearances over total bases plus the Strawberry Differential (lack of apparent intensity divided by inches of height) to the negative power of times picked off second—from which is derived something like Total Percentage. Abstruse formulas are good for shifting the burden of worrying about the economy from the taxpayer to tax-exempt think tanks, where it belongs. Economists could speak of Total Money, a figure that would surely not be reducible (thanks in no small part to baseball salaries), but here's the beauty of it: total Money doesn't sound like anything we would want to reduce.

Just thinking out loud here. But maybe I have found the heart of the problem. Maybe instead of trying to come up with something we can realistically reduce, we should stop thinking reductively. When we think national indebtedness, perhaps we should think growth. What other country in the history of the world has been able to run such a munificent tab?

Back when we were trying to figure out how to end the Vietnam War, Senator George Aiken of Vermont suggested that we declare victory and then get out. Perhaps it is time, now, to declare solvency: our debt is gravy, our deficit is profit, our long struggle against incursions of capital from the north to the south of the break-even line is ended.

Or is that a leap already taken by knowledgeable moneypersons, dating at least as far back as, I don't know, around 1984?

STICKING IT

ON THE

GIPPER SIDEWAYS

The imminent legacy of Reaganism: an America governed so effectively by fatcats and imagemongers that the Constitution is abandoned, the District of Columbia is obliterated by a private-sector nuclear device, royalty is instituted, and the figurehead chief of state is Caesare "Chay" Appleton, a Reaganesque and Ollie Northern hero of the Nicaraguan Conflict, whose trademark is a homburg hat worn—even into battle—sideways.

Richard Condon has a new novel out, *Emperor of America.* Its premise is the above, all of which I buy, except for the hat.

In my view, a popularly tenable vision of national Republicanism as both ludicrous and menacing is at least ten years overdue. And who better to provide such a vision than Condon, whose witty and highly readable novels have included *The Manchurian Candidate, Winter Kills* and *Prizzi's Honor,* all three of which have been made into memorable movies? I welcomed this book with open arms.

Then, after bringing those arms somewhat closer together (as befits a reviewer), I started reading. The first thing that tempted me to open my arms again, and drop the book, was a bit of military communications confusion caused by someone's name being Roger Over. That sounds like a joke Reagan might *tell.*

The second thing was the hat.

How can the same man who created Maerose Prizzi have also created a mediagenic man-on-horseback character who wears a homburg sideways? Surely such a trademark would look dumb and forced, to any viewer however credulous, and would wobble.

I regret to report that the hat characterizes the book.

Of Wambly Keifetz IV, the greedhead power broker whose machinations shape the new America, Condon writes:

"He was ardently committed to the Flag to which he referred affectionately as 'Old Tootsie,' and he led the sixty-seven-person staff at Keifetz Hall, Greenwich, each morning in singing the national anthem, controlled by pitch pipe, followed by a massed Pledge of Allegiance in Latin, the original form of the oath as it had been taken daily by the Roman legionaries under Julius Caesar in 40 B.C. with: 'I pledge allegiance to the balance of trade and to the Export-Import Bank for which it stands. For tax loopholes indivisible with a kiss-off and a promise for all.' "

This is high-school-level sardonicism, and not at its most accessible. In this book, for some reason, the heretofore deft Condon becomes not only heavy-handed but airily hard to follow. Only professional doggedness kept this reviewer wading back and forth through sentences like "Jon's fiancée, Elizabeth, had moved him even beyond his own belief in any conceivable extent that a woman had ever moved any man."

Occasionally, out pops an arresting, Chandleresque line—"a jaw like a hammock filled with fat people." Other passages have their own peculiar charm: " 'I am not a politician,' he said with the odd sincerity of the overweight."

But how do you like this for an image: "Chay used his expressive eyes for television. . . . With the right television makeup, they seemed to leak out of his face like pieces of canned fruit"?

Here is a sentence that I can't get out of my mind, somehow: "She experienced the terror of possibly falling out of the chaise lounge." I wish I could.

The plot, in my judgment, is too slapdash to go into.

The hell of it—well, part of the hell of it—is that Condon makes some good points. The big-money forces behind Emperor Appleton supply him with a self-image consultant, formerly an assistant to Michael Deaver, whose job is to convince Appleton, as the aforementioned Keifetz puts it, "that his magic came to him in the form of his immeasurable luck. If he believes that, everything has to come out right and he will do anything we tell him because he won't be interested in thinking for himself, he'll let his magical luck come up with the solutions. . . . And God knows that if they are told about his magic, the people will absolutely believe in him, and we'll stay where we belong, in the driver's seat." I don't think I have encountered anywhere else such a plausible sinister analysis of the Reagan dynamic.

In our time, this book insists, the consent of the governed is best obtained and retained by what we might call govertainment. Or in the words of Keifetz, "Television! The key to all minds and all hearts because it permits the people to be entertained by their government without ever having to participate in it. . . . Representation is fiction."

This fiction, however, is not representative—of Condon's litertainment or, I like to think, of anti-Reaganism. Can it be the work of some imposter, a Republican dirty trickster?

Other possible explanations:

■ What the author refers to nicely as Reagan's "Harold Teen manner" somehow scuttles satirical attacks on the old phenom. Only Garry Trudeau slashed away at Reagan steadfastly throughout the Eighties, and as a result "Doonesbury" was widely criticized (though not by me) as no longer funny.

■ Condon has given vent to a kind of nausea brought on by the corruption of political discourse in the Reagan-Bush years. Consider this outburst, which has to do with the unhealthy magic of television viewing: "Does it not seem passing strange? The mayhem there, the palmistry of lewdness produced at such low cost? A pod of wattage for a chair, to enjoy, in congress, busts of stellar consequence? Villains into shining heros, tailored changelings by the magic wands of light? But wait! Keyholes for pain are not all it reaches. It proves that the possession of money, reason for such Eden, is why we're here." Surely no one who has ever written well could write this badly except on purpose. Can it be a hint that the novel's opening scene is in a town called Almodovar, which is the name of the director of *Women on the Verge of a Nervous Breakdown*?

■ Condon decided he was going to be wildly fanciful in this one, and therefore didn't have to be rigorous. Actually, of course, the wildly fanciful has to be more rigorous than anything.

■ Condon, like his Manchurian candidate, was programmed years ago by the Republicans to establish himself as a trenchant observer and then, when the time came, to render the truth about Reaganism in self-discrediting form.

■ Luck.

FREE
SPEECH,
MY FOOT

The redundantly named Lucky Roosevelt, chief of protocol during the Reagan administration, has authored a book containing (according to Maureen Dowd's report in *Mirabella*) this revelation:

"The Chinese became upset when an American diplomat talked about feet, a grave faux pas in China."

It is not, however, a grave faux pas in China to shoot college students. To be fair, it is probably not acceptable in China for college students to be shot by foreign visitors; but feet, we are to believe, are not to be discussed by anyone there, nor is anyone to discuss feet with Chinese visitors here.

Well, I'm sorry. I would like to visit China myself, but if someone at the border asks me, in a roundabout way, whether I intend to get into the area of feet, I don't feel I can rule it out. If Chinese people themselves don't want to talk about feet, fine. But I am an American. *Bound* feet, okay. I am more than willing not to bring up bound feet. Or anyone's mother's feet, say. But what if mine hurt? Surely it is not unheard of for a foreign visitor to find that a Chinese person is standing on one of his or her, the visitor's, feet. In that case, as far as I am concerned, all bets are off.

The first time a friend of mine was allowed to help serve coffee at a reception in her home, her mother made it very clear to her that she was not to mention Mrs. Ogle's nose, which had been getting gradually lower on one side than the other, for some reason, over the years. In the event, my friend heard herself (with, I am inclined to believe, some satisfaction) saying in her most mannerly voice, "Would you like some sugar in your nose, Mrs. Ogle?" In China I might be that way with feet. "In our country we have an old football expression—woops, I guess I've put my foot in my—woops." A writer, after all, should be like a cat, whose instinct is to sit in the lap of the one person in the room who hates cats. Hey, people *shouldn't* hate cats, right?

How *can the Chinese not* talk about feet, *ever*? How do they buy shoes? Over the centuries, presumably, they have worked out euphemisms, little knowing looks, traditional ways of tiptoeing around feet. ("Pardon me, Ms. Ambassador, you seem to have put your you-know-what in some dogshit.") But I am not at all ashamed to say that in this country, we haven't.

In fact *The New York Times* reported not long ago that "references to men's genitals—their images and functions—have been permeating the popular culture." The *Times* dispatch went on and on, bringing in Regis Philbin (though not Robert Mapplethorpe) and the face of the camel in the cigarette ads (though not the old joke, "Look at the schmuck on that camel"). And you're telling me the Chinese won't talk about *feet*?

In the Persian Gulf there are different taboos. The Pentagon has advised American servicepersons not to talk to Arabs about heterosexual dancing, Christianity (as in "Where in Christ's name can I go to find a little heterosexual dancing?") or anything Jewish.

This is the New World Order? If Kuwait and Saudi Arabia and all those other oil nations over there are so quick to take offense, and so rich, how come no one expects them to defend their own borders? Evidently they couldn't even afford enough radar or spies to warn themselves that the Iraqis were coming. I guess they exhausted their resources protecting themselves against *discussion*, even, of the lambada, ecclesiastical hats and Barbra Streisand. If there is to be a massive American presence in the Middle East, it ought to be on this basis: here we are and we talk about *anything*.

The world, I realize, is not one big Sally Jesse Raphael show. Someone told me the other day that she once traveled on a boat, in an African country, in the company of several men who believed so devoutly in fasting at the time of year in question that they would not even swallow their own saliva, and so they spat constantly, on some bags of dates that the boat was transporting to market. She did not seize the opportunity to discuss this practice with these men. When in Rome, I might in fact avoid the subject of ecclesiastical hats. Unless I were officially instructed by my government to avoid it, in which case I would feel patriotically obliged to say what I believe, which is how can the American Way be reconciled with such instructions, and how can Jesus *possibly* have inspired *those hats*?

I speak of the American Way. And yet Lucky Roosevelt tells us that she, who favors abortion rights, never got up the nerve to raise that issue with the anti-choice president she chose to serve for seven years: "Truthfully, I could not imagine ever raising an unpleasant subject with Ronald Reagan."

Not even, "Some sugar in your mind, Mr. President?"

NATIONAL GRIPER'S DAY
═══════IS JUST LIKE═══════
EVERYTHING ELSE
THESE DAYS

America was not built on self-reassurances. Do you know what fully two thirds of the Declaration of Independence amounts to? Pure griping. Against "a long train of abuses and usurpations." The English king "has refused his assent . . . He has forbidden . . . He has utterly neglected . . . He has dissolved . . . He has obstructed . . ." And on and on, rousingly.

And yet two hundred and some-odd years later, no one will stand up for National Griper's Day. Two years ago, it was listed in Chase's Annual Events, an accepted, reliable guide to special observances around the nation. Today, National Griper's Day is defunct. In Russia, the people are griping, and getting a kick out of it. In America, President Bush—who got elected by means of such tactics as impugning his opponent's patriotism with regard to the Pledge of Allegiance—hugs puppies and is popular.

"Grumbling is the death of love," said Marlene Dietrich, but she was a femme fatale. Femme fatales don't want to hear it. And anyway, that's grumbling, a low, disconsolate drone. I'm talking about griping. As a matter of fact, "Grumbling is the death of love" is a gripe.

Gripe originally meant *grip.* Anybody who has a grip on things has a gripe, and is the cause of gripes. Griping implies a gut-level feeling. Griping concerns things that ain't right and ought to be. Griping, I will argue, is something that Ronald Reagan (a sort of butch fatale) and other factors conspired to suppress in the 1980s.

Remember the Johnson and Nixon years, when presidents weren't nice guys and we had protest and dissent? In the Eighties, protest and dissent were replaced by "WE'RE NO. 1." I don't have any polls to back me up on this, but I am going to assert anyway that among the millions who watched the gloating and vainglory at the 1984 Olympics (in the convenient absence of Eastern-bloc competition) there must have been a few viewers, surely, who felt that Americans in the Eighties have tended to give self-esteem a bad name.

I daresay April 15 was chosen for this short-lived negativism festival because of the income-tax deadline. But how can we gripe wholeheartedly about unjust taxation, as the original patriots did, when we know politicians are too timid to mention taxation as a creditable source of income, and yet the country is spending billions of dollars more than it takes in? And if we've got no room to gripe about taxes, the same goes for the deficit.

Oh, maybe we could blame the over-leveraging of America on the Japanese, or more specifically on the introduction into this country of sushi. When we began to eat snippets of raw marine life, according to this analysis, we began to break down the age-old American taboo against eating your bait—more often referred to by economists as eating your seed corn. But if it's sushi that has led us into a sea of red, then why aren't the Japanese themselves undercapitalized?

We can't gripe about what we've brought on ourselves. We can, actually, but what's the use, when Eighties Republicans are in charge? Eighties Republicans don't believe in government, so why come to them?

If anyone is responsible for national problems, Eighties Republicans believe firmly, it is Seventies Democrats, that is to say, all Democrats. And Eighties Democrats just gripe among themselves—no, just grumble—which is why they aren't in the White House. To be a hot party today you can't have negative thoughts. If the Democrats kicked out the jams and griped full-bore the way the chairman of the Republican Party plays the blues, it would make them come off as even more out of step with the national mood than they already come off as.

Oh, sure, a few people still feel free to gripe. The rich. Darryl Strawberry walked out of baseball's spring training (probably the least onerous paid activity known to humanity) because he was making only $1.4 million, plus endorsements, for playing below his potential.

"I don't want to have to be negotiating once the season starts," he said, "because they're going to be basing it on how I play. I don't want to be distracted like that."

There's a gripe the average person can get behind! So what is the average person going to do? Identify with management? It's bad form for management to gripe, management can only caution or view with alarm.

A while back, I mentioned the national mood. So I guess you're going to insist that I characterize it for you. Me with no pollsters at my disposal. Actually, if I did have pollsters I would dispose of them. Here's a gripe: I'm sick and tired of reading about what 47.9 percent of Americans are inclined to believe this week. The public should come to the media wondering "What happened?" Not, "What do 38.7 percent of us suppose?"

Kinder and gentler do-nothingism mixed with dread.

That is the national mood.

You may have thought I was going to say that the national mood was "Don't Worry, Be Happy." But by now a plurality of you, by my calculations, have heard that song one too many times. It has ceased to bridge the gap between the Reagan Era and what is coming next.

After all, kids are bringing guns to school. A violence-inducing drug appropriately called crack is rampant. The news has lately been of poisoned apples. And there are other things going around that may go beyond griping but also, at least, beyond insouciance.

Ronald Reagan, the soul of the Eighties, seemed to feel sincerely that griping—unless he was doing it himself—was un-American. But he discouraged griping more powerfully by serenely waiving a grip on things. By the end of his tenure, all he seemed to be on top of was those popularity polls. After attending a space agency affair last year, Mr. Reagan was asked whether he had ever thought of going into outer space himself. "I've been there for several years," he said. But we no longer have President Reagan to sustain a confident belief that being out of touch is a virtue.

Will George Bush be more conducive to griping than Ronald Reagan was?

It gripes me to say this, but I don't know. Let me say, however, that I have just turned up this quotation:

"When people cease to complain, they cease to think."

Inconveniently, the person who said that was not someone who bears comparison to George Bush. The person who said that was Napoleon Bonaparte.

But let's give Napoleon credit; he said that while he was Emperor. There's real assurance: affirming that griping is healthy while you are the world's greatest power. That's the kind of assurance this country used to have.

I'm going to say one more thing in Napoleon's behalf. I don't know whether Napoleon ever wrote a conciliatory letter to a former supporter who had opposed him on a crucial issue, as Mr. Bush did to the conservative activist Paul M. Weyrich after Weyrich helped block the nomination of John G. Tower as secretary of defense. But if

Napoleon ever did write such a letter I'll bet he never signed it, as Mr. Bush signed his, "Sincerely, and I mean sincerely."

If President Bush ever moves on to "Sincerely, and I *sincerely* mean sincerely," then he may at least give rise to a national revulsion against accentuating the positive into the ground.

THE CEO BLUES

The man in the next seat had eyes the color of money. He looked at me as if he figured I'd been slipped into first class because I had something on the pilot. (Actually, the plane to where I'd been going had been overbooked, and the woman at the gate had asked me whether I'd be willing to fly somewhere else instead, and since I'd recently taken a seminar to improve my negotiating skills, I'd said, well, okay, but only if she'd upgrade me.) But when I told him my first name, he regarded me differently. And by the time I realized that he thought I'd said I represented an outfit called ROI (an acronym for Return on Investment), he had finished four martinis and his story.

In high school, Anson Skedmark (for that was his name) was CEO of his senior class. He was elected as president, but his first official act was to change the name of the office. He loved the ring of it, CEO. He was determined to be one in business before he was forty.

His father was a curio salesman, door to door; his mother a wet-nurse. No one in his family had ever had a desk. In the Sixties, when others were running naked with flowers in their hair (not only other members of his generation but also his father, who was in many ways not the role model he might have been), Skedmark was wearing a suit. Reading *Winning Through Intimidation.* And learning to smoke large cigars.

It paid off. Three days after he turned thirty-nine he was in fact named chief executive officer of a small marketing-enhancement design-consulting firm. In three years under Skedmark its revenues went from $39,500 to $268 million. His clients included COMSAT, the entire lawn-implement industry and the nation of Bolivia. His nine executive assistants stayed on duty at various posts around the clock, in shifts (one of them lived in a Lincoln in Skedmark's driveway), in case he woke up (he slept only four hours a night anyway) feeling like barking instructions to someone who earned in the six figures. His own annual compensation was in the low eight. He married a Liechtensteinian heiress, who collected art and raptors (large birds) and gave him four children. He produced a ghost-written book entitled

Optimizing Excellence, which was on the *New York Times* best-seller list for thirty-nine weeks. At the 1988 company show, a chorus of two hundred performers donned masks of his face to dance a musical tribute. And he had a helipad.

It was good.

But then things began to change. First his banker, T. Charles Divvy, who had made some large-hearted real-estate loans around the great Southwest, jumped out of a window. A limousine window, at a speed of only about thirty miles an hour; but still, in traffic. Divvy was changed.

"The man had vision!" Skedmark exclaimed. "I'd get him on the horn and say, 'Cholly, I need an injection of cash,' and he could see collateral in . . . in a grain of sand! Now he's joined Leverageaholics Anonymous!" Skedmark's debt-to-capital ratio, it turned out, was 174 percent, which I guess (I don't know anything about finance myself) is pretty impressive but only as long as everyone remains large-hearted.

Skedmark's board did not. "I got them appointed!" Skedmark exclaimed. "I worked with them! Every three months I called in a consultant who concluded that they were underpaid, and I did something about it, and every six months I threw in a new table. Bigger. Nicer wood. But that's not enough for them anymore. Now they all want *gavels.* Well, I'm not *giving* them gavels!"

Instead he's accepted cutbacks. Had to. His parent firm has been merged with a larger firm which is fighting a hostile takeover effort mounted by a company that Skedmark had thought he owned. It's a painful, belt-tightening time. Not only has Skedmark had to stop stabling his horse at the office, but he's down to three executive assistants, the one in his driveway is down to a Mercury, and none of them makes more than the vice president of the United States.

And they have attended a seminar in which they learned that yes men aren't really good for their boss—whatever *he* may say. "So they've become no men!" Skedmark cried. "I *like* yes men."

Revenues for 1990 were projected at $680,000—well up from where they were when Skedmark took over, but well down from where they were at his peak. Under pressure from his comptroller, Skedmark accepted the Shiite religion as a client. His own creative department picketed corporate headquarters, and one of his no men has been leaking confidential information to Salman Rushdie.

His chief operating officer brought in a humor consultant. When Skedmark asked the COO why the Table of Organization chart was hanging upside down and several rolls of toilet paper had come flying in through the boardroom window, the COO consulted some notes and said, "You know what you call a fly when you pull his wings off?"

"*WHAT!?*" Skedmark cried.

"A walk."

Clients who feel that their marketing design has not in fact been enhanced have found that they can sue. Skedmark has had to take out $42 million worth of consultancy liability insurance.

For some reason that he can't quite get straight, Skedmark must meet three times a week with representatives of the Serbo-Croatian community, to hear their grievances.

People threw floppy disks at him recently at a work-station closing.

Certain public-sector commitments oblige him to supply fifteen buses and as many port-a-potties for a Free Neil Bush rally next month in Washington.

He has long since given up large cigars (hardly anyone will tolerate being in the same room with them anymore, even other CEOs), cold turkey. If he'd sought help, the market would have found out about his addiction and his company's stock would have plunged.

"I'm a CEO," he said. "An *American* CEO. And what does it add up to? I never have time anymore to read Clausewitz. I can't remember the last time I had a free moment to pop *Patton* into the VCR. In fact . . . the last time I looked at George C. Scott in that helmet . . . I had to look away. Because I felt that if he knew what I put up with, he would look away from me. There. That's the truth of it. Old McDonald had a farm, C-eye, E-eye, O."

"Oh, come on," I said. "After all, work isn't everything. Your family life must be a great consolation."

He gave me such a look.

"My wife," he said, "got tired of being traditional and started her own business. Now she wants us to move to Seattle. Because *she* can run *her* business from a houseboat, which she thinks will be good for the children. She studied with a Sufi holy man who convinced her that when you practice 'not-being,' everything will fall into place. '*Our* Sufi told you that?' I said to her. She *laughed.* She said the whole notion of '*our* Sufi' or anybody's Sufi was antithetical to Sufism. *She went to a competitor's Sufi.* She has written a book entitled *Being a CEO in Your Spare Time.*"

"Has it made the best-seller list?"

"Don't you *read?* It knocked my book out of first place! And I find out the bi—"

He caught himself, and glanced guiltily at the flight attendant. "I just had to take an encounter group with all my female employees," he whispered to me. "Every damn . . . blessed one of them. Yattata-yattata-yat . . . Expressing their feelings.

"And I find out the *woman* . . ." This time he glared at the flight attendant, but sulkily. ". . . used *my writer.*"

"Gosh," I said. "Well, hey. You're in the fast lane. There are bound to be peaks and valleys. Things can't get much worse than this."

"Oh, no?" he said. "Just before I boarded this flight, I learned two things.

"One: my father, who was certified insane in 1979 and it cost me half a million dollars to get him de-certified and set him up in some kind of research in 'cyberspace' to get him off my back—my father, who is sixty-four years old and wears dreadlocks—has developed a 'virtual reality' program that enables any Tom, Dick and Harry to put on a vest wired to a computer that enables him to feel like a CEO!

"Two: my lawyer makes more than I do."

"Oof," I said. (Though to my ears, frankly, that last bit sounded like part of the human condition.) "That is hard to take. It makes you wonder, in a free country, how could things go so wrong?"

"There's a flaw in the system," he said. "One deep fundamental flaw."

"What is that?" I asked.

"Insufficient CEO empowerment," he said. " 'Empowerment,' I hear from the women. 'Empowerment,' I hear from the Serbs and the Croats. 'Empowerment,' I hear from *OSHA*. Did you know they've got *OSHA* cranked up again? The *Republicans*! They've got a new guideline out now, it's psychologically unhealthy to require a marketing-enhancement design-consulting employee to engage in company practices that do not empower the employee to enhance his or her own self-images. 'Empowerment, empowerment.' But never empowerment for *me!*"

"What kind of empowerment exactly do you have in mind?" I asked.

He gave me an impatient look, as if he knew that I knew perfectly well what he had in mind, what anybody in his position would have in mind.

"A chief executive officer," he said, "under our present laws and system of government, is not empowered to execute anyone."

FORGIVE THEM, FOR THEY
HAVE TOLD US
HOW THEY DID IT

To be an egregious sleazehead is human. To forgive is an option that we, the relatively virtuous, might (while we are kicking the shameless greedbucket in question around) want to kick around.

Let's face it: one reason we feel that the scandalous should burn in the lawcourts and the tabloids is envy. Not everyone has the opportunity, or the energy, or the vision, or the breathtaking hardshell trashiness, to carry original sin to broad public extremes. Most of us improve our lie a little bit here and there, but few of us dare to slip around and holler "Hi Mom" at the same time or to double-deal ourselves an empire.

When someone gets caught ripping off millions in the name of Jesus, or acquiring cartoon-hero speed through steroids, or running for president and after party girls at the same time, we compare them to ourselves. We, we conclude with some justice, are more sociable. Sinners of truly scandalous proportions tend to have no one with whom to gossip about other people. And we have better sense. We know better than to think we can get away with such things.

So we cluck. It is small of us. If we were bigger mountebanks ourselves, we would forgive. I'll bet Gary Hart has forgiven Jim and Tammy Bakker (though he may well have declined invitations to appear with them on *Donahue* or *Oprah*), and vice versa.

We *aren't* big mountebanks, though. We haven't had the fun of it. Gloating over the fall of the mighty-unlike-a-rose is too spontaneous a human pleasure to be healthily repressed. The most deplorable tendency of the American public in the Eighties, surely, was its *tolerance* of prominent fraudulence. Ronald Reagan and many members of his administration spring to mind.

Let he who is without sin cast the first stone? If that rule prevailed, the only people who would get to cast stones would be the very people who most deserve to have stones cast at them: those who feel that they are, or can pass for, sinless.

But once we have hooted and deplored, it is time to consider forgiveness.

So is it "Go, and sin no more," that we want to say to, for example, Jimmy Swaggart? Surely not. Swaggart's holiness was so overbearing that I would love to see it built back up and then redragged through the mud.

Ivan Boesky is a different case. Would I want him to do something else monumentally shady, and get caught again, and, this time, have to pay fines amounting to considerably more than the ones he had to pay last time? On the one hand, yes, because Boesky (give him credit, so to speak) was not unentertaining. He showed me a lot when he was photographed, on furlough from jail, in a wild white beard that would not have seemed out of place on Jeremiah, the prophet, or on Howard Hughes in his hermit period.

On the other hand, it is probably the fault of Boesky—taking him to stand for what we might call the metastatically rich—that I have such a hard time staying solvent. What a Boesky can afford trickles down to raise the level of what it costs the rest of us to get by. No fine or jail sentence can undo that social consequence.

So I hesitate to lump the scandalous together. Then too, I hesitate to take them one at a time, because all I know about any of them is what I have learned through the media.

Well, I do have three bits of scandal-related information that I have picked up word-of-mouth and have not revealed until now.

One: the host of a talk-radio show in Atlanta told me a couple of years ago that he had introduced—because they were his consecutive guests—the Jimmy Swaggart hooker to Jimmy Carter. Carter was gracious. The hooker (to whom I apologize for forgetting her name) said, "Gosh. When I first met Jimmy Swaggart I never dreamed it would lead to meeting the former president of the United States."

Two: I sat next to an oil-tanker bosun's mate on an airplane recently, and when I asked him about the *Valdez* oil spill he said that oil tankers were underregulated and that the captain of the *Valdez* should not be the scapegoat for that tanker's gunking of Alaska because captains mostly handle paperwork and *"everybody* on oil tankers drinks. There's nothing else to do."

Three: my friend Bruce Tucker, who wrote James Brown's autobiography (*James Brown, the Godfather of Soul*) with James Brown, tells me that he talked to James Brown shortly after James Brown was put in jail, and James Brown said, "If America can stand for James Brown to be in jail, then James Brown can stand for James Brown to be in jail." If only Leona Helmsley could find it in herself to be so gracious.

But then I guess the main reason I, personally, speaking as an American, could readily stand for Leona Helmsley to be in jail is that she isn't so gracious. Nor can she sing "Papa's Got a Brand New Bag" and dance the mashed potatoes as no one else ever could. Also her hair isn't as much of a contribution as James Brown's is.

I don't know that these bits of information carry us very far toward general standards for forgiveness of the scandalous. It may be that genuine bits seldom do.

Let me say this: however unduly scandal figures have soared, aren't they people who put their pants on one leg at a time just like us?

I don't know. Conceivably, they have enjoyed the pants-putting-on process more: "Mmm, I am pulling on *Pete Rose*'s pants, boogity-boogity—the pants of a man who will always have *plenty* of legs to stand on." Or maybe they have enjoyed it less: "Quickly, quickly, get these pants up before anybody catches *Michael Milken* with a limb out."

We don't know. No one can look into the heart and soul of another human being and say either "Poor baby" or "Aha!"

Before I dither off into scandalous inconclusiveness, let me tell you a story with a moral. I had a friend in college, a fraternity brother, who was cool. He was so cool that he not only played varsity football and basketball, he also rode around vividly on a motorcycle. If you ever saw Burt Reynolds in *Deliverance*—this friend of mine was cool like that.

And one day this friend of mine was turning a corner, coolly, on his motorcycle, and he forgot to put his leg out, and he leaned over too far, and the motorcycle tipped over and pinned him to the pavement in the middle of the street.

As it happened, a young and timorous pledge of our fraternity was crossing the street when this happened. There lay my friend, at the feet of this young man, who didn't know what to say.

My friend, though pinned, did.

"If you'll get this thing off me," he said coolly, "I'll teach you how to ride it."

So here's what I propose that we require of scandal figures: that they instruct us in how they went about doing what they did. I don't mean, "I regret that the unfortunate incident occurred because I didn't ride herd hard enough on my staff, being the soft-hearted person that, as my old mother used to say, I am."

I mean, "Okay. Here's how I pulled off those outrageous things you've heard about, and here's how good I felt when everything was going my way, and here's how silly I felt when it all collapsed upon me. Wait till you hear about how I convinced those girls to be video-taped with me—actually I had to *tell* them I was Rob Lowe, but then they said, 'Oh, yeah, we were just saying you looked like *somebody*'— and then, here's a tip that I picked up in the White House when President Reagan was telling me stories about Errol Flynn. . . .''

You know what I mean? They have to tell us all the *good, inside* stuff.

And then we will all sit down and write them letters, saying, "Well, after hearing exactly how you went about doing that awful stuff you did, we realize that you are human, you put your pants on one leg at a time like anybody else (though maybe you linger over the process longer than most or maybe you race through it more hastily than most). We realize that what you did was not all that big a deal, actually, and maybe we would have done it, too, if we hadn't had any more sense than you. We are all brothers, aren't we, only you are on proba-tion. We forgive you."

Oh, they'll hate it.

A CHRISTMAS CAROL

(FOR THE EIGHTIES)

Our indebtedness to Scrooge,
It seems to me, is huge.
What if every human heart were pure as Tiny Tim's,
And all it took to bless us were a bit of goose and hymns?
No extravaganzas, just inertia,
No galloping commercia-
Lization to deplore?
Snore.

Scrooge, you know,
Was the one who was so
Non-commercial Noel-wise he wouldn't venture tuppence,
Till he got his comeuppance.
Then, however, urged
To *go with* things, he splurged.
It's the new Scrooge whom we emulate today.
Hey,

Look,
Would man have been given the coffee-table book
If Christmas belonged to the Cratchits?
Wouldn't savvy publishers be cruising on their yatchits
Off some balmy isthmus,
Disregarding Christmas
Like Scrooge before he saw the light?
Right.

Would folks invest in farming
Evergreens abundantly with prices all alarming,
Prodding us in turn to make our own demanding deals,
If the bottom line of Christmas were the way one *feels*?
Don't bet a dime on it.
"Yuletide supply-side ride—you can betcha *I'm* on it"—
Now Scrooge needn't hide his greed beneath a bushel.
Push'll

Get you shove
That most of what we're mindful of
At Christmas would be crowded out
Of our attention span if all about
Us, marketing
Did not praise and sing
And give us what redeems us from the urge to be retentive—
Incentive.

Till purse-relaxing dreams improved his humor,
Scrooge was no consumer.
Today it sounds funny,
But Scrooge *saved* his money—
Then he converted, from merely being rich
To spending like it, which
Is why I say that we're in Scrooge's debt
Yet.

Of course we also owe
Billions to ourselves and other countries, so
Scrooge will have to wait in line.
By grace, perhaps—surely not design—
We've become a wealthy moocher
Nation. So, does Christmas Future
Haunt us like the specter of it old Scrooge saw?
Naw.

If we owe too many dollars, why we'll lower
The dollar's value, and pinch some more
Pennies from the federal budget shares
Of those who live on prayers.
Or so it looks from here, and who am I to say
That conceivably the way
It looks from heaven sickens
Dickens?

CHRISTMAS DWINDLES

W
e had full-blown, giblet-gravied, bright-eyed and bushy-treed, predominantly merry Christmases when I was growing up in Decatur in the Forties and Fifties, although one year Mother was sick in bed, another year Susan and I pulled the tree over onto ourselves, and another year Criselle came over and sat in my drum.

I don't remember minding too much about the drum; old Santy had brought plenty of other good stuff. I would assimilate as much of this stuff unto my person as I could at once and go down the street to show it off to my friends who had also gotten a lot. We lived in a neighborhood of modest-sized homes, but kids would come flying out of them pumping new bikes, sporting new football helmets and cowboy jackets, and waving new BB guns and Bunsen burners. Our parents had grown up without things and didn't want us to. It would be several days before my sense of abundance wore thin and gave way to a sense of enough.

When I was seven, Santa Claus brought me our family's first television set, so that I no longer had to walk all the way through the woods to Julian's house to watch Woody Willow. This show, the Atlanta area's answer to Howdy Doody, was something I watched nearly every afternoon for several formative years, but I don't recall much about it. I had my birthday party on it once. (Are any shows that local anymore?) It advertised Peter Paul chocolate coconut pecan candy bars. It had, besides Woody himself, a character named Tilly the Termite. How an explicitly wooden boy and a termite can have sustained a long relationship, I don't know. The candy is what stands out.

Little did I reflect back then how abruptly I would grow up to father children of my own, post-marionette-era children, who would genuinely desire for Christmas every blessed thing, except antifreeze and milk, that they saw advertised on TV: little plastic placekickers that propel little plastic footballs over little plastic goalposts, little bendable rubber outdoorsmen that dress up like commandos and have jungle adventures, little plastic subdebs that put on bras and have dates. These children wouldn't say, "Do you reckon Santa Claus can find a little man I can whittle a little cutlass for and make up stories about?" They would say, "I want Six Million Dollar Man." And when they got him, he wouldn't be as animated as he was in the commercials.

It was before these children entered the picture that I spent my first Christmas away from home—in the army, on Governors Island, New York, just off the isle of Manhattan. I reached Governors Island on December 23, so I had to get a Christmas tree at the last minute. At the Quartermaster Filling Station, which was where people on the post got their trees, I saw laid out before me some of the wretchedest greenery I had ever seen, up to that time.

We are all familiar with that sad scene of early January—those prone, used, residually entinseled, faded, and broken Christmas trees out in the street, awaiting the callous hands of the trash man. That was the scene, minus entinselment, that confronted me on December 23 in the Governors Island U.S. Army QM Filling Station. "Do you have any with needles on them?" I asked the attendant. "Back home," I told him, "you see more festive greens than that on a stalk of collards."

He looked sympathetic. "Yeah," he said. "We had four hundred trees come in this year. Ninety-five percent of 'em stunk."

At length I found one that was at least three-dimensional. I inveigled a few extra branches to graft onto the trunk. At the post fire station I had everything dipped in fireproofing fluid pursuant to post regulations, though none of it seemed much of a threat to ignite.

The next day, Christmas Eve, I went to Macy's, where, just before closing time, I found myself in the toy department, which was a shambles. Very like Bourbon Street at 4:00 A.M. the last night of Mardi Gras. Presiding over one of the central counters was a jerkily oscillating plastic Santa Claus, showing wear, with a sign on him reading SANTA IS FOR SALE.

I didn't buy him. I did buy some especially gaudy tree ornaments, partly because I was brought up to impute pathos (especially at Christmas time) not only to folks but also to animals, plants and some inert objects, and these untaken bold spangles struck me as being, figuratively, out on a limb.

Bedecked, the tree looked as though it had sold its hair to buy someone a watch fob, and in return had received combs, ribbons, barettes, tiaras. It becomes a problem to reconstruct Christmas when you're grown.

TOMORROW
═══════════════WILL NOT═══════════
WAIT

Asked to foresee three major trends that will characterize where we are headed in the Nineties and beyond, today's established futurists may be expected to glance more and more characteristically over their shoulders and foresee . . . three major trends, according to a recent, rather smirky, "post-futurist" study.

Sometimes four.

Since these major trends are not always the same three, or four, from futurist to futurist, there has been a tendency until recently to dismiss, on grounds of getting on with it, the last several trends cited overall, say emerging experts in the rapidly expanding field of critiquing prescience as such. But a growing demand for less predictable, more overtake-resistant trends has led leading futurists to take a closer look at—well, at their reflections the next morning, for one thing.

Futurists. . . . The thing is, you'd have to know futurists. I might have been a futurist myself, but I married young, had children to support. I chose trade journalism and occasional plain-talk commentary. No regrets. Let me tell you something about futurists.

Futurists aren't accustomed to being dwelled on, as such. And when they are, they are just like anybody else, believe me: a long time getting over it. Especially when it comes to futurists (don't call them prognosticators), a breed unto themselves. A kind of frontier ethic . . . and then when you start breaking it down to the neo- or near-futurists, the nextualists, the due-time crowd, the by-and-by boys (not all of them boys anymore)—the squabbles, the hurt feelings, the things best left unsaid.

■ Continued overdiversification of software.

Is usually one of them. One of the major trends. In the view of futurists. These young Turks see it a little differently. To them, *everything* can be reduced to . . .

■ **277**

Let me ask you something. Do you recall a time when all there was was hardware?

You may well be too young. You perhaps belong to that class of people which one well-known eventualist terms "teenage lawyers." Plugged into some manner of metaleverage mergerware deal where already you are conjuring buying power out of thin air, to a far greater degree than the recognized experts or frankly (I have never sought to capitalize on what's coming) I am, aren't you? It's all right. No, it is.

The days of only hardware. Literal nuts and bolts. You're too young. Even to imagine.

Ah, but that's just it: in those days we *had* to imagine, we didn't have the dreamware, the museware. Used to go down into the basement, take a chisel or a twenty-penny nail, and stir around in Pop's toolbox, making a noise like

scrarglesgggrklblnk glgnk,

until something emerged. Something magical, because our minds made it so.

Unless what emerged was Pop. He didn't like us in his tools. And see what that leads to. New tools.

Warmware, dourware (which isn't all that dour, if you knew dour in the old days), wistfulware (which . . . oh, well), sweetware, hotware. You take for granted wares that experts in the field only a few years ago could not have predicted without feeling queasy for a moment.

But those blushful days are gone forever, say the post-futurists (let's call them that, for now).

That's what the futurists said, in another time, about bathing suits with skirts and navel coverage. You can forget about ever seeing big bathing suits again, they said, and how warmly that foresight was received! Talk about your backslaps after work, in the bar downstairs! That you may not know. I was there.

You do know of course that navel coverage, broader coverage generally, in swimwear is resurgent. Oh, yes. Baby Boomers spreading, and learning shame. A waist, as they say, is a terrible thing to mind. And now: affluent people *younger* than Boomers.

Here is where it gets interesting.

Trends in the future, some of the new breed are suggesting, will not just loop back upon themselves, as in the past, but will tend to shimmy.

Shimmer is the term some seem to favor, but that is as may be. The market, as always, will be the judge of *shimmer*.

But shimmy, now.

Grownups don't shimmy. Not grownup men.

Of course, more and more, as we know, trends are gender-vague, and so be it. But I'm just saying. I suppose professional male dancers shimmy when so directed, in the workplace, but—we won't get anywhere, here, going into sex differences, because we know what that leads to. Many of the most provocative post-futurists, in fact, *are* female, and far be it from me.

But I'm just saying, as one who has been around for a while, when you talk shimmy, strictly speaking, you're talking one of two things: the front end of a motor vehicle or the hips and shoulders of her sister Kate.

But you wouldn't remember that song. I don't remember it either. I remember people who remembered it.

I spoke with one futurist insider the other day, I won't give his name, but it would be familiar to anyone who wasn't born yesterday. And he tossed a copy of the new counterjournal *Seer Seen* onto the table with such force that it overturned the pork skins. And he said, "I should have seen it coming. Right? Right? So sue me. I don't need this. Right? What do I *need* with this?"

I studied the face of that man, who had said so many then-unheard-of things before, and it occurred to me to hope that we will not lose sight of the good old seat-of-the-pants feel for what it looks like down the road a piece, as best we can say from where we stand.

The other day I asked a man how old he was and do you know what he said?

"I'm seventy-two years old *already.*"

Things happen.

In closing:

■ A greater need for essential trust, mixed with readiness to forgive, in the eyes of the beholder (and a corresponding shortage of it), than ever before.

■ A recognition, in terms of the market, of the need to lead the bitter to the sweet—as we used to say—rather than, as in the past, the other way around. Though back before that, it was the same way around then too, but that's going *way* back, oh, I don't rightly know how long. It would've been before Binnie died, because he was with Tocomeco and they had that logo back then, remember, old man Blodwold *drew* it? With a felt-tip pen? No, wait, we didn't *have* felt-tip pens. Drew it with an old smudgy Paper Mate ballpoint that you clicked in and out.

You don't see those much anymore, do you, those wonky ballpoints that click in and out. Little spring in there. I remember one time in school, I was sitting next to Bird Noles and he sat behind Lianne McGehee, who was so prissy, and Bird, you know, he talked like he had his finger up his nose—excuse me—even when he didn't, and Lianne was wearing this summer dress that revealed quite a lot of her back and I could see old Bird looking at it, and looking at it, and thinking to himself, and thinking to himself, and clicking that old ballpoint pen of his—they were new then—in and out, and finally he just couldn't stand it any longer. He tapped on old Lianne's bare shoulder and she rolled her eyes the way she did and kind of halfway looked around at him and he said, "Err. *Snrrk.* Kin I draw uh eeeagle on your back?" Said it just like that, you know. "Kin I draw uh eeeagle on your back?"

The things we remember. Of course she didn't let him. Not Lianne McGehee. She would be forty-eight now.

■ Buy. Buy something. It doesn't have to be much. That's where a lot of people get sidetracked. It can be just a tiny handful of microcircuit-breakers, or whatever you call them, no larger than an active person's hand. But if you don't buy, I don't buy, then she doesn't buy, he doesn't buy, and it snowballs and builds until there goes the future. Let's don't say a handful of microcircuit*breakers.* Let's say a handful of dreams. I don't think I can impress this upon you enough. By that I mean I believe I can say with confidence that if I end on this note, with a rising intonation, you will like it.

AND NOW

FOR THE

RESURRECTION (BLUB)

Synchronized swimmers scream at each other underwater, and they are sick and tired of hearing about Esther Williams. People don't realize these things about synchronized swimming.

In fact, a lot of people who don't know anything about synchronized swimming, and even some who do, feel that the sport could stand an injection of something. A man who ran into synchronized swimming in college one evening right after biology lab says that it inspired in him a great ambition: some night when the lights went out for a climactic floating-torches-in-the-darkness number he would slip down to the side of the university pool and spike it so heavily with Gentian Violet, a dye used to stain slides in biology labs, that when the lights came back on, the girls would resurface purple.

But that would be gilding the lily. To be sure, such an idea may have occurred to some synchronized swimming team in earnest, and who knows that it won't be tried this weekend in the AAU indoor nationals. A sport that has seen, in recent years, the Shamrock Hilton Corkettes perform *The Highest—a Religious Pilgrimage* and the Newark Nereids in *Thieves of Ali Baba*—not to mention Sydonia Fisher and Linda Howerton of the Hayward (California) Recreation Flying Fins in *Roumania, Roumania—Soul of the People*—is accustomed to bold effects. But traditionalists in the sport would frown on purple girls, and with reason. Anyone who has really looked into what is referred to as "the synchro picture"—certainly anyone who has become acquainted with Mrs. Margaret Swan and the San Antonio (Texas) Cygnets—knows that synchronized swimming has color enough already.

The Cygnets are forty-nine girls in all, ranging in age from five to seventeen. The Cygnets' A team—eight girls aged thirteen to seventeen—is the third best in the country, behind the Santa Clara Aquamaids and the San Francisco Merionettes. Mrs. Swan, the team's coach and owner, has derived its name from her own (the Merionettes named themselves for their coach, Mrs. Marion Kane, changing a letter to work in the mermaid angle). There are other noteworthy team names: the Buffalo Swimkins, the Kansas City Sea Sprites, the Minneapolis Fairview Synkers, the Paso Robles Roblettes, the Oakland Moose (Club) Naiads, the Walnut Creek Aquanuts, the Town of Tonawanda (New York) Aquettes, the (Cuyahoga Falls, Ohio) Waterworks Flippers and the Garland (Texas) Park and Recreation Department Garlettes.

Mrs. Swan lives in—and trains the Cygnets in a yellow-and-white-striped plastic bubble adjacent to—a haunted house. The ghost in this house has a penchant for tucking in beds. Jo Clare Oliverio, fourteen, who is in her ninth year under Mrs. Swan, once spent the night in this house with another Cygnet and no one else. "We got up in the morning and left the bed all yuck," she recalls, "and went into the kitchen and fixed ourselves breakfast. When we went back we looked at the bed. It was *all made up.*" Mrs. Swan has psychic friends who tell her that when they enter the house they "think 'strangled.' They have a sense of someone being strangled in this house."

But that is a side matter; synchronized swimming is eerie in its own right. Its practitioners can walk on subsurface water. That is, while holding their arms entirely out of the water and upraised in a series of graceful attitudes, they appear for all the world to be walking smoothly across the bottom of the pool through water that comes up only to their rib cages, when in fact they are suspended in water ten feet deep. They are keeping themselves unbobbingly afloat and processional, with several feet of water between their feet and the bottom, by means of a feverish activity from the knees down known as "the eggbeater kick." Can Arnold Schwarzenegger do that?

The eggbeater kick, which is like the goalie's kick in water polo, has in recent years played a larger and larger role in synchronized swimming. Before it gained prominence among other techniques of defying gravity and water pressure, the sport had tended to resemble, in the words of one coach, "ballet with the curtain halfway down" because the head, arms, and upper body were so often underwater, busily keeping the legs on display. What ballet was visible was also upside down. Now the upper body is big in every routine. Mrs. Swan's swimmers can eggbeater kick themselves so high that they are out of the water from the waist up. It may not be long before some soloist does Botticelli's *Venus*—unfortunately with a suit and presumably without a shell—with only the toes doing any treading, and everything else acting out the number *Hey Venus, Goddess of Love That You Are* or, rather, something classical with the same theme.

None of which is to take anything away from the other fundamentals of synchronized swimming. From the basic ballet leg (which is the extending of one leg, poised as though for toe dancing, up in the air while the swimmer glides along on her back) to the open spin 180-degree back pike somersault gaviata, there are 114 officially recognized stunts, each graded according to its level of difficulty. In AAU competition a solo, duet or team number must include five of these standard stunts, plus any number of hybrid or improvised stunts (a dolpholina, for instance, is a cross between a dolphin and a catalina, and a swordalina is a cross between a swordfish and a catalina, but these are official stunts; hybrids are even richer syntheses). "We have a film of us in last year's nationals," says Cygnet Jeanie Hayden. "We run it backward, and if we see anything cute, we use it for a hybrid." All of these movements must not only be performed with great poise and body control, as much below as above the water, but also be woven into a composition and synchronized with the accompanying music, which is generally semiclassical, background-type, or classical. Asked whether rock music has ever been used, Cygnet Margo Hernandez, thirteen, says, "No, but one team used the Mickey Mouse Club song." Mrs. Swan has gone so modern as to work in a little Erik Satie. Points are awarded by judges (as many as eighteen at once) to each stunt and to the routine as a whole, in such finely computed totals as 112.4875.

In the course of a competitive number, a team or an individual will range far and wide. Mrs. Swan likes a team number to cover the length of a twenty-five-yard pool three or four times in five minutes, so good form and speed in the basic swimming strokes are required. But each stunt must be performed in a strict compass comparable to that of gymnastics, only without a bar to swing from. The technique that gives the swimmer controlled lift, and a sort of purchase on the stunt's ideal pattern in the water, is an impressively efficient, hard-to-define use of the hands and arms known as sculling.

Sculling is differentiated from paddling or finning, which is what most people, not to mention fish, do when treading water or swimming. Paddling is "a direct push by the palm along the line of propulsion," according to an article on the subject of sculling by an early expert named George Gordon Hyde. "Every drive stroke must be followed by a recovery stroke in the opposite direction . . . ," he wrote. "[Paddling's] power is therefore necessarily intermittent. . . . When rapidly performed it is sporadic and jerky in appearance."

And when you are doing a shark circle, or an eight-girl float, or a 360-degree spinning heron or even something so simple and functional as an oyster—especially when it is all part of *Ching Ming the Coming of Spring* or *The Tragedy of Donner Pass* or *Paris in Pink* or *Maiden of Hiroshima* or *Accentchu-ate the Positive* or *Goya's Famous Duchess* or *The Hundred Gates of Thebes* or *Saturday Matinee in Slipt Disc, Montana* or *Impressions of Imperial Russia* or *Pride of the Piranhas (Devil Cannibals of All Fish)*—you can't afford to be sporadic and jerky. So you scull. "Sculling," wrote Hyde, "employs the same basic principle as the airplane propeller, whose blade moves crosswise to the direction of travel and which gets its driving power from the angle of the blade. . . . However, nature did not give us rotary joints like the propeller; so we must scull by a series of hand sweeps back and forth across the direction of push, changing the palm angle at the beginning of each sweep so that the push will always be in the same direction. The resulting hand motion is very similar to that of the blade of a wind-shield wiper." Leave it that sculling is a wondrous unobtrusive wigwag motion of the hands and forearms, the pitch and vectors of which the swimmer can adjust with great subtlety according to her position and course in the water and which enables the rest of the body to do everything a ballerina could do if she could hang in the water like a trout.

Or it might be better to say a gymnast or a diver instead of a ballerina. The above-mentioned treatise by Mr. Hyde is contained in a book entitled *Aquatic Art,* but that is a term now shunned by synchronized swimming people. "It takes synchro out of competition," says Mrs. Swan, "and puts it into an arty context. Also we despise the term water ballet. That denotes something just done with a musical background. It doesn't denote the fact that these girls are real athletes." Synchronized swimmers think that if gymnasts, divers, and figure skaters can be Olympic athletes, then why can't they?

Margaret Swan's primary goal is competitive—to break the hold on first and second place in the AAU's held for years by California teams. But she is a showwoman. Not only has she developed or overseen such vivid competitive numbers as the duet *Blitzkrieg!!—1939,* in which, in 1968, Cygnets Angie Taylor and Betsy Hart formed a floating swastika with their bodies, but she keeps the club afloat financially by augmenting its repertoire with entertainments. These are mammoth production numbers and lively popular-music and comedy routines to be performed for one hundred dollars a show (or occasionally for free as a community service) at military bases, country clubs, state park openings and conventions. For such appearances the Cygnets are currently preparing what Mrs. Swan describes as "a Gay Nineties 'Don't tie me to the railroad, little Nell' affair called *Laughing Raymond.* Raymond is the villain." (Raymond is a name that will recur in this story in a supernatural context.) "Audiences would really rather see a lot of legs on top of the water than the most intricate thrusting movements," says Mrs. Swan, and the girls enjoy a chance to throw in a little poolside cancan before jumping in, or swimming to Herb Alpert or Broadway tunes instead of the heavy classical stuff favored by AAU judges. Then, too, there are higher-toned exhibitions. The Cygnets have been invited to perform with the Dallas Civic Ballet, and in May 1969 they did a show in the San Antonio River, between an amphitheater on one bank and a stage on the other, from which the San Antonio Symphony played in accompaniment. "We had some special problems with that show," says Mrs. Swan. "Like dead rats floating by and beer cans. And riverboats coming around the corner during practice. Girls who just held torches and didn't have to show their feet got in with tennis shoes on so they wouldn't get cut."

"There was this real mushy stuff on the bottom," says Cygnet Kathy Jansen, "and you'd go down to your knee in it. Then you'd go back up, put up a ballet leg, and mud would go streaming down."

That is not the kind of thing that makes synchronized swimmers scream underwater. The term for such vocalization is "blub." A blub is rather than a cry of despair, a signal used in team numbers. But if you ask Mrs. Swan or a given Cygnet what a blub is exactly, she will say, "Oh, just a scream underwater." For each pivotal moment in a routine, such as the time for a spin to begin, one girl is appointed the blubber. Everyone starts off together on her blub. "It's just *'bwaaah,'* says Margo Hernandez. "It depends on who it is. Gaye Lynn's got a high, high-pitched one." "Once in Sacramento," says Mrs. Swan, "they suddenly took off faster than I'd ever seen them. The blubber had said, underwater, 'Swim like hell!'"

Apparently such cries are perfectly audible underwater, but not a peep rises above the surface. It wouldn't do for *The Miracle of the Lame Prince* or *Belles of Captain Jimmie's Showboat* or *The Colosseum— Spectacle of Terrors at the Circus Maximus* or *Fantasy of the Redbirds* or even *The Soul of Poland* or *Portrait of Satan* to be punctuated with "bwaaah" or "swim like hell." It wouldn't do, either, for there to be much roiling of the surface; a swimmer on her back sculling often produces small vortices, but anything bordering on splash is bad form. Grimacing is also frowned upon. "You have to look nice when you breathe," says Jeanie Hayden. "When you're dying underwater, you can't come up and look like it. You have to look pleasant. I get panicky sometimes when we're holding our breath for a long time. You're under there and your blood is pounding, but you know you have to stay under. Sometimes you can't see anybody, and it all closes in on you. Sometimes in a meet you wonder what's going to happen if you're upside down underwater and your noseclip comes off. Sometimes your nose gets oily and . . .

"Also you can get turned around. Once I did a stunt and ended up on top of the water instead of under. We did last year's team number at a local meet in a pool with no lights, and the pool was on a slant and there were no lines on the bottom. You know you're out of formation, but you don't know where. You can't talk and say, 'Scoot over that way, y'all?' You go into a spin and everybody's swimming into each other. That's when it gets embarrassing."

The Cygnets embarrass themselves rarely, but they suffer year-round. They work out three hours every day of the summer, every day during Christmas holidays and at least three times a week the rest of the year. A workout may entail as many as three thousand yards of sculling and swimming back and forth. They get very little recognition. When they tell people they are synchronized swimmers, people always bring up Esther Williams—which isn't too hip because in her movies Esther Williams tended to do very simple tricks, often propelling herself by pushing up from the bottom, which is considered cheating today. " 'Oh, Esther Williams the Second,' people say," sighs Kathy Jansen, "and you want to say *'uhhhhh,'* because here she did this *dolphin.'* "

"Synchro is terribly demanding," says Mrs. Swan. "Girls never go steady. We've had some very popular girls, and they date—Betsy Hart is Miss San Antonio. We've had cheerleaders, student council presidents and exceptional students. But you seldom call the home of a synchronized swimmer and find the line busy for hours.

"We push these kids to the limits of their abilities. We demand outrageous things of them. If I have a show and I can't do without a girl, and she's sick, she just has to swim, that's all. The first year we had our own pool we swam outdoors without the bubble until February—there were icicles on the fence. That was the year we had the fewest colds."

"She drives you," says Jeanie Hayden. "She's two different people. When we make trips, she cracks jokes and is fun to be with, but in the pool you don't cross her."

"When we got to the nationals," says Kathy Jansen, "everybody else called their coach by her first name; but we just . . . 'Margaret?' 'Margaret'—we just couldn't. Here we were saying, 'Mrs. Swan,' 'Mrs. Swan.' We didn't mean it to sound formal or anything, but . . . 'Margaret' just sounded so . . . So we called her 'Duck.' "

So it is that Mrs. Swan, a petite fifty-one-year-old grandmother of five and an assistant professor of physical education at San Antonio

Junior College, has had made up for herself a sweatshirt that says MOTHER DUCK which she wears to workouts.

"When I was growing up in Texas," she says, "we didn't have chlorinated pools. I was always kept out of the water, or when I did get in, I had to keep my head out. I had had measles, which caused some hearing loss. Still, I loved swimming.

"In 1950, in Houston, at the Shamrock Hilton I saw Joy Cushman and Ernestine Mignone, two of the earliest synchronized swimmers, do a duet. I went back home to Dallas and did some experimenting with it myself. When I moved to San Antonio in 1955 a woman had just started a class in the YWCA here. I became their coach and called them the Silver Fins. When I quit the Silver Fins because of parental interference, I started Cygnets. It's probably the only synchro club that's owned and directed by an individual instead of being run by a parents' governing board or a recreation center. It makes for a benevolent dictatorship, I guess you'd call it."

The Cygnets were organized in 1963, and by 1966 they had won the junior national championship (an indication of the agreeable casualness of the Swan ménage is that someone has placed a rubber nose on the peaked hands of a winged gilt bathing girl who is poised atop the '66 trophy in Mrs. Swan's crowded study). The Cygnets have won a special trophy awarded to distinguished teams outside California every year it has been offered. "I don't know of any girl who, if she dedicates herself, can't be successful in synchro," says Mrs. Swan. "I have had kids who were just blobs of jelly who with application became part of a championship team."

A brochure that Mrs. Swan sends out to parents of prospective Cygnets says, "We believe that we can give your girl a reason for not smoking, drinking or indulging in drugs because we offer her a group that stands for clean living and offers tangible rewards for clean living. We believe in competition and in strenuous physical activity and a consuming measured interest for every girl. Swimming is a wonderful exercise. It is feminine, it builds beautiful bodies, it develops poise and it saves lives. We offer your daughter the experience of sports competition. We can and will take her as far as she is willing and able to go—from beginner to champion—from inside the city limits to halfway around the world . . . ! She will learn to make sacrifices and decisions; to plan her time and to schedule herself. She will have fewer colds (we can prove this statistically) and she will have something special to cling to when she is trying to find herself as a woman."

Mrs. Swan no longer sends these brochures out except on request. Word of mouth is sufficient to keep membership high, despite a considerable rate of attrition as girls decide that they have had enough or their families decide that synchro is too much for them. "Your family has to put up with a bunch," says Jeanie Hayden. "Family vacations and dinner times have to be planned around you." It costs ten dollars a month dues to be a Cygnet, and each Cygnet family has to agree to sell or buy five dollars' worth of tickets to Cygnet performances every month. These revenues pay travel and pool expenses; Mrs. Swan doesn't take a salary, but Cygnets pays the mortgage on the pool, which the Swans rent to a neighborhood swim club in non-Cygnet hours. "I've worked with the YWCA," says Mrs. Swan, "and I'm sympathetic with girls who want to do these things and don't have the money. So we've given some scholarships to Cygnets. But these girls haven't all appreciated it." She sighs and shakes her head. "Finally, last year, I said I don't care if I never see another poor girl."

Most Cygnets, then, come from upper-middle-class families, but the club is fairly diverse ethnically. There are Anglo-Saxon, Spanish, Jewish and Italian names among the ranks, and there have been two black Cygnets. "One black girl, who dropped out, would have been on the A team this year," says Mrs. Swan, "and she would've been the first black girl ever in the national championships."

Making friends is one of the "tangible rewards" referred to in the Cygnets' brochure. "When I started at five," says Jo Clare, "I was the only girl that little. I'd just sit down at the shallow end of the pool and just freeze." "But then you go on and get to know a lot of people," says Jeanie, "and you don't want to quit. And when I stop synchro for a while, it makes me feel like I'm getting fat."

"You feel like you're not *doing* anything," adds Kathy.

"When we're swimming we can eat anything we want and not get fat," says Jeanie. "Most of our friends understand now, so when we're shoveling it in they don't say anything."

"Like they don't say, 'Pig!' " says Jo Clare.

"And trips," says Jeanie. "You say, 'I'll be going to California in a few weeks,' to other kids in school, and they say, 'Really?'

"Synchro takes a lot of discipline. But you get out there with a stunt you hate, and somebody works on it with you, over and over for hours, *uhhhhhh*—and then it starts getting *better*. That makes you feel good."

Jeanie adds that national competition confirms that feeling. "You know you're good, but you don't know how good," she says. "When we got third in the nationals last year it was so neat."

Everything considered, synchronized swimming can still be a grind. Santa Clara's Kim Welshons, now retired after winning or helping to win ten senior national solo (*The Taming of the Shrew*, etc.), duet (*Spell of the Gypsy,* etc.) and team (*Rosh Chodesh—Israelean Festival,* etc.) championships and being nominated for the 1970 Sullivan Award, told an interviewer last summer, "Sometimes, with the work and the performances, I feel like a thing instead of a person. I get on a plane, I get where I'm going, and I go into the water. In many cases the hotel and the road are all I see."

The career of a good AAU synchronized swimmer usually stretches from age eleven to age seventeen. After that there is college competition, which is not so stiff, but very rarely does a girl go on to swim in a professional water-ballet troupe, either in residence at a place like Cypress Gardens or Marineland (where some years ago the Vero Beach Dolphinettes performed with trained porpoises) or traveling around with a portable pool. "Once these girls get through competition, they've had it," says Mrs. Swan with a gleam in her eye. "They're sick of it."

"What we want this year in the nationals is a standing ovation," says Jeanie Hayden. "the Merionettes got one with a patriotic routine in Oklahoma three years ago. They had a flag in it—they formed a flag and rotated from side to side like a flag waving. We considered a patriotic number this year, but there have been so many of them done recently. The judges get sick of *The Battle Hymn of the Republic* over and over. So we decided on a religious one. The indoor finals will be on the day before Easter. We're going to do *Resurrection.* When you go out there and do something like that it really makes you feel good."

"Supposedly, your theme doesn't count in the scoring," says Mrs. Swan. This principle would appear to be borne out by a study of past national results—in the 1968 outdoor solo competition Sherrill Gonterman of Shaw Park, St. Louis, with *Jazz-A-Ma-Dazz,* finished one point ahead of Kay Ruenzel of the Berea (Ohio) Swim Club Aquateens, with *Freedom from Behind the Iron Curtain,* and Sharon Lawson of the Merionettes placed far above either of them with *Powers from Beelzebub.* Another index to the austerity of the judging is this guideline from a 1968 seminar led by Dawn P. Bean of Santa Ana, California:

WHAT WE DON'T JUDGE
Where does it say "smile"?
Her costume is beautiful, so suitable, etc.
She has so much "showmanship."
Her music is terrible.
I don't believe Spaniards dance like that.

"But when you're pushing for the top," says Mrs. Swan, "you want something spine-tingling."

It took her from November 1 until just before Christmas to put together the five minutes of music for *Resurrection*. This music comprises seven different selections from records as various as *Handel's Greatest Hits* and *The Hallelujah Album* by Carmen Dragon, which includes passages from the soundtrack of *The Robe*. A single cymbal clash is picked up from one record—"on that they do a tuck and roll and go under like crazy"—and then there is a snatch of the "Hallelujah Chorus," something from Respighi's *St. Michael the Archangel*, and so on. "We wanted to use the traditional 'Palms' you hear on Palm Sunday, so we're using that from *The Robe*," says Mrs. Swan. "Then we carry out the whole idea of Gethsemane, and carry through the Crucifixion, the Resurrection and then the "Hallelujah Chorus." It *is* spine-tingling.

More spine-tingling than the Swans' ghost stories, in fact. Though they aren't bad. "I was a skeptic," says Mrs. Swan's husband George, who runs a rent-all agency in San Antonio, "until I moved into this house." That is the ninety-six-year-old, single-story home of Alphonse W. Perrin, who built it himself in 1875 after moving down from New York in search of a better climate. It is made of quarried limestone, the same material used to build the Alamo, which is also located in San Antonio, and it is hard to describe architecturally, especially now that the Swans have added to it here and there. It has high ceilings, knee-high doorknobs and several nice, heavy pieces of old Spanish furniture. "We hear the windows rattling at night when there is no wind," says Mr. Swan. "A contractor who came out to the place before we moved in heard the windows rattling one night when there was no wind and not even any *windows*. Just the opening was there in the wall."

On another night, before they moved in, the Swans held a séance in a back bedroom. All twelve people in attendance, say the Swans, heard footsteps enter the house, go toward a hall closet and then stop. These steps have been heard a few times since, and they always wind up at the closet. "I'm not the kind of man who is afraid to get up and check on a noise at night," says George Swan, who is heavily built, "but I heard those steps one night when I was here alone, and I got a gun and got in bed and stayed right there."

"We'd heard from our real-estate agent that people had been mistreated here," says Mrs. Swan vaguely. Then there were the psychic friends to whom the house said "strangled"—one of these let the house's spell sink in for a while and declared, says Mrs. Swan, that "there was a Raymond" in the background. "We had found all the old family letters, and there was no Raymond mentioned in any of them. We couldn't figure it out." But then the Swans discovered the old Perrin graveyard on a piece of adjoining property. There was a headstone for Raymond Perrin, dead at the age of thirty-eight. Further inquiries revealed that Raymond had been an afflicted child—possibly with brain fever—and "he had to be cared for like a vegetable," says Mrs. Swan.

If there was a strangulation, though, it has not come to light. Nor can the Swans explain the tucking-in phenomena that have occurred in the house. There was what happened to Jo Clare's bed, and then there was the experience of another female guest. "She had to have everything loose over her body," says George. "All the covers had to be very loose. Well, she woke up in the night with everything tucked in solid on all three sides."

Who can explain such things? But on the other hand, why linger over them when the Cygnets are outside in the bubble working out?

There are to be run-throughs of the B-team number, which is to the tunes of a medley of the national anthems of World War I and is entitled *In Flanders Fields the Poppies Blow,* and then of the big one, *Resurrection.*

Mrs. Swan says a few words to the B-team over the sound system; one speaker is underwater so that the girls can hear the music while submerged. In fact they tend to submerge while Mrs. Swan addresses them because they can hear her more clearly down there than above the surface, where everything echoes vibrantly around and around the bubble. The smell of chlorine is in the air. On the inside the bubble's stripes look orange rather than yellow, and the sun shining through them onto the choppy surface colors the water a fluctuating marbled orange and white.

"One of the big problems in this sport," Mrs. Swan says in an aside, as the girls loosen up, "is how to denote the choreography. We write all kinds of strange things down. Like overarm crawl and a pull to the back and a roll to the side . . . Do it again," she says to a Cygnet, "and watch your feather."

The sun casts the shadow of a four-hundred-year-old oak tree onto the walls of the bubble, and also the shadows of scraggly mesquites. The girls are going through individual stunts. They call to mind Hedy Lamarr in *Ecstasy,* Ophelia afloat and the Lady of the Lake. Here and there through the orange-and-white, oak-and-mesquite-shaded surface there occurs a girl's single pointed foot, slowly ascending, like Excalibur only rounded and fetching.

"Different teams are known for different things," Mrs. Swan is saying. "We are known for our flamingo 360-degree spins. And we are known for the floats we do. In *Symbols of British Majesty—Orb and Scepter,* eight girls, some with their feet together, some with their heads to-gether—girls holding feet with feet—went down underwater, latched together, and made a ball. Then they rolled. It looked like an orb."

The B-team routine is beginning. Now the girls have all submerged, and you know, although you can't hear her, that one of them is screaming. "In a thing we called *Ode to the Dawn,*" adds Mrs. Swan, "they made a shark circle, lying on their sides, and went around once. Then three made a smaller circle in the center, and three piked out and resurfaced with their legs split so the whole thing looked like the sun with rays. In *Resurrection* we do a Celtic cross."

The B-team is well into its number. Girls are oystering out of a swastika into a flamingo position with *Deutschland, Deutschland, Über Alles* building into a crescendo in a yellow-and-white-striped bubble with the shadows of trees, in San Antonio, Texas, and now "a long way . . . to Tip-per-ra-ry," and the finale is *The National Emblem March.*

Then on into *Resurrection* with a blub on the drop-under, and there is a period during which the Cygnets are underwater for twenty-seven seconds, while first one shift and then another comes up—projecting only legs out of the water—and executes a hybrid "with a half-spin at the top," as Jeanie Hayden has explained it, "then spin down to where the legs are even, another spin at the ankles and sink."

They sink. They come back up. They form the cross. Says Mrs. Swan: "When a girl is holding another girl's foot in a float, while they're all sculling on their backs, she is taking two fingers and hold-ing onto her neighbor's Achilles' tendon and lifting."

Clash! go the cymbals, the girls go under again, "And He shall reign for . . . He shall reign for e-ver and e-ever. Hallelujah! Hallelujah! Hallelujah!" ringing all around the orange-and-white water through which young girls' heads are sprouting at last, and if a ghost were to come sculling along through the bubble in midair, blue in the face with a pair of disembodied hands around its neck, how much would it add?

GOSPEL RAP

Fella saw a woman coming down the street,
She looked so good he was indiscreet—
Said, "Hey there, Mama, you're a mover.
If that ain't so, I'm Herbert Hoover."

"Mm-Mm," she said.

He said, "I swear,
You got such sweet long legs and hair.
I doubt I've seen the likes of you."

"Well," she said, "that may be true."

"Hey," he said, "I've got some sheer
Long fine black silk stockings here.
I'd like to help you slip them on."

"Whoa," she said, "you hold the phone.
We got to talk about—you know—religion."

"What's that got to do with it, Pigeon?"

"*Ev*-ry-thing for a girl like me."

"Well," he said, right casually,
"I recognize *no* higher power."

"Our . . . *acquaintance* has gone sour,"
She said—"Your legwear may be great,
But listen here while I quotate
[As she stepped off on her heels and toes]:
'There are no fixes in atheists' hose.' "

=AFTERNOON WITH=

A BUCK

This is a true story. That's the trouble with it. Not that it's true, but that I feel the need to tell people it is. Three days after these events happened to me—three days, that is, after I became the first person I have ever heard of who wrestled, physically, with an apparently lust-driven deer—I visited a movie set, where I told the story to everyone who would listen. Everyone looked professionally dubious. A prominent screenwriter was on hand to help punch up this movie's script from day to day, make it track better, give the characters clearer motivation. Two-thirds of the way through my story, the screenwriter frowned.

"Where would he get a brick?" he said.

"Not *he*," I said, "*me*. This happened to me. I just reached down, and there was a brick there, on the ground."

"What would a brick be doing there?" he wanted to know.

"I don't know," I said. "This *happened*. See, here are the scars."

I shouldn't have said that then, because—well, for one thing because it was too dramatic a thing to say on a movie set, since I wasn't in the movie. But also because it wasn't time in my story yet for the scars—I hadn't established how a person would get such scars from wrestling with a deer. Which is something that no one I have told this story to has ever heard of happening. It is a great story, in that sense.

Actually they weren't scars yet, they were cuts. But they looked as though they might become scars, if I kept picking at them. (Today, I regret to say, they are almost gone.) The scriptwriter wasn't motivated to do more than glance at them. I pushed on through to the end of the story. Except that I didn't have a good ending for it yet. I'm not sure that I have one now, but I do have an aftermath, which I lacked then.

"I thought you were going to do more with the red-sequin thing," the screenwriter said. "If not the pants."

If this were not a true story, I dare say I would do more with the red-sequin thing, because it was certainly a crucial element: Jessie Betts's skating dress. If not the pants.

Some backstory (I believe they call it in the movie industry): I divide my time between New York City and the country, western Massachusetts. So do my close friends, the Betts family. But they weren't coming up to the country on the weekend of September 22–23, 1990, because Jessie, their twelve-year-old daughter, had a big ice-skating competition in the city on the afternoon of Sunday the twenty-third. If she finished in the top three, she would go on to a higher-level competition at Lake Placid. And Jessie had left her red-sequin skating dress in their country house. So her mother, Lois, asked me whether I could possibly bring it in to the city in time for the competition.

I was more than happy. Here is something that I don't go into, usually, when I tell this story to people, but something that is true: I have always felt vaguely at fault with regard to women's clothes. I don't buy the right ones as presents, I don't compliment women on them sufficiently, I don't even notice them often enough, except to the extent that I find them provocative.

That is just the truth. And if it causes the woman reader of this story to turn against me as a narrator—as I say, I have always felt at fault with regard to women's clothes. And here was a chance to do a perfectly wholesome, positive, supportive, non-ulterior, clothes-affirming favor for a fine young woman of whom I am avuncularly fond.

I went to the Bettses' house and picked up Jessie's dress before noon. That gave me time to play tennis with my friend Jon Swan on the Bettses' court, which lies in a clearing in the woods behind their house.

I have a good first serve, when I get it in, but otherwise my tennis game is not, I like to believe, a reflection of my character. Jon is a decade or so older than I am and has a bad leg and a worse racket, but his play is clever, steady and amicably intent, whereas my groundstrokes fluctuate back and forth from overhit to tentative, my concentration is feverish one moment and miles away the next, I am often preoccupied with trying to think of some way to dissociate myself from my last shot (if not from my character) as I hit the next, and I lack (on those rare occasions when it might become an issue) a killer instinct.

In my day I have pressed strong opponents, however, and as someone who used to make a living as an interviewer I like to believe that when I hit a stretch of semiconsistent competence I at least draw something interesting out of more natural players, perhaps by dint of what Keats called (not in a tennis context) negative capability. Over the years I have mellowed to the point that I no longer scream and throw my racket.

And this was the first set I had played since the previous summer, so when I lost to Jon six–love without having got loose yet, and noticed that it was time to head toward the city, I was philosophical. After all, I was about to spend the rest of my afternoon coming to the aid of a promising young American figure skater.

Knowing the importance of my mission, Jon volunteered to sweep the court. I hustled up the path and emerged from the woods into the Bettses' backyard.

Where a deer stood.

Just stood there. About halfway between me and the Bettses' driveway, where my car was parked.

Deer abound in western Massachusetts. Once after a heavy rain I looked out the window of my own house and saw a big deer rushing downstream in the river. I thought maybe it was being swept away by the swollen current, but when I ran out and hollered *"Hey,"* the deer hooked a quick U-turn, swam back upstream a few yards and then jumped out of the water and ran through the middle of the village into the trees behind the general store.

That's what you expect a deer to do—flash into view and then modulate soundlessly off on tiny hard feet.

Or people kill them. One night on the road a big doe leapt out of the darkness and my right front fender hit her a glancing *whap.* I backed up and there she was in the middle of the road, on her knees and haunches, too stunned to be shooed out of harm's way. I ran to the nearest house, whose owner said, "Must've been thirty grazing out back the house at fresh dark," and called the state police. When we went back to check on her she was gone, and then we heard a *whump* and *crunch* up the road. A woman driving a pickup full of rocks had done for her, or another deer just like her, this time.

"Awww, I *hit* my brakes," the woman told us. "You'd miss 'em if they stopped, but they stop-and-start—aww, jumped right into me, well, here if you get the front feet and you get the back feet and just swing 'er up"—and she drove away with venison on the rocks.

The deer of my story, as I say, was just standing there. In the Bettses's backyard. I glanced at my watch, saw that I had a little leeway timewise, and thought to myself, "I believe I'll see how close I can get to this deer."

I crept toward him. He didn't move. I crept closer. He didn't move. He almost looked like he was looking right at me, but I couldn't tell for sure. To the extent I could actually see his eye, it looked as if it might have a faraway look in it. It was black. I crept closer, then I relaxed, stood up straight, walked right toward him. He didn't move.

At this point in the story people suspect a trick. "Stuffed, right?" some say. "You're going to tell me this was a stuffed deer." My agent, Esther Newberg, to whom I told this story the day after it happened— at that point I was still so stirred by the story that I thought her first reaction was going to be an eagerness to sell the movie rights. But no, what she said was, "Right, right, the Woody Allen moose, right? Wakes up on the bumper of the car."

And my own sister, Susan, said: "Is this going to be like the time in New Mexico we took that old dried-up deer carcass that the dogs drug up and we put it in your bed to see what you'd say when you pulled the covers back?" (Which is something my own sister actually did to me, years ago, when we were younger and more sportive.)

But no. This deer was not stuffed, nor temporarily stunned, nor dead. He actually shifted his stance a bit, but not much. I was only six feet away from him. I thought to myself, "I believe I am going to be able to *touch* this deer."

Which is something I've always wanted to do. To make physical contact with an independent wild animal. I guess everybody has a certain desire to do that, if it can be done safely. And a *deer!* A deer doesn't snarl, isn't off-putting, yet is almost the essence of wildness as in *there-it-is-vwoop-there-it-goes.*

I took two steps and put my hand between his horns.

He didn't mind. Not very soft to the touch: ridged coarse hair on hard skull, like a cow's head.

I scratched. He seemed to *like* it. In fact he butted forward slightly, as if appreciatively, moving into my stroke as a cat will. But unlike a cat's, this deer's head wasn't very pettable from my point of view. As opposed to his, evidently.

I thought: This is neat. Then I thought: This is weird.

Childish thoughts. But linking up with a wild animal is something I have been thinking about since childhood, when stories led me to identify with so many rabbits and bears. (And how about *Bambi?* I came to the end of that book and I said to myself, "Wait a minute. The *mother dies?* I'm a little kid! Why would they give me a book where the mother dies? Are they trying to tell me something? She looks healthy. . . ." And in *The Yearling,* the boy had to shoot his pet deer. Damn.)

And then I thought: These *horns* I'm scratching between. They're horns. Altogether four points. It seemed to me that I had probably been scratching this deer's head long enough. I couldn't see that it was leading anywhere. "Okay, then," I said briskly (the only time either the deer or I spoke). I made to take my leave.

The deer wouldn't let me. That is to say, as soon as I took my hand away he took a step forward, pushing his head into my midsection. I grabbed his horns, close to his head. He took another step.

I didn't want to back up. It wasn't a big issue with me, I didn't feel that I had anything to prove, exactly, to this deer or to myself. But everything considered I didn't like the idea of backing down. The deer pressed forward.

I was wondering, why is this deer doing this? It didn't accord with any deer behavior I had ever observed or heard about. He was so intent on it. As though it was just something that he'd always wanted to do. He of course had no responsibilities, it meant nothing to him that Jessie needed her red-sequin dress.

Then I noticed he was drooling.

Could you get rabies from a deer? But he wasn't showing any interest in biting me. I had never in fact heard of deerbite. You could get Lyme disease from a deer tick, I knew, but I had never heard of anyone getting deer ticks directly from a deer.

At any rate, there we were. I felt strong enough to hold him at . . . well, "at bay" didn't seem to be the expression. To a standstill. But for how long?

Enough. I had things to do. I gave the deer a brisk shove, freed my hands and flapped my pants at him.

I was wearing shorts. From the tennis. I had my long pants tucked under my arm. Waving my pants at him required that I push off and do a quick snatch-and-wave, and I didn't get a very good grip on my pants, and my tennis racket—which was also tucked under my arm— slipped down between my elbow and my hip, and what with one thing and another, my pants wound up on the ground. The deer, recoiling slightly, glanced down at them.

I didn't feel secure about bending down to pick them up. The deer butted at them tentatively. Then he lifted his head. My pants were hooked on one of his horns.

Oh, Lord, I thought. This deer is going to run off into the forest with my pants. Containing my wallet. And my car keys. Which means, how can I get Jessie's red-sequin skating dress to her in time for her competition?

I grabbed my racket and hit at my pants. They came loose. I didn't feel secure about bending down to pick them up, though. The deer surged forward. I grabbed his horns again, in the process dropping my racket.

And there we were. I was reminded of the story of an Irish soldier who, in a battle against the Turks, cried out to a comrade, "I've caught a Tartar!"

"Bring him along then," said the comrade.

"He won't come."

"Then, come along yourself."

"Arrah, but he won't let me."

If you are attacked by a shark or a bear, I had heard, your best bet is to punch it in the nose. But it is hard to get a blow to the head in when you're in a clinch. I did manage to frap the deer's nose with my knuckles. It felt like—well, you don't get any gratification from hitting a deer in the nose. And the deer didn't seem to mind it. I twisted his head one way, and then the other. He seemed actually to relish this.

I decided to bulldog him down. I pushed his head all the way to the ground—lowering myself, in the process, to one knee. I didn't get his head turned over, though, the way rodeo guys do a steer's. His head was on the ground, but the rest of him was under no pressure to follow it. All four of his feet remained planted. And what if I did get him tumped over—those sharp toes thrashing around . . . Then I noticed that his points were now pointing at my groin. I stood up again, and his head came with me. And there we were.

This was not like anything I had experienced before. I guess you could say the same about anything you haven't experienced before. But this was like—well it wasn't like having a coatrack come alive in your hands, and it wasn't like getting entangled with a stranger's umbrella while trying to get off the subway, and it wasn't like being proffered a lion's foot and seeing a thorn in it. Maybe it was something like quitting smoking; but I never have smoked.

Either I was tiring, or he was pushing harder. I gave some ground. I had the feeling that the deer, if he wanted to, could push harder still. And he had more traction than I did, and his horns were harder than my hands—I wasn't holding the points, but the parts I was holding were rough, almost like coral, and what if he got a temper up . . .

"Were you scared?" I was asked by people to whom I told this story early on.

"Yes," I answered, until my friend Vereen Bell said, "That's hard to imagine, being scared of a deer."

"Not so much *scared,*" I have told people since. "I mean, I knew he wasn't going to kill me. But what if he got frightened and started slashing around? Deer use their horns to fight off wolves, right? I could imagine getting gouged enough that I'd have to go to the emergency room. You don't mess around with a wild-animal puncture. And then how would I get to New York in time with Jessie's red-sequin skating dress?"

I was scared. I was backing up bit by bit to keep my arms extended; every bit of extension I lost, the deer took it up like slack.

I *could* have called out to Jon, who was down in the woods sweeping the court. But I didn't want to. Maybe if he hadn't just beaten me six–love I would have, but I don't think so. I felt this was something I ought to be able to deal with myself. Anyway, what would I have called out, exactly?

"Jon! Could you come up here quick? I . . . I'm . . . I've got ahold of a deer and he won't let me turn him loose!"?

No. Jon is a writer too, and this was my story. I tried to put myself in the deer's place. What did deer do with their horns, usually? Beside fight wolves. Bump and rub them off on trees. Did this deer think I was a tree? Maybe he was wondering why this tree was behaving like this.

I decided to shift him off onto a real tree. He might be relieved. I backed around in the yard, looking over my shoulder for trees, finding a couple of little ones. What did he need with them, he had me.

I backed further, into some bushes. This felt like a bad move. I minded being in these bushes more than the deer seemed to. And now I didn't have anywhere further to back. I looked down.

That's when I saw the brick.

Several women I have told this story to have had a real problem with the brick. Not on narrative grounds, but because they disapprove of violence to deer. So do I, I assure them. But Jessie was waiting . . .

If this were fiction maybe I would have the red-sequin dress under my arm. Maybe the dress would be what attracted the deer. Maybe the deer would knock me down and make me wear it. But no. The dress was waiting in the car.

And the brick came to hand. People have bricks in their yards, right?

I turned loose with my right hand long enough to pick up the brick and bonk the deer on the nose with it. The deer seemed startled, in a tentative way. The brick didn't feel good in my hand, but I hit him harder with it—not *hard* hard, but hard enough that he pulled back, somewhat.

He looked at me, noncommittally. I was tired of this! I needed space! I wanted my pants! I wanted to get rid of the brick, get rid of the deer. I threw the brick at him. That did the trick, he sprang away.

"Jon!" I yelled. "Come up here! The strangest thing!"

I saw that my right hand was bleeding. I ran to the Bettses' swimming pool and stuck it in.

Jon witnessed the deer, standing a few yards away looking enig-
matic, and he also saw my wounds. You could write him care of the
Columbia Journalism Review, where he is an editor. Would I make that
up? I'm an old journalist myself. Jon also recalls that I was flushed and
breathing hard, which I suppose is true enough but I feel he puts too
much emphasis on it. Of course he didn't see any of the actual wrestling itself.

I went to the Swans' house and Marianne Swan bandaged the cuts
and I drove to the city holding my hand above my heart—all the way,
for two hours, so it wouldn't bleed anymore (Marianne's idea). I got
the dress to Jessie in time.

And the rest of this story is telling it to people, most of which I have
already told you about. The Bettses said the deer must have been the
same one they'd seen lurking around in their yard the previous weekend. Their bulldog, Max, an amiable and forthright animal, had run
him off twice. (Once when the Betts were at my house I carelessly
shoved an armload of wastepaper into the fireplace, the fire blazed out
into the living room, and Max jumped up and *attacked the fire.* It backed
down.) The Bettses had been told that the deer was probably one of
several that another family in the area had been feeding all summer.
So he'd lost his fear of people.

My friend Jim Seay, a deer hunter, put in that it was rutting season.
At that time of year hunters sometimes clack two old racks of antlers
together and male deer come running, looking to butt heads. "Your
deer was horny," Jim said. "I never knew heard of one hooking up
with a person like that, though." I thought he might sound more
envious, somehow. He sounded . . . sympathetic.

Here is my son John's response to the story: "I'd probably have
done the same thing myself." A generous thing for a son to tell a
father. I feel bad that I didn't think to tell him in return, "I'd probably
have done, myself, all the things I've given you a hard time about."
I might say that there seemed to be a note of *resignation* in his voice.
When something happens to your father you can't help thinking, deep
inside, "Ah. Yes. This is the kind of thing the men of my family do."

Actually John might well have handled the deer better than I did.
He can beat me in tennis, and he has always had a way with animals.
When he was little he told his mother, "I go up to dogs I don't even
know and whisper, 'I love you.' "

Maybe I should have whispered something to the deer, or chanted
something, or jumped on his back and ridden him off into the woods.
This story could use a transcendant moment. But I had to get away,
there was Jessie's dress. Which, as I say, I got to her on time. She

skated with aplomb. She missed, by one point, making the top three and Lake Placid, but that didn't get her down.

A couple of weeks later, the deer approached a man who was doing some work on the Bettses' house. The man called the game warden, who shot the deer with a tranquilizer dart and took his horns off with a chainsaw. Nobody has reported seeing the deer since. Maybe he was cured of being a people animal, or maybe he let a hunter get close to him during deer week this winter and died wondering what he may also have wondered when he and I parted: Hey, what is the *story* here? But that is just speculation on my part.

FADE OUT, freeze frame, whatever works. How often does a true story end satisfactorily? In the end you throw a brick at it.

GOOD AND OVER

Toothache's deep-rooted but bliss is a rover—
A time comes to bid it so long.
It's better for something to be good and over
Than rotten and still going strong.

> Good-bye-aye-aye,
> Good-bye and yoo-hoo.
> Life does not wait for us,
> Let's not be late for a
> Seat on the ongoing choo-choo.

Rapture is fine, then it's smoke up the chimney,
A lawsuit is longer by far.
How brief was our glorious weekend in Bimini
Compared to the Thirty Years War.

> Good-bye-aye-aye,
> Good-bye and yoo-hoo . . .

The longer we dwell on the music that's faded,
The more it gives way to what's wrong.
Celebrate late companions, for that is what they did,
And live for wine, persons and song.

> Good-bye-aye-aye,
> Good-bye and yoo-hoo . . .

How sweet are the moments when we are in clover.
Sometimes we don't know till they're gone.
So long live the things that are so good and over,
And *plpp* to what ought not go on.

ABOUT
——————THE——————
AUTHOR

ROY BLOUNT, JR., is now the author of eleven books, if you count the two versions of his book about the Pittsburgh Steelers twice and the two halves of his double book of verse only once. But these are matters of interest largely to scholars. The thing that most people come away with is a sense that he is about as tall as they expected, give or take an inch or two, one way or the other. Otherwise he is a total contradiction, on the one hand serving as his own harshest critic (" *'Spine-tingling'*? Oh, please"), on the other hand agreeing with Dr. Samuel Johnson that "no man but a blockhead ever wrote, except for me."

WAR
21